The Political Economy of Capital Cities

Capital cities that are not the dominant economic centers of their nations – so-called 'secondary capital cities' (SCCs) – tend to be overlooked in the fields of economic geography and political science. Yet, capital cities play an important role in shaping the political, economic, social and cultural identity of a nation. As the seat of power and decision-making, capital cities represent a nation's identity not only through their symbolic architecture but also through their economies and through the ways in which they position themselves in national urban networks.

The Political Economy of Capital Cities aims to address this gap by presenting the dynamics that influence policy and economic development in four in-depth case studies examining the SCCs of Bern, Ottawa, The Hague and Washington, D.C. In contrast to traditional accounts of capital cities, this book conceptualizes the modern national capital as an innovation-driven economy influenced by national, local and regional actors. Nationally, overarching trends in the direction of outsourcing and tertiarization of the public-sector influence the fate of capital cities. Regional policymakers in all four of the highlighted cities leverage the presence of national government agencies and stimulate the economy by way of various locational policy strategies.

While accounting for their secondary status, this book illustrates how capital-city actors such as firms, national, regional and local governments, policymakers and planning practitioners are keenly aware of the unique status of their city. The conclusion provides practical recommendations for policymakers in SCCs and highlights ways in which they can help to promote economic development.

Heike Mayer is a Professor of Economic Geography at the Institute of Geography and a member of the Center for Regional Economic Development at the University of Bern in Switzerland.

Fritz Sager is a Professor of Political Science at the KPM Center for Public Management at the University of Bern in Switzerland.

David Kaufmann is a Postdoctoral Researcher at the KPM Center for Public Management at the University of Bern in Switzerland.

Martin Warland was a Postdoctoral Researcher from August 2016 until January 2017 at the Institute of Geography and the Center for Regional Economic Development at the University of Bern in Switzerland.

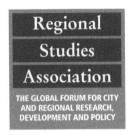

Regions and Cities

Series Editor in Chief
Joan Fitzgerald, *Northeastern University, USA*

Editors
Maryann Feldman, *University of North Carolina, USA*
Gernot Grabher, *HafenCity University Hamburg, Germany*
Ron Martin, *University of Cambridge, UK*
Kieran P. Donaghy, *Cornell University, USA*

In today's globalised, knowledge-driven and networked world, regions and cities have assumed heightened significance as the interconnected nodes of economic, social and cultural production, and as sites of new modes of economic and territorial governance and policy experimentation. This book series brings together incisive and critically engaged international and interdisciplinary research on this resurgence of regions and cities, and should be of interest to geographers, economists, sociologists, political scientists and cultural scholars, as well as to policy-makers involved in regional and urban development.

For more information on the Regional Studies Association visit www.regionalstudies.org

There is a 30% discount available to RSA members on books in the *Regions and Cities* series, and other subject related Taylor and Francis books and e-books including Routledge titles. To order just e-mail Joanna Swieczkowska, Joanna.Swieczkowska@tandf.co.uk, or phone on +44 (0)20 3377 3369 and declare your RSA membership. You can also visit the series page at www.routledge.com/Regions-and-Cities/book-series/RSA and use the discount code: RSA0901

124 The Rural and Peripheral in Regional Development
An Alternative Perspective
Peter de Souza

123 In The Post-Urban World
Emergent Transformation of Cities and Regions in the Innovative Global Economy
Edited by Tigran Haas and Hans Westlund

122 **Contemporary Transitions in Regional Economic Development**
Global Reversal, Regional Revival?
Edited by Turok et al.

121 **The Illicit and Illegal in Regional and Urban Governance and Development**
Corrupt Places
Edited by Francesco Chiodelli, Tim Hall and Ray Hudson

120 **The Political Economy of Capital Cities**
Heike Mayer, Fritz Sager, David Kaufmann and Martin Warland

119 **Data and the City**
Edited by Rob Kitchin, Tracey P. Lauriault and Gavin McArdle

118 **The Unequal City**
Urban Resurgence, Displacement and The Making of Inequality in Global Cities
John Rennie Short

117 **Urban Transformations**
Geographies of Renewal and Creative Change
Edited by Nicholas Wise and Julie Clark

116 **The Scottish Economy**
A Living Book
Edited by Kenneth Gibb, Duncan Maclennan, Des McNulty and Michael Comerford

115 **Reanimating Regions**
Culture, Politics, and Performance
Edited by James Riding and Martin Jones

114 **Territorial Policy and Governance**
Alternative Paths
Edited by Iain Deas and Stephen Hincks

113 **Economics of Planning Policies in China**
Infrastructure, Location and Cities
Wen-jie Wu

112 **The Empirical and Institutional Dimensions of Smart Specialisation**
Edited by Philip McCann, Frank van Oort and John Goddard

111 **EU Cohesion Policy**
Reassessing performance and direction
Edited by John Bachtler, Peter Berkowitz, Sally Hardy and Tatjana Muravska

110 **Geography of Innovation**
Edited by Nadine Massard and Corinne Autant-Bernard

109 **Rethinking International Skilled Migration**
Edited by Micheline van Riemsdijk and Qingfang Wang

108 **The EU's New Borderland**
Cross-border relations and regional development
Andrzej Jakubowski, Andrzej Miszczuk, Bogdan Kawałko, Tomasz Komornicki, and Roman Szul

107 **Entrepreneurship in a Regional Context**
Edited by Michael Fritsch and David J. Storey

106 **Governing Smart Specialisation**
Edited by Dimitrios Kyriakou, Manuel Palazuelos Martínez, Inmaculada Periáñez-Forte, and Alessandro Rainoldi

105 **Innovation, Regional Development and the Life Sciences**
Beyond clusters
Kean Birch

104 **Unfolding Cluster Evolution**
Edited by Fiorenza Belussi and Jose Luis Hervás-Olivier

103 **Place-based Economic Development and the New EU Cohesion Policy**
Edited by Philip McCann and Attila Varga

102 **Transformation of Resource Towns and Peripheries**
Political economy perspectives
Edited by Greg Halseth

101 **Approaches to Economic Geography**
Towards a geographical political economy
Ray Hudson

100 **Secondary Cities and Development**
Edited by Lochner Marais, Etienne Nel and Ronnie Donaldson

99 **Technology and the City**
Systems, applications and implications
Tan Yigitcanlar

98 **Smaller Cities in a World of Competitiveness**
Peter Karl Kresl and Daniele Ietri

97 **Code and the City**
Edited by Rob Kitchin and Sung-Yueh Perng

96 **The UK Regional–National Economic Problem**
Geography, globalisation and governance
Philip McCann

95 **Skills and Cities**
Edited by Sako Musterd, Marco Bontje and Jan Rouwendal

94 **Higher Education and the Creative Economy**
Beyond the campus
Edited by Roberta Comunian and Abigail Gilmore

93 **Making Cultural Cities in Asia**
Mobility, assemblage, and the politics of aspirational urbanism
Edited by Jun Wang, Tim Oakes and Yang Yang

92 **Leadership and the City**
Power, strategy and networks in the making of knowledge cities
Markku Sotarauta

91 **Evolutionary Economic Geography**
Theoretical and empirical progress
Edited by Dieter Kogler

90 **Cities in Crisis**
Socio-spatial impacts of the
economic crisis in Southern
European cities
*Edited by Jörg Knieling and
Frank Othengrafen*

89 **Socio-Economic Segregation in
European Capital Cities**
East meets West
*Edited by Tiit Tammaru, Szymon
Marcińczak, Maarten van Ham,
Sako Musterd*

88 **People, Places and Policy**
Knowing contemporary Wales
through new localities
*Edited by Martin Jones, Scott
Orford and Victoria Macfarlane*

87 **The London Olympics and
Urban Development**
The mega-event city
*Edited by Gavin Poynter, Valerie
Viehoff and Yang Li*

86 **Making 21st Century
Knowledge Complexes**
Technopoles of the world
revisited
*Edited by Julie Tian Miao, Paul
Benneworth and Nicholas A.
Phelps*

85 **Soft Spaces in Europe**
Re-negotiating governance,
boundaries and borders
*Edited by Philip Allmendinger,
Graham Haughton, Jörg Knieling
and Frank Othengrafen*

84 **Regional Worlds: Advancing
the Geography of Regions**
*Edited by Martin Jones and
Anssi Paasi*

83 **Place-making and Urban
Development**
New challenges for contemporary
planning and design
*Pier Carlo Palermo and Davide
Ponzini*

82 **Knowledge, Networks and
Policy**
Regional studies in postwar
Britain and beyond
James Hopkins

81 **Dynamics of Economic Spaces
in the Global Knowledge-based
Economy**
Theory and East Asian cases
Sam Ock Park

80 **Urban Competitiveness**
Theory and practice
Daniele Letri and Peter Kresl

79 **Smart Specialisation**
Opportunities and challenges for
regional innovation policy
Dominique Foray

78 **The Age of Intelligent Cities**
Smart environments and innova-
tion-for-all strategies
Nicos Komninos

77 **Space and Place in Central and
Eastern Europe**
Historical trends and
perspectives
Gyula Horváth

76 **Territorial Cohesion in Rural
Europe**
The relational turn in rural
development
*Edited by Andrew Copus and
Philomena de Lima*

75 **The Global Competitiveness of Regions**
Robert Huggins, Hiro Izushi, Daniel Prokop and Piers Thompson

74 **The Social Dynamics of Innovation Networks**
Edited by Roel Rutten, Paul Benneworth, Dessy Irawati and Frans Boekema

73 **The European Territory**
From historical roots to global challenges
Jacques Robert

72 **Urban Innovation Systems**
What makes them tick?
Willem van Winden, Erik Braun, Alexander Otgaar and Jan-Jelle Witte

71 **Shrinking Cities**
A global perspective
Edited by Harry W. Richardson and Chang Woon Nam

70 **Cities, State and Globalization**
City-regional governance
Tassilo Herrschel

69 **The Creative Class Goes Global**
Edited by Charlotta Mellander, Richard Florida, Bjørn Asheim and Meric Gertler

68 **Entrepreneurial Knowledge, Technology and the Transformation of Regions**
Edited by Charlie Karlsson, Börje Johansson and Roger Stough

67 **The Economic Geography of the IT Industry in the Asia Pacific Region**
Edited by Philip Cooke, Glen Searle and Kevin O'Connor

66 **Working Regions**
Reconnecting innovation and production in the knowledge economy
Jennifer Clark

65 **Europe's Changing Geography**
The impact of inter-regional networks
Edited by Nicola Bellini and Ulrich Hilpert

64 **The Value of Arts and Culture for Regional Development**
A Scandinavian perspective
Edited by Lisbeth Lindeborg and Lars Lindkvist

63 **The University and the City**
John Goddard and Paul Vallance

62 **Re-framing Regional Development**
Evolution, innovation and transition
Edited by Philip Cooke

61 **Networking Regionalised Innovative Labour Markets**
Edited by Ulrich Hilpert and Helen Lawton Smith

60 **Leadership and Change in Sustainable Regional Development**
Edited by Markku Sotarauta, Ina Horlings and Joyce Liddle

59 Regional Development Agencies: The Next Generation?
Networking, knowledge and regional policies
Edited by Nicola Bellini, Mike Danson and Henrik Halkier

58 Community-based Entrepreneurship and Rural Development
Creating favourable conditions for small businesses in Central Europe
Matthias Fink, Stephan Loidl and Richard Lang

57 Creative Industries and Innovation in Europe
Concepts, measures and comparative case studies
Edited by Luciana Lazzeretti

56 Innovation Governance in an Open Economy
Shaping regional nodes in a globalized world
Edited by Annika Rickne, Staffan Laestadius and Henry Etzkowitz

55 Complex Adaptive Innovation Systems
Relatedness and transversality in the evolving region
Philip Cooke

54 Creating Knowledge Locations in Cities
Innovation and integration challenges
Willem van Winden, Luis de Carvalho, Erwin van Tujil, Jeroen van Haaren and Leo van den Berg

53 Regional Development in Northern Europe
Peripherality, marginality and border issues
Edited by Mike Danson and Peter De Souza

52 Promoting Silicon Valleys in Latin America
Luciano Ciravegna

51 Industrial Policy Beyond the Crisis
Regional, national and international perspectives
Edited by David Bailey, Helena Lenihan and Josep-Maria Arauzo-Carod

50 Just Growth
Inclusion and prosperity in America's metropolitan regions
Chris Benner and Manuel Pastor

49 Cultural Political Economy of Small Cities
Edited by Anne Lorentzen and Bas van Heur

48 The Recession and Beyond
Local and regional responses to the downturn
Edited by David Bailey and Caroline Chapain

47 Beyond Territory
Edited by Harald Bathelt, Maryann Feldman and Dieter F. Kogler

46 Leadership and Place
Edited by Chris Collinge, John Gibney and Chris Mabey

45 **Migration in the 21st Century**
Rights, outcomes, and policy
*Kim Korinek and Thomas
Maloney*

44 **The Futures of the City
Region**
*Edited by Michael Neuman and
Angela Hull*

43 **The Impacts of Automotive
Plant Closures**
A tale of two cities
*Edited by Andrew Beer and
Holli Evans*

42 **Manufacturing in the New
Urban Economy**
*Willem van Winden, Leo van
den Berg, Luis de Carvalho and
Erwin van Tuijl*

41 **Globalizing Regional
Development in East Asia**
Production networks, clusters, and
entrepreneurship
*Edited by Henry Wai-chung
Yeung*

40 **China and Europe**
The implications of the rise of
China as a global economic power
for Europe
*Edited by Klaus Kunzmann, Willy
A Schmid and Martina Koll-
Schretzenmayr*

39 **Business Networks in
Clusters and Industrial
Districts**
The governance of the global
value chain
*Edited by Fiorenza Belussi and
Alessia Sammarra*

38 **Whither Regional Studies?**
Edited by Andy Pike

37 **Intelligent Cities and
Globalisation of Innovation
Networks**
Nicos Komninos

36 **Devolution, Regionalism and
Regional Development**
The UK experience
Edited by Jonathan Bradbury

35 **Creative Regions**
Technology, culture and
knowledge entrepreneurship
*Edited by Philip Cooke and
Dafna Schwartz*

34 **European Cohesion Policy**
Willem Molle

33 **Geographies of the New
Economy**
Critical reflections
*Edited by Peter W. Daniels,
Andrew Leyshon, Michael
J. Bradshaw and Jonathan
Beaverstock*

32 **The Rise of the English
Regions?**
*Edited by Irene Hardill, Paul
Benneworth, Mark Baker and
Leslie Budd*

31 **Regional Development in the
Knowledge Economy**
*Edited by Philip Cooke and
Andrea Piccaluga*

30 **Regional Competitiveness**
*Edited by Ron Martin,
Michael Kitson and
Peter Tyler*

29 Clusters and Regional Development
Critical reflections and explorations
Edited by Bjørn Asheim, Philip Cooke and Ron Martin

28 Regions, Spatial Strategies and Sustainable Development
David Counsell and Graham Haughton

27 Sustainable Cities
Graham Haughton and Colin Hunter

26 Geographies of Labour Market Inequality
Edited by Ron Martin and Philip S. Morrison

25 Regional Innovation Strategies
The challenge for less-favoured regions
Edited by Kevin Morgan and Claire Nauwelaers

24 Out of the Ashes?
The social impact of industrial contraction and regeneration on Britain's mining communities
Chas Critcher, Bella Dicks, David Parry and David Waddington

23 Restructuring Industry and Territory
The experience of Europe's regions
Edited by Anna Giunta, Arnoud Lagendijk and Andy Pike

22 Foreign Direct Investment and the Global Economy
Corporate and institutional dynamics of global-localisation
Edited by Jeremy Alden and Nicholas F. Phelps

21 Community Economic Development
Edited by Graham Haughton

20 Regional Development Agencies in Europe
Edited by Charlotte Damborg, Mike Danson and Henrik Halkier

19 Social Exclusion in European Cities
Processes, experiences and responses
Edited by Judith Allen, Goran Cars and Ali Madanipour

18 Metropolitan Planning in Britain
A comparative study
Edited by Peter Roberts, Kevin Thomas and Gwyndaf Williams

17 Unemployment and Social Exclusion
Landscapes of labour inequality and social exclusion
Edited by Sally Hardy, Paul Lawless and Ron Martin

16 Multinationals and European Integration
Trade, investment and regional development
Edited by Nicholas A. Phelps

15 **The Coherence of EU Regional Policy**
Contrasting perspectives on the structural funds
Edited by John Bachtler and Ivan Turok

14 **New Institutional Spaces**
TECs and the remaking of economic governance
Martin Jones, Foreword by Jamie Peck

13 **Regional Policy in Europe**
S. S. Artobolevskiy

12 **Innovation Networks and Learning Regions?**
James Simmie

11 **British Regionalism and Devolution**
The challenges of state reform and European integration
Edited by Jonathan Bradbury and John Mawson

10 **Regional Development Strategies**
A European perspective
Edited by Jeremy Alden and Philip Boland

9 **Union Retreat and the Regions**
The shrinking landscape of organised labour
Ron Martin, Peter Sunley and Jane Wills

8 **The Regional Dimension of Transformation in Central Europe**
Grzegorz Gorzelak

7 **The Determinants of Small Firm Growth**
An inter-regional study in the United Kingdom 1986–90
Richard Barkham, Graham Gudgin, Mark Hart and Eric Hanvey

6 **The Regional Imperative**
Regional planning and governance in Britain, Europe and the United States
Urlan A. Wannop

5 **An Enlarged Europe**
Regions in competition?
Edited by Louis Albrechts, Sally Hardy, Mark Hart and Anastasios Katos

4 **Spatial Policy in a Divided Nation**
Edited by Richard T. Harrison and Mark Hart

3 **Regional Development in the 1990s**
The British Isles in transition
Edited by Ron Martin and Peter Townroe

2 **Retreat from the Regions**
Corporate change and the closure of factories
Stephen Fothergill and Nigel Guy

1 **Beyond Green Belts**
Managing urban growth in the 21st century
Edited by John Herington

The Political Economy of Capital Cities

Heike Mayer, Fritz Sager, David Kaufmann, and Martin Warland

Routledge
Taylor & Francis Group

LONDON AND NEW YORK

First published 2018 by Routledge

2 Park Square, Milton Park, Abingdon, Oxfordshire OX14 4RN
52 Vanderbilt Avenue, New York, NY 10017

Routledge is an imprint of the Taylor & Francis Group, an informa business

First issued in paperback 2019

British Library Cataloguing in Publication Data
A catalogue record for this book is available from the British Library

Library of Congress Cataloging in Publication Data
Names: Mayer, Heike, 1973- author. | Sager, Fritz, author.
Title: The political economy of capital cities / Heike Mayer, Fritz Sager, David Kaufmann and Martin Warland.
Description: New York : Routledge, 2018. | Includes index.
Identifiers: LCCN 2017020530| ISBN 9781138681439 (hardback) |
    ISBN 9781315545837 (ebook)
Subjects: LCSH: Capitals (Cities)—Economic aspects. |
    Capitals (Cities)—Political aspects. | Policy sciences.
Classification: LCC JF1900 .M39 2018 | DDC 330.9173/2—dc23
LC record available at https://lccn.loc.gov/2017020530

ISBN: 978-1-138-68143-9 (hbk)
ISBN: 978-0-367-87800-9 (pbk)

Typeset in Times New Roman
by Swales & Willis, Exeter, Devon, UK

Contents

List of figures   xiv
List of tables   xvi
About the authors   xvii
Preface   xix
Acknowledgements   xx
List of abbreviations   xxii

1   Introduction   1

2   Framework for analyzing secondary capital cities   14

3   Setting the scene   43

4   The economic geography of secondary capital cities   76

5   Locational policies in secondary capital cities   118

6   Conclusion: Deal with it – ten recommendations to
    ensure secondary capital cities thrive   154

    Appendix   170
    Index   176

Figures

2.1	Main structure of public-procurement-driven CC-RIS	16
3.1	The picturesque historic old town of Bern is a UNESCO World Heritage Site and represents Bern's former wealth and power	44
3.2	View from the Washington Monument, looking down the National Mall, with the United States Capitol in the background	45
3.3	Centre Block of the Parliament of Canada, with the Peace Tower on Parliament Hill in Ottawa	48
3.4	Map of the Bern metropolitan area and its location in Switzerland	50
3.5	Map of the Ottawa-Gatineau metropolitan area and its location in Canada	52
3.6	Map of The Hague metropolitan area and its location in the Netherlands	54
3.7	Map of the Washington, D.C. metropolitan area and its location in the United States	55
3.8	The Dutch government shapes The Hague's cityscape: The Binnenhof complex of buildings with the Prime Minister's office is seen at the front. At the back, from left to right: The Ministry of Education, Culture and Science, the Ministry of Health, Welfare and Sport, the Ministry of Security and Justice, and the Ministry of the Interior and Kingdom Relations	58
3.9	Swiss parliament building in Bern	59
3.10	Percentage of public procurement of KIBS compared to all goods and services, Canada	67
4.1	K Street is a preferred location for firms seeking proximity to Congress and the White House	77
4.2	Arlington County, Virginia is a preferred location for firms working on DoD and DHS contracts	78
4.3	Avoiding Ottawa's traffic jams: Firms in Kanata	79
4.4	SBIR awards by MSAs, 2000–2010	97
4.5	Formerly state-owned firms located in Bern	101
4.6	Maintaining strong partnerships with federal agencies: George Mason University	103

4.7	Investigators digitalize a crime scene in the CSI laboratory in The Hague	106
4.8	The 1776 premises provide co-working space for start-ups in government-dominated industries	110
5.1	Parts of the old psychiatric hospital of St. Elizabeths are to be transformed into an innovation campus	120
5.2	One example of a large real estate development project in Washington, D.C. is The Wharf waterfront revitalization project, located in the southwest of the District	126
5.3	View from the Peace Tower of the Parliament of Canada overlooking the Ottawa River. The City of Gatineau is in the background	130

Tables

1.1 Cases based on the population of SCCs in OECD countries 8
1.2 Overview of interviews conducted 9
2.1 Capital city regional innovation system failures and stages of development 24
2.2 Categorization of locational policies 26
2.3 Combining RIS failures and locational policy frameworks 34
3.1 Population dynamics in the four capital city regions 51
3.2 Overview of clusters in the four secondary capital cities 62
3.3 Number of employees in knowledge-intensive sector for selected regions in Switzerland, Canada, USA, and the Netherlands, 2012 63
3.4 Composition of KIBS sector, 2012 64
3.5 Public-procurement spending in Switzerland, the Netherlands, Canada, and USA, 2014 68
4.1 Case study regions at a glance 113
5.1 Explanatory factors for locational policies 133
5.2 Institutional explanatory factors for locational policies 139
5.3 Case study regions at a glance 149

About the authors

Heike Mayer is a Professor of Economic Geography at the Institute of Geography and a member of the Center for Regional Economic Development at the University of Bern in Switzerland. Her primary area of research is in local and regional economic development, with a particular focus on the dynamics of innovation and entrepreneurship, place making and sustainability. Mayer began her career in the United States, where she completed a Ph.D. in Urban Studies (Portland State University) and held a tenured professorship at Virginia Tech. She is the author of *Entrepreneurship and Innovation in Second Tier Regions* (Edward Elgar) and co-author of *Small Town Sustainability* (with Prof. Paul L. Knox, Birkhäuser Press).

Fritz Sager is a Professor of Political Science at the KPM Center for Public Management at the University of Bern in Switzerland. He specializes in policy studies, public policy analysis, and program evaluation. His main fields of research are urban politics and policy, metropolitan governance, public health and prevention, land use, and transport policies, with a special focus on implementation. He is co-author of *Policy-Analyse in der Schweiz* (with Prof. Karin Ingold and Andreas Balthasar, NZZ Libro) and co-editor of *The European Public Servant* (with Prof. Patrick Overeem), *Evaluation im politischen System der Schweiz* (with Prof. Thomas Widmer and Andreas Balthasar, NZZ Libro), and *Moving Beyond Legal Compliance: Innovative Approaches to EU Multi-level Implementation* (with Dr. Eva Thomann, Taylor & Francis).

David Kaufmann is a Postdoctoral Researcher at the KPM Center for Public Management at the University of Bern in Switzerland. He specializes in urban policies and urban politics, as well as the analysis of migration and asylum policies. David Kaufmann studied at the University of Zurich, the University of Lund in Sweden, and the University of Bern. He has also been a guest researcher at Leiden University in the Netherlands, Virginia Polytechnic Institute and State University in the USA, and the University of Ottawa in Canada.

Martin Warland was a Postdoctoral Researcher from August 2016 until January 2017 in the Institute of Geography and the Center for Regional Economic Development at the University of Bern in Switzerland. He holds a Ph.D. in Economic Geography from the University of Bern and currently works as a research and data project manager at Livit AG Real Estate Management. Prior to joining our research project on capital cities, he studied economic geography, law, and business administration at the Humboldt University of Berlin in Germany, and at the University of Illinois at Urbana-Champaign in the USA. His research focuses on the knowledge economy from a spatial perspective and has been published in journals such as *Cities – The International Journal of Urban Policy and Planning* and *The Service Industry Journal*.

Preface

The Political Economy of Capital Cities studies the dynamics that influence economic development in Bern, Ottawa, The Hague, and Washington, D.C. These four cities represent capitals that are not the dominant economic centers of their nations; we refer to them as 'secondary capital cities' or SCCs. Secondary capital cities tend to be overlooked in the fields of economic geography and political science, and there is a lack of research describing their political economy. More specifically, this book examines capital city regional innovation systems and highlights the role played by public procurement in advancing innovation. Local economic development is the goal of locational policies. We show how the four capital cities use these policies to diversify their economies.

In contrast to traditional accounts of capital cities, this book conceptualizes the modern national capital as an innovation-driven economy influenced by national, local, and regional actors. Nationally, overarching trends in the direction of outsourcing and tertiarization of the public-sector influence the fate of capital cities not just in the United States, but also in Canada, the Netherlands, and Switzerland. As a result, the capital city economy follows the logic of a regional innovation system and is driven by public procurement dynamics, as well as by concrete policy choices. Regional policymakers in all four cities leverage the presence of national government agencies and stimulate the economy by way of various locational policy strategies. Capital cities' positioning strategies can be allocated to two dimensions, with one being focused on the nation state and the other on interurban competition. Our empirical insights are based on four in-depth case studies that employ both qualitative and quantitative data.

While accounting for their secondary status, the book illustrates how capital city actors such as firms, national, regional, and local governments, policymakers, and planning practitioners are keenly aware of the unique status of their city. By taking this approach, the book helps us understand contemporary dynamics in knowledge-based urban economies and, more specifically, how they play out in the context of capital cities. Based on our findings, the conclusion provides practical recommendations for policymakers in secondary capital cities and highlights ways in which they can help to promote economic development.

Acknowledgements

This book is about a set of capital cities that all of the authors have called home at some point or other. In Bern, we are familiar with the sight of politicians walking freely across the plaza in front of the Parliament Building; We experienced Ottawa as a bilingual capital city where people speaking French and English intermingle on a daily basis. We remember The Hague as an international town where you can find important international organizations, the palace of the Dutch Royal Family as well as the North Sea; We have walked along the National Mall and visited the numerous museums, as well as various sporting events, in Washington, D.C. From these experiences, we know that capital cities are wonderful places to live in and visit. The four capital cities we examine in this book are also fascinating subjects to study from an interdisciplinary perspective. Discussions were held with all four cities concerning their status compared to the much stronger economic centers of their respective nations. In Switzerland, these discussions began in 2008, when the federal government published the first drafts of its national spatial development strategy and Bern was not registered as a metropolitan region on the national map. This caused alarm among local and regional policymakers, who began lobbying for better treatment. In Washington, D.C., discussions about how to strengthen the US capital have been ongoing for some time, and particularly since the Home Rule Act of 1973. Ottawa and The Hague have experienced similar debates in recent years. As observers of these debates, we started to think about a larger research project, within which we could systematically analyze and compare such dynamics. In 2013, we launched a multi-year research project, which was supported by the Swiss National Science Foundation. As economic geographers and political scientists, we embraced an interdisciplinary approach in this project and developed a research design that drew on our respective fields, but also combined them. David Kaufmann and Martin Warland began their dissertation projects and were each able to live and work in each capital city for several months. This embeddedness provided an in-depth, first-hand understanding of the political economy dynamics at work in the four secondary capital cities.

The financial support provided by the Swiss National Science Foundation (Grant Number 143784) allowed us to pursue this research, particularly with regard to extended research visits in each capital city. We also enjoyed great hospitality in each of the cities, where the local institutions helped us with collegial and administrative support. We are hugely grateful for the support given by Leiden University at its campus in The Hague, by Virginia Tech`s National Capital Region campus in Arlington County in the Washington, D.C. region, and by Ottawa University's Center on Governance. Many individuals also provided help with contacts, gave feedback, inspired our work, helped with research, and helped add the final touches to this book. We would especially like to thank Carl Abbott, Caroline Andrews, Frederike Asael, Fabian Bauer, Elanor Best, Jim Bohland, Regula Buchmüller, Eric Champagne, Margret Cowell, Michael Daniels, Ulrike Dietz, David Doloreux, Silvan Duner, Angela Franovic, Steven Fuller, David Gordon, Antoine Habersetzer, the late Terry Holzheimer, Livia Jakob, Lorenz Joss, Kristina MacVicar, Paul Messerli, Anna Minta, Afroze Mohammed, André Nietlisbach, Patrick Overeem, Georg Tobler, and Nicholas Velez.

We would also like to sincerely thank all of the interview partners in Bern, Ottawa, The Hague, and Washington, D.C. who took the time to talk to us and share their insights.

Heike Mayer, Fritz Sager, David Kaufmann, and Martin Warland
Bern, April 11, 2017

Abbreviations

ACT-IAC	American Council for Technology and Industry Advisory Council
ARWG	Acquisition Reform Working Group
BCIP	Build in Canada Innovation Program
BRICC	Basic Research Innovation and Collaboration Center
CBD	Central business district
CC-RIS	Capital city regional innovation system(s)
CRS	Capital Region Switzerland
DARPA	Defense Advanced Research Projects Agency
D.C.	District of Columbia
DHS	Department of Homeland Security
DoD	Department of Defense
EPFL	École polytechnique de l'Université de Lausanne
ETH	Swiss Federal Institute of Technology
EU	European Union
FDA	Food and Drug Administration
FDI	Foreign direct investment
GDP	Gross Domestic Product
GGBa	Greater Geneva Bern Area
GSA	General Service Administration
GSIN	Goods and Services Identification Number
GTSC	Government Technology & Services Coalition
GWBoT	Greater Washington Board of Trade
GWI	Greater Washington Initiative
HEI	Higher education institution
HSD	The Hague Security Delta
ICT	Information and communications technology
IT	Information technology
KIBS	Knowledge-intensive business service(s)
MEC	Mason Enterprise Center
MRTH	Metropolitan Region of Rotterdam The Hague
MWCOG	Metropolitan Washington Council of Governments
NACE	Nomenclature statistique des activités économiques dans la Communauté européenne

NAICS	North American Industry Classification System
NCC	National Capital Commission
NCPC	National Capital Planning Commission
n.e.c.	not elsewhere classified
NFI	Netherlands Forensic Institute
NFIA	Netherlands Foreign Investment Agency
NGO	Nongovernmental organization
NIH	National Institutes of Health
NOGA	Nomenclature générale des activités économiques (General Classification of Economic Activities – Switzerland)
NRC	National Research Council
NSF	National Science Foundation
NTIA	National Telecommunications and Information Administration
NVTC	Northern Virginia Technology Council
OECD	Organisation for Economic Co-operation and Development
OSME	Office of Small and Medium Enterprises
PIA	Partnership Intermediary Agreement
PIANOo	Professional and Innovative Tendering Network for Government Contracting Authorities
PILT	Payments in lieu of tax
PPI	Public procurement for innovation
PSC	Professional Service Council
PTT	Post-, Telefon- und Telegrafenbetrieb
PWGSC	Public Works and Government Services Canada
R & D	Research and development
RIS	Regional innovation system(s)
SBI	Standard Industrial Classifications (The Netherlands)
SBIR	Small Business Innovation Research
SCC	Secondary capital city
SCC-RIS	Secondary capital city regional innovation system(s)
SFDF	Swiss Federal Department of Finance
SGE	Swiss Global Enterprise
sitem-Insel	Swiss Institute for Translational and Entrepreneurial Medicine
SME	Small and medium-sized enterprise
TandemNSI	Tandem National Security Innovations
TNO	The Netherlands Organization of Applied Scientific Research
TU Delft	Delft University of Technology
US(A)	United States (of America)
WFIA	WestHolland Foreign Investment Agency
WTO	World Trade Organization

1   Introduction

Capital cities play a crucial role in shaping the identity of a nation. As the seat of power and decision-making, capital cities represent the nation not only through their symbolic architecture, but also through the presence of important political and economic institutions. However, factors such as the decline of the nation state, the rise of transnational institutions, and the ascendancy of global cities have challenged the traditional role and centrality of capital cities. These trends have eroded the customary functions of capital cities, particularly in those capitals that are not the primary economic centers of their nations. While London, Paris, and Tokyo seem to have relegated the capital city function in favor of their ongoing transformation into global cities (Sassen, 1991), capitals like Bern, Ottawa, The Hague[1], and Washington, D.C. proactively strive toward harvesting the benefits of being a political center, albeit in a variety of ways. The economic and political changes we examine in this book relate to their unique regional innovation systems (RIS) and the set of locational policies formulated in secondary capital cities (also referred to throughout as SCCs). All four cities take advantage of a specialized economy, which benefits from close interactions between government agencies and the firms that do business with these agencies. This form of contracting, referred to as public procurement, has become a driver of regional knowledge dynamics in SCCs. In addition, SCCs formulate a diverse set of locational policies not only to promote themselves and to develop their regional economy, but also to ensure their status in the national urban system. This book examines the factors and forces at play in SCCs such as Bern, Ottawa, The Hague, and Washington, D.C. with the focus on their political economy.

Research on capital cities is relatively sparse, resulting in a lack of a coherent set of theories about the political economy of this specific type of city (Campbell, 2000). One reason for the lack of attention afforded to this topic may be the tendency of urban researchers to focus instead on world or global cities (Sassen, 1991), global city regions (e.g. Scott, 2001), polycentric megacity regions (Hall & Pain, 2006) or megaregions (Florida, Gulden, & Mellander, 2008). Along those lines, Gordon notes that capital cities slipped off the radar of scholarly attention because they became a "casualty both to fashionable enthusiasm for 'global cities' against national centers, and to a shift of interest toward less formal and monolithic kinds of institution" (Gordon, 2006, p. 3). There is clearly a need for comparative research about the political economy of capital cities since we know very little about SCC economies and how they function as RIS. Moreover, there is a lack of knowledge about the ways in which the institutional setting and the political processes at work in these cities shape the formulation of locational policies. Therefore, this book does not focus on capital cities in terms of an examination of the unique environment in which the capital serves as the seat of government of a nation; instead, we are interested in examining specific economic and political arrangements shaped at the local and regional level by actors such as government agencies, firms, economic developers, and politicians with the aim of increasing the capital city's competitiveness. We refer to this as an actor-centered approach to capital city research. Our objective is to shed light on the identity of these actors at the local and regional levels in a capital city, to determine their motivations, and how they shape the capital city economy. As we will show, capital city actors strategically use capital city functions to leverage the capital city status. While this book intends to fill a gap in the literature on capital cities, we also provide practical, feasible recommendations for the various actors who shape the capital city economy.

Defining (secondary) capital cities

A focus on the SCC and its surrounding political and economic structure presupposes a clear definition of this type of capital. In general, capital cities can be defined as the

> seat of power and a place of decision-making processes that affect the lives and future of the nation ruled, and that may influence trends and events beyond its borders. Capitals differ from other cities: the capital function secures strong and lasting centrality; it calls for a special hosting environment to provide what is required for the safe and efficient performance of the functions of government and decision-making characteristics of the place.
>
> (Gottmann & Harper, 1990, p. 63)

Existing research highlights different types of capital cities (Campbell, 2000; Hall, 2006; Zimmermann, 2010). Hall (2006), for example, distinguishes seven types of capital cities based on their role and function. He describes multifunctional capitals that combine the majority of national higher-level functions (e.g. London, Paris, Madrid, Stockholm, Tokyo). Then there are global capitals that also play a role beyond their respective nations (e.g. London, Tokyo). A third category encompasses political capitals, which were established to focus on their role as the national seat of government (e.g. The Hague, Ottawa, Washington, D.C., Canberra, Brasilia). Former capitals are another category, representing capital cities that lost their role as seats of government, but retain some historical functions (e.g. St. Petersburg, Philadelphia, Rio de Janeiro). Similarly, ex-imperial capitals were once important as colonial centers (e.g. London, Madrid, Lisbon, Vienna). Provincial capitals once functioned as capitals and still have some importance (e.g. Milan, Stuttgart, Toronto). The final category encompasses so-called 'super capitals', which are centers of international organizations (e.g. Brussels, Geneva, Nairobi). While Hall's categorization is not mutually exclusive, it provides a useful way to highlight the heterogeneity in the roles and functions of capitals.

Campbell (2000) provides additional characteristics that distinguish capitals in terms of their size, the form of national government, or the timing of the founding of the capital. He distinguishes between "the capital as the dominant economic city in the nation" (such as Montevideo, Paris, London, Copenhagen) and "the capital as a secondary city" (such as Ottawa, Bonn Canberra, Ankara), pointing to the economic status and relative position of the capital within the nation concerned. This division implies a lack of higher national-level or even international-level economic functions of SCCs (Hall, 2006), compared to cities with a strong economic and internationally important base (such as global information and finance in London or Tokyo). Similarly, Zimmermann (2010) distinguishes between capital cities that are or are not the primary economic centers of their nations.

In this book, a *secondary capital city (SCC)* is defined as the *capital city of a nation where there is at least one city within the respective nation that is more important to the country economically than the capital city*. SCCs are more often found in federal states than in other systems. Capital cities in these nations were often chosen as a compromise, to balance power relationships, but also to separate economic and political power or to serve as independent, alternative sites to the traditional commercial centers (Gottmann, 1977; Gottmann & Harper, 1990; Harris, 1995; Mayer, Sager, Kaufmann, & Warland, 2016; Nagel et al., 2013; Slack & Chattopadhyay, 2009; Spate, 1942). For these reasons, SCCs are not infant capitals. Often, they were deliberately chosen to exert a regulative role with the original idea that they should refrain from aspirations of becoming an economic powerhouse (Mayer et al., 2016). Yet, as we will show in this book, SCCs nowadays also have ambitions to compete with other cities through the development of a dynamic regional economy.

Examining SCCs and their economies requires an interdisciplinary perspective that has been lacking in the literature to date. By contrast, the literature on capital cities is dominated by disciplinary inquiries. For example, a large group of scholars has examined issues regarding the urban planning and architecture of capital cities, particularly as they relate to the history, urban design, and planning of capital cities and how they relate to the representation of power (Clark & Lepetit, 1996; De Frantz, 2006; Hall, 2006; Hall, 2010; Sohn & Weber, 2000; Till, 2006). In this realm, monographs about the history or urban morphology of specific capital cities dominate. Another set of authors has examined capital cities as places that represent national identity, where a nation's memory and symbols are staged (Cochrane, 2006; De Frantz, 2006; Till, 2006). More recent literature in the field of urban studies focuses on social inequalities within capital cities (Tammaru, Marcińczak, van Ham, & Musterd, 2015) and also on the relocation of capital cities (Rossman, 2017). In the aforementioned studies, however, each capital is treated as a unique case and generalizations are almost impossible. Furthermore, this kind of research is characterized by fragmented inquiries from specific disciplinary perspectives, and a more comprehensive or even comparative interdisciplinary perspective of the political economy of capital cities is largely absent.

Studies in economic geography and political science may offer a more useful way of systematically examining the political economy of capital cities. The urban studies/economic geography literature, for example, conceptualizes capital cities as "information cities" (Castells, 1989), "national information brokers" (Abbott, 1999, 2005), or "transactional cities" (Gottmann, 1977). Capital cities that are conceptualized in that way are places where complex relationships between government, private-sector, and third-sector actors form a distinctive economic system, which is spatially manifested through their interactions, which, in turn, produce information and knowledge (Abbott, 1999; Feldman, 2001; Gerhard, 2007; Markusen, Hall, Campbell, & Deitrick, 1991). To examine these interactions in the capital city context, we utilize the RIS approach (Braczyk, Cooke, & Heidenreich, 1998; Doloreux & Parto, 2005; Tödtling & Trippl, 2005). The political science perspective examines the ways in which capital city actors resolve the tensions between local and national responsibilities. Moreover, this literature examines how capital cities are embedded in the multilevel governance institutions of their nation states (Harris, 1995; Rowat, 1968a, 1968b; Slack & Chattopadhyay, 2009; Wolman, Chadwick, & Karruz, 2006). In this book, the political science perspective makes use of neoinstitutional theory to explore how economic orientations and political institutions constrain or enable the formulation of local policies (Hall & Soskice, 2001; Hall & Taylor, 1996; Scharpf, 1997). We outline a locational policy framework to capture the wide variety of policies that cities and regions formulate to strengthen their economic competitiveness.

These two research strands combine to provide a political economy perspective, which will allow us to examine the modern capital city and highlight the complex interdependencies between public and private actors. To that extent, Campbell (2000) argues that

> though all cities experience the interaction – both cooperative and conflicting – of government and private interests, nowhere do these interests intersect with such power as in a capital: the government–market interactions are more complicated in a capital, and the national government has greater influence over the local economy, labor markets, and land markets. This creates a distinctive political economy of capital cities.
>
> (Campbell, 2000, p. 10)

Traditional capital city research in political science and public administration (such as Harris, 1995; Nagel et al., 2013; Slack & Chattopadhyay, 2009) for the most part follows the work of the Canadian political scientist Donald Rowat (1968; 1973). He compared the central–local relationship in 17 federal capitals and particularly emphasized the underlying conflict of capital cities: to serve both the interests of the nation as a whole and the interests of the local residents. This conflict was later coined the classical capital city conflict, the challenge of dual democracy, or simply the Rowat thesis (Harris, 1995; Nagel et al., 2013).

This traditional capital city research conceptualizes capital cities as objects of the nation state and does not tell us much about how their political economies function, what kind of economic interactions are prevalent in capital city regions, or what kind of policies are formulated by local actors. We adopt an actor-centered perspective on capital cities that attempts to answer the questions outlined in the foregoing. However, we do not postulate that capital cities are coherent actors that do not have to deal with differing economic orientations of their RIS or a variety of political interests in the policy formulation process. While our unit of analysis is capital cities, we examine the specific economic and political arrangements shaped by actors such as government agencies, firms, economic developers, and politicians at the local and regional levels to increase the capital city's competitiveness. The aim of such an actor-centered perspective is to go beyond classical capital city research by studying actors in capital cities that operate within the settings of their regional economy and the nation state, but are not constrained by these economic and political structures.

Why study SCCs? Some globalization scholars would argue that capital cities in general, but even more so these SCCs, have lost importance and that global or world cities (Salet, Thornley, & Kreukels, 2003; Sassen, 1991) are far more critical to the functioning of the global economy because they coordinate and control capital flow. However, capital cities still play an important role because global capital flow continues to be regulated within the context of nation states (Rodrik, 2011) and nation states are governed through institutions that, for the most part, are located in capital cities. In addition, the rise of transnational institutions such as the EU, WTO, etc. has led to the emergence of a new type of political city (e.g. Brussels, Strasbourg, Geneva), which indicates that the spatial concentration of public and private institutions and agencies may produce certain agglomeration advantages. In addition, the current economic crisis has shown that important decisions about rescuing banks or bailing out firms like large-scale automobile manufacturers were taken not in New York City, Zurich, or Detroit, but in Washington, D.C. or Bern. Finally, against the backdrop of the uncertain nature of today's political regimes and the current leanings toward parochial nationalism, we have to wonder what the future holds for capital cities.

Given the lack of comparative research and general theorizing about capital cities and in view of their continued importance going forward in the 21st century, we examine the factors responsible for the economic success of SCCs. As we show in this book, there is a need for a systematic, comparative analysis of the political economy of different SCCs, particularly in regard to their economic dynamics and positioning strategies. We are interested in explaining the political economy of SCCs for two reasons: First, we conceptualize capital cities as knowledge-based economies that function as RIS. The RIS concept allows us to analyze how the overall shift in the economy toward knowledge, information, and services may have created a new type of economy. It is not merely the presence of the public sector and political institutions that define the capital city economy; rather, it is the complex interplay between firms in political consulting, special interest lobbying, IT, and defense – all of which can be considered 'knowledge-intensive business services' (KIBS) – on the one hand, and national institutions and the political process that define a capital city economy in the modern era on the other. In addition, capital cities are often highly dependent on the nation states. Gordon notes that

> capital cities […] face in an exaggerated form the common urban problem of lacking autonomous control over the resources required to maintain their economic roles and satisfy the social needs of their citizens. Coping effectively with this situation demands of their leaders a governance strategy, which weaves together the management of both internal and external political relationships.
>
> (Gordon, 2003)

Thus, we conceptualize capital cities as metropolitan areas that are not isolated from the national urban system. Rather, capital cities position themselves within these urban systems. This is more relevant nowadays because SCCs can no longer rely on a comfortable dependence on the nation state for their development. These SCCs now face urban competition, just like any other metropolitan area. Therefore, their political leaders are active in repositioning the capital city in urban networks through the formulation of locational policies.

Compared to urban centers that are the primary economic motors of their nations, SCCs may not play an important role in international and national urban economic networks. Nevertheless, in recent years, they have specialized and their economies may function as RIS. As these economies have become more specialized, policymakers and politicians in these capital cities have started to proactively work toward positioning the city in national and urban networks. Thus, it may be that the traditional view of the capital city as the domesticated host city of the nation state, mired by a comfortable dependency of the very state it was hosting, no longer holds up.

Research questions and basic tenets of this book

This book is guided by three research questions, derived from our respective disciplines:

(a) Economic geography: How do public-procurement-driven innovation activities function as drivers for knowledge dynamics in capital city RIS?
(b) Political science: What kinds of locational policies are formulated in SCCs and why are these locational policies formulated?
(c) Overarching interdisciplinary question: How do SCCs respond economically and politically to their changing role within the historical transformation of the nation state and increasing trends toward a knowledge-based economy? Which mechanisms are at work in the mutual relationship between economy and politics? In what ways does the development of a specialized RIS influence the locational policies of an SCC? And vice versa: In what ways does the locational policy influence the economic dynamics of a SCC?

The book rests upon the following five basic tenets concerning the political economy of SCCs:

1   National governments increasingly rely on the private sector for the delivery of products and services. This process is referred to as public procurement and has the potential to create economic dynamics in the form of innovation. This was first evident in the tertiarization of the defense industry and the rise of defense-services complexes in the Washington, D.C. region (Markusen et al., 1991). This process is not confined to the United States and is also found to influence capital city economies in other nations such as Canada, the Netherlands, Switzerland, etc. Because of this process, national government agencies increasingly rely on external knowledge provided by private sector firms. As a result, interactions between the public and private sectors follow a unique spatial pattern and dynamics, which can be understood using the concept of RIS.
2   The RIS of capital cities are characterized by complex patterns of interaction between public demand and private supply: Public demand, on the one hand, is often associated with constraining procurement procedures, a culture of bureaucracy, arm's-length relationships, nonprofit incentives, and risk-averse government officials (Mergel and Desouza 2013; Roodhooft and Van den Abbeele, 2006). Private supply, in the form of IT government contractors, on the other hand, is usually associated with rapidly-changing technologies, collaborative strategic relationships, and risk-taking entrepreneurs (Trippl, Tödtling, & Lengauer, 2009). Such perspectives are, however, often overly stylized and do not incorporate the dynamics we observed in SCCs. Through public procurement, capital cities become crucial places where both sectors meet and firms interact with other firms and government agencies. Thus, capital city RIS can function as bridges between the public and private sectors.
3   Regional policymakers in capital cities can leverage the presence of federal agencies for knowledge generation and innovation by stimulating systemic knowledge flows between public and private actors. Moreover, capital city economies can function as seedbeds for start-ups and spin-offs, helping to advance the region's entrepreneurial dynamics.
4   Capital cities are not objects of their nation states, that is, they are not there merely to serve the nation state, for example by hosting legislative and executive functions, but they can also develop their own economic development strategies and not be dependent on the nation state. Capital cities make strategic use of their capital city function because this function represents a unique selling proposition in the national urban system. A variety of locational policies build on the capital city function. Using this approach, the capital city function can be used to strengthen the economic competitiveness of capital cities.
5   Capital cities have the advantage of being able to formulate two-dimensional positioning strategies in their efforts to withstand and perform in interurban competition. On the one hand, capital cities may position themselves

as the capital city of a nation, and, on the other hand, capital cities can position themselves as business centers that feature a very specialized political economy. As regards the latter positioning strategy, capital cities can leverage their highly-regulated sectors and the presence of national governmental organizations. This two-dimensional positioning strategy thus targets multiple types of actors, ranging from KIBS firms, international investors, tourists, and residents, to higher-tier governmental units.

Methodology

To examine the political economy of SCCs, we conducted a comparative study of the RIS and locational policies of Bern, Ottawa, The Hague, and Washington, D.C. Our study built on an interdisciplinary approach that draws on theories and methodologies in economic geography and political science. The four cities were chosen because they represent secondary capitals in the context of democratic cultures (Europe, North America) and are located within the context of the Organisation for Economic Co-operation and Development (OECD). There are ten SCCs in the 34

Table 1.1 Cases based on the population of SCCs in OECD countries

Country	Capital city	GDP metropolitan region (US$) % of national GDP	Primary city	GDP metropolitan region (US$) % of national GDP
Australia	Canberra	n/a	Sydney	199,970 20.10%
Canada	Ottawa	56,323 3.94%	Toronto	271,449 18.99%
Germany	Berlin	165,376 4.92%	Munich	184,701 5.49%
Israel	Jerusalem	n/a	Tel Aviv	n/a
Italy	Rome	189,919 9.44%	Milan	234,523 11.65%
The Netherlands	The Hague	39,517 5.31%	Amsterdam	121,289 16.31%
New Zealand	Wellington	15,423 13.51%	Auckland	39,792 34.87%
Switzerland	Bern	n/a	Zurich	77,011 18.63%
Turkey	Ankara	74,936 8.52%	Istanbul	243,277 27.65%
United States	Washington, D.C.	442,758 2.86%	New York City	1,215,233 7.86%

Sources: OECD GDP metropolitan areas for Australia, Canada, Germany, Italy, the Netherlands, Switzerland, and the United States. Data from 2012 in million US$. Australia and Switzerland – data for only the primary city available. OECD GDP regional database TL3 regions for New Zealand and Turkey. Data from 2012 in million US$. Turkey data from 2008. Israel – no available data.

OECD countries (see Table 1). Bern, Ottawa, The Hague, and Washington, D.C. are four prime examples of economically-inferior capital cities. In all four cases, primary cities such as Zurich, Toronto, Amsterdam, and New York City overshadow the SCCs in terms of their share of national gross domestic product (GDP).

From an economic geography perspective, we explored how the four capital cities function as RIS driven by public-procurement activities that engage the public and private sectors. RIS encompass knowledge dynamics among and between various groups of actors, such as government, industry, and research institutions. The political science perspective examined the locational policies that are formulated in these four capital cities. Based on this, we developed a locational policies framework that allows us to capture the variety of policies formulated by cities and regions to strengthen their economic competitiveness. The locational policies framework incorporates various bodies of literature from economic geography, political science, and urban studies.

Data for this book were collected using a variety of methods and from a diverse set of sources (see also the Appendix). To facilitate meaningful comparative insights, the empirical part of the study was based on a nine-month field study in The Hague, Ottawa, and Washington, D.C. in addition to several months of fieldwork in the authors' hometown of Bern. During this time, the researchers were embedded as guests in local academic institutions (Leiden University, Campus, The Hague from September to November 2014, Virginia Tech's National Capital Region campus in Arlington County from December 2014 to February 2015, the University of Ottawa's Centre on Governance from March to May 2015). The close interactions with experts, who were familiar not only with the capital city but also with our respective disciplinary perspectives, allowed for deep immersion in the field and a balanced interpretation of the data.

Table 1.2 Overview of interviews conducted

Category	Bern	The Hague	Ottawa	Washington, D.C.
KIBS firms in federal procurement	22	10	20	10
Regional development organizations	3	3	5	5
University institutes	2	4	5	8
Sector associations	0	2	2	4
Federal procurement officials	1	2	2	2
Local or regional policymakers	4	7	1	6
Higher-tier governmental officials	2	3	5	1
Local or regional private interest groups	2	2	3	5
Financial organizations	1	1	0	3
Major employing firms other than KIBS firms	4	2	2	0
Law firms	0	1	1	1
Others	2	2	3	3
Totals	43	39	49	48

Source: Authors' analysis.

A total of 179 semistructured, face-to-face expert interviews provide the main data source for this study. Interview partners included KIBS firms involved in public procurement, public-procurement officers, representatives from national associations, local and regional politicians and policymakers, public officials from higher-tier government organizations, representatives from local or regional private interest groups, economic developers, and experts from local higher education institutions.

Synopsis of chapters

Given that this book has an interdisciplinary focus, we intend to stimulate research in the fields of geography, political science, and urban studies. Scholars will find the book interesting because the political economy perspective combines a set of theories that have not hitherto been integrated. RIS concepts, for example, do not integrate a locational policy perspective. Similarly, to date there has not been any locational policy framework that would allow for comparative studies of cities or regions. The locational policy framework outlined in this book facilitates such comparison and also allows the RIS concept and locational policies to be interlinked through innovation policies.

Policymakers and planning practitioners will find the insights instructive because we formulate specific recommendations on how best to foster RIS and show how firms, policymakers at the city level and decision-makers at the national level can engage with the capital city economy.

In Chapter 2, we present our theoretical framework linking the economic and innovation dynamics with the ways in which SCCs attempt to develop and position themselves through the formulation of locational policies. We put forward an interdisciplinary perspective that is informed by theories of economic geography and political science because processes of economic development and political positioning are interrelated and need to be examined together. By linking two different theoretical strands – the RIS approach and the concept of locational policies – this chapter presents a framework for the subsequent chapters and the study of economic and political dynamics in SCCs.

Chapter 3 presents the four case study regions. Despite some obvious differences in size, we focus on the specific political environment characterized by the presence of all state levels and interactions of public and private actors seeking spatial proximity to national government organizations. In a capital city, politics has to serve the interests of the nation as a whole, as well as its local residents. It is thus interesting to examine what kinds of governing arrangements have been created to balance these interests and how those arrangements affect policy formulation in capital cities. Furthermore, we show that the four capital cities have unique preconditions for innovation dynamics. The economic profile of the four cases is deeply rooted in their function as capital cities. We identify distinguishing features of the case studies by comparing the knowledge-based economy of the four SCCs with the three largest cities in their respective countries.

Chapter 4 presents an analysis of the distinctive knowledge dynamics of SCCs. As national governments increasingly outsource services, private sector firms become more involved in governmental tasks, such that one of the main drivers of knowledge dynamics in SCCs is the public-procurement process. We highlight the ways in which public procurement shapes knowledge interactions between public and private actors by focusing on KIBS firms. Moreover, we outline how regional and national organizations leverage the presence of government agencies for innovation by bringing together public and private actors.

In Chapter 5, we focus on the locational policies formulated in the four cities under scrutiny. For each of the four categories of locational policies – innovation policies, attracting money, coordination, asking for money – we discuss the locational policies empirically observed. Building on this systematic description, we postulate three broad lines of inquiry to explain the formulation of locational policies, namely, institutional factors, the characteristics and development of the RIS, and local and regional political factors. Overall, we show that SCCs have started to leverage both their capital city status as well as their RIS through the formulation of locational polices.

The conclusion takes a somewhat different perspective. Here, we draw on the case study findings and develop a set of recommendations for firms, local policymakers, and national decision-makers. The recommendations are intentionally practice-oriented because we think that actors in SCCs need to be aware of their potential for leverage. However, it should be noted that our recommendations are not meant to be a one-size-fits-all recipe for all capital cities. No single factor is responsible for the economic fate of an SCC – quite the contrary: As our case studies illustrate, various actors at different levels are developing strategies that depend on the unique context of the capital city. Our recommendations thus need to be adjusted to the specific SCC context in each case. However, our conclusions are intended to provide reasonable pointers as to how to ensure that SCCs prosper once this adaptation has been completed.

Note

1 The Constitution of the Netherlands states that Amsterdam is the capital city. However, all three branches of the Dutch state, as well as the Royal Family, are located in The Hague. This anomaly can be explained by the French occupation of the Netherlands. Napoleon Bonaparte preferred to settle in Amsterdam, and thus made it the permanent capital. Following Napoleon's withdrawal in 1813, the Dutch decision-makers returned the seat of government to The Hague, but left the capital city status to Amsterdam, as it was not considered to be very important (Meijers et al. 2014, 93) and/or it was a compromise because it "met both the feelings of self-esteem of the burghers of Amsterdam and the fears of other provinces of a renewed dominance by Holland and Amsterdam in particular" (Donner 2008, p.201).

References

Abbott, C. (1999). *Political Terrain: Washington, D.C., from Tidewater Town to Global Metropolis*. Chapel Hill: The University of North Carolina Press.

Abbott, C. (2005). Washington and Berlin: National Capitals in a Networked World. In A. W. Daum & C. Mauch (Eds.), *Berlin – Washington, 1800–2000: Capital Cities, Cultural Representation, and National Identities*. New York: Cambridge University Press.

Braczyk, H.-J., Cooke, P., & Heidenreich, M. (1998). *Regional Innovation Systems: The Role of Governance in a Globalized World*. London: UCL Press.

Campbell, S. (2000). *The Changing Role and Identity of Capital Cities in the Global Era. Annual Meeting of the Association of American Geographers*. Pittsburgh, PA.

Castells, M. (1989). *The Informational City: Information Technology, Economic Restructuring, and the Urban-regional Process*. Oxford: Blackwell Publishers.

Clark, P., & Lepetit, B. (1996). *Capital Cities and Their Hinterlands in Early Modern Europe*. Aldershot: Scolar Press.

Cochrane, A. (2006). Making up meanings in a capital city power, memory and monuments in Berlin. *European Urban and Regional Studies, 13*(1), 5–24.

De Frantz, M. (2006). KulturPolitik im Wandel: Hauptstadtsymbolik in Wien und Berlin. *Österreichische Zeitschrift für Politikwissenschaft, 3*, 237–253.

Doloreux, D., & Parto, S. (2005). Regional innovation systems: Current discourse and unresolved issues. *Technology in Society, 27*(2), 133–153.

Donner, P. H. (2008). Residence or Capital? In D. Vriesendorp, F. Nelissen, and M Wladimiroff (Eds.), *The Hague Legal Capital? Liber in Honorem W.J. Deetman* (pp.197–206). The Hague: Hague Academic Press.

Feldman, M. (2001). The entrepreneurial event revisited: Firm formation in a regional context. *Industrial and Corporate Change, 10*(4), 861–891.

Florida, R., Gulden, T., & Mellander, C. (2008). The rise of the mega-region. *Cambridge Journal of Regions, Economy and Society, 1*(3), 459–476.

Gerhard, U. (2007). *Global City Washington, D.C.: Eine Politische Stadtgeographie*. Bielefeld: transcript Verlag.

Gordon, D. (2006). *Planning Twentieth Century Capital Cities*. London, New York: Routledge.

Gordon, I. (2003). Capital needs, capital growth and global city rhetoric in Mayor Livingstone's London plan. Paper presented at the Association of American Geographers Annual Meeting, New Orleans.

Gottmann, J. (1977). The role of capital cities. *Ekistics: The Problem and Science of Human Settlements, 44*(264), 240–243.

Gottmann, J., & Harper, R. (1990). *Since Megalopolis: The Urban Writings of Jean Gottmann*. Baltimore, Maryland and London: The Johns Hopkins University Press.

Hall, P. A., & Soskice, D. W. D. (2001). *Varieties of Capitalism: The Institutional Foundations of Comparative Advantage*. Oxford: Oxford University Press.

Hall, P. A., & Taylor, R. C. R. (1996). Political science and the three new institutionalisms. *Political Studies, 44*(5), 936–957.

Hall, P. G. (2006). Seven types of capital city. In G. D. L. A. (Ed.), *Planning Twentieth Century Capital Cities* (pp. 8–14). New York: Routledge.

Hall, P. G., & Pain, K. (2006). *The Polycentric Metropolis: Learning from Mega-city Regions in Europe*. New York: Routledge.

Hall, T. (2010). *Planning Europe's Capital Cities: Aspects of Nineteenth Century Urban Development*. New York: Routledge.

Harris, C. W. (1995). *Congress and the Governance of the Nation's Capital: The Conflict of Federal and Local Interests*. Washington, D.C.: Georgetown University Press.

Markusen, A., Hall, P., Campbell, S., & Deitrick, S. (1991). *The Rise of the Gunbelt: The Military Remapping of Industrial America*. New York: Oxford University Press.

Mayer, H., Sager, F., Kaufmann, D., & Warland, M. (2016). Capital city dynamics: Linking regional innovation systems, locational policies and policy regimes. *Cities, 50*, 206–215.

Mergel, I., & Desouza, K. (2013). Implementing open innovation in the public sector: The case of challenge.gov. *Public Administration Review*, *73*(6), 882–890. https://doi.org/10.1111/puar.12141.Open

Nagel, K.-J., Andrew, C., Gilliland, A., Obydenkova, A., Van Wynsberghe, C., & Zimmermann, H. (2013). *The Problem of the Capital City: New Research on Federal Capitals and Their Territory*. Barcelona: Generaltat de Catalunya, Institut d'Estudis Autonomics.

Rodrik, D. (2011). *The Globalization Paradox: Democracy and the Future of the World Economy*. New York and London: W.W. Norton.

Roodhooft, F., & Van den Abbeele, A. (2006). Public procurement of consulting services. *International Journal of Public Sector Management*, *19*(5), 490–512. https://doi.org/10.1108/09513550610677799

Rossman, V. (2017). *Capital Cities: Varieties and Patterns of Development and Relocation*. New York: Routledge.

Rowat, D. (1968a). *The Government of Federal Capitals*. Toronto: Univeristy of Toronto Press.

Rowat, D. (1968b). The problems of governing federal capitals. *Canadian Journal of Political Science*, *1*(3), 345–356.

Rowat, D. (1973). *The Government of Federal Capitals*. Toronto: University of Toronto Press.

Salet, W., Thornley, A., & Kreukels, A. (2003). *Metropolitan Governance and Spatial Planning: Comparative Case Studies of European City-regions*. New York: Taylor & Francis.

Sassen, S. (1991). *The Global City: New York, London, Tokyo*. Princeton: Princeton University Press.

Scharpf, F. (1997). *Games Real Actors Play: Actor-centered Institutionalism in Policy Research*. Boulder, Colorado: Westview Press.

Scott, A. (2001). *Global City-Regions: Trends, Theory, Policy*. Oxford: Oxford University Press.

Slack, E., & Chattopadhyay, R. (2009). *Finance and Governance of Capital Cities in Federal Systems*. Montreal, Quebec and Kingston, Ontario: McGill-Queen's University Press.

Sohn, A., & Weber, H. (2000). *Hauptstädte und Global Cities an der Schwelle zum 21. Jahrhundert*. Bochum: Winkler.

Spate, O. H. K. (1942). Factors in the development of capital cities. *Geographical Review*, *32*(4), 622–631.

Tammaru, T., Marcińczak, S., van Ham, M., & Musterd, S. (2015). *Socio-economic Segregation in European Capital Cities: East Meets West*. New York: Routledge.

Till, K. (2006). *The New Berlin: Memory, Politics, Place*. Minneapolis: University of Minnesota Press.

Tödtling, F., & Trippl, M. (2005). One size fits all?: Towards a differentiated regional innovation policy approach. *Research Policy*, *34*(8), 1203–1219.

Trippl, M., Tödtling, F., & Lengauer, L. (2009). Knowledge sourcing beyond buzz and pipelines: Evidence from the Vienna software sector. *Economic Geography*, *85*(4), 443–462.

Wolman, H., Chadwick, J., & Karruz, A. (2006). *Capital Cities and Their National Governments: Washington, D.C. in Comparative Perspective*. George Washington University, Institute of Public Policy.

Zimmermann, H. (2010). Do different types of capital cities make a difference for economic dynamism? *Environment and Planning C*, *28*, 761–767.

2 Framework for analyzing secondary capital cities

To be able to comprehensively analyze the economy of secondary capital cities (SCCs), an interdisciplinary perspective is required. In the following, we outline an economic geography and a political science approach to studying SCCs. We first review the concept of a regional innovation system (RIS) and adapt it to the context of capital cities. Specifically, we highlight the role of public procurement and its influence on innovation dynamics in SCCs. We then turn to locational policies and show how inward- and outward-oriented policies target different spatial scales and how locational policy strategies address different target groups, such as firms and political entities, at various levels. In the final section of this chapter, we link the two approaches and argue for a combined perspective.

Regional innovation systems in capital cities

We conceptualize capital city economies as RIS and recognize that the concept has not been utilized to any great degree in this context (Asheim, Smith, & Oughton, 2011; Cooke, 2001; Doloreux & Parto, 2005). Most studies of RIS have examined regions where private-sector industry clusters are located (e.g. the automobile cluster in Stuttgart, high-technology industry in Silicon Valley). A focus on RIS where public-sector activities dominate is missing. Yet thinking about capital city economies from a territorial innovation perspective is particularly insightful when we take growing trends toward outsourcing and tertiarization of public-sector activities into account (Cowell & Mayer, 2014; Feldman, 2001; Markusen, Hall, Campbell, & Deitrick, 1991). Facing immense pressures to cut expenditure, governments have turned to private firms in the course of their public-procurement efforts. As a result, firms – particularly those that provide knowledge-intensive services – have become more involved with government agencies.

According to Doloreux and Parto (2005), an RIS is "typically understood to be a set of interacting private and public interests, formal institutions, and other organizations that function according to organizational and institutional arrangements and relationships conducive to the generation, use, and dissemination of knowledge" (p. 134). An RIS consists of two subsystems that are embedded in a regional socioeconomic and cultural setting (Tödtling & Trippl, 2005). The first subsystem, the so-called *knowledge application and exploitation subsystem*, encompasses companies, their customers and suppliers as well as their competitors and collaborators. The second subsystem consists of the *knowledge generation and diffusion subsystem*, which includes public research organizations like universities and research institutes, intermediary organizations such as technology transfer offices, as well as workforce and educational organizations.

The application of the RIS concept to the context of capital cities requires some adjustments: National government organizations, such as ministries, departments and agencies, have a strong presence in the *knowledge application and exploitation subsystem* of a capital city regional innovation system (CC-RIS). Whereas in a private sector-oriented RIS, demand comes from a specialized industry and various interactions between customers, suppliers, and competitors are constituted by interfirm relationships, in a capital city RIS, the biggest demand for goods and services is usually from the national government. Markusen (1996), for example, argues that national government organizations operate as anchors for private sector firms, and, as a result, regions that are home to large military installations, public-sector institutions like universities, or – as we describe in this book for SCCs – government agencies function as state-anchored industrial districts. In these districts, the dominance of the national government as the main buyer of goods and services creates a distinctive RIS, in which customers, suppliers, and collaborators interact. In such a system, businesses adapt to the specific needs of public-sector clients, which differ fundamentally from those of private sector clients. Firms that contract with government agencies tend to locate in close proximity to government organizations in order to take advantage of the specific capital city agglomeration economies (Feldman, Francis, & Bercovitz, 2005). While firms that produce standardized goods and services have less incentive to be located in the capital city, knowledge-intensive business service (KIBS) firms in particular may benefit from spatial proximity to national government clients. KIBSs are defined as "services that involve economic activities which are intended to result in the creation, accumulation or dissemination of knowledge" (Miles, 2005). Muller and Doloreux (2009) add that KIBS firms "are mainly concerned with providing knowledge-intensive inputs to the business processes of organizations, including private and public sector clients" (p. 65). Consequently, the private sector in a capital city is composed largely of KIBS firms (Aslesen & Jakobsen, 2007; Wood, 2006), and, as result, national government agencies that demand specialized services from KIBS firms dominate the knowledge application subsystem in a CC-RIS.

The *knowledge generation subsystem* in a capital city consists of national research laboratories, but also universities. For example, Ottawa has 44 federal research laboratories focusing on government-related topics such as military, security, telecom, etc. In addition to national research laboratories, the capital city is also home to numerous other research-oriented organizations, such as think tanks, nonprofits and nongovernmental organizations, that provide strategic knowledge to public- and private-sector actors. The original RIS concept views technology-mediating organizations as important diffusers of knowledge (Tödtling & Trippl, 2005). When we think about such mediating organizations in

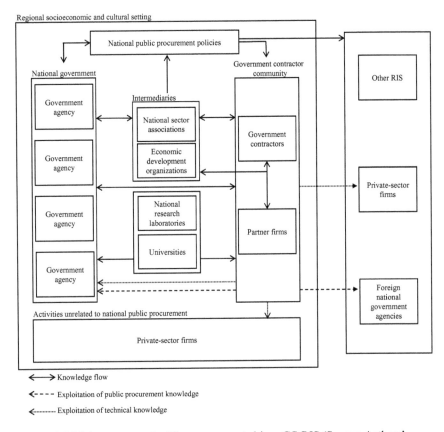

Figure 2.1 Main structure of public-procurement-driven CC-RIS (Source: Authors' analysis, inspired by Tödtling & Trippl (2005)).

the capital city context, we find them in associations focused on nationally important industry sectors, for instance. Examples include so-called information and communication technology councils, which engage in public relations to advocate nationally on behalf of their member firms. As frequent hosts of business network events in the capital city, they also facilitate informal knowledge linkages within the capital city economy.

The two subsystems are embedded in a specific socioeconomic and cultural regional context (see Figure 2.1). CC-RIS are driven by national public-procurement policies. They also do not exist in a vacuum as they are connected not only to other RIS, but also to foreign national governments.

Actors and linkages

As outlined above, a CC-RIS encompasses a unique set of actors (Gordon, 2013). From a regional economic perspective, firms that do business with government agencies are at the center of this RIS. These government contractors mediate knowledge between other government contractors and government clients and serve them as either partners or competitors. A common practice in public procurement – particularly for knowledge-intensive services – is teamwork, whereby a prime contractor collaborates closely with one or more subcontractors and solutions are developed through a collaborative team effort. Teams are organized around a particular issue and include individuals and firms with different capabilities and skills. As a result, public-procurement projects can provide a stimulating environment for collective learning processes, something that economic geographers have observed for other industries such as the software industry (Ibert, 2004). The selection of partner firms is therefore critical to a government contractor's business success (Sedita & Apa, 2015).

Another set of actors in a CC-RIS are associations that serve as mediators between the public and the private sector and therefore have the potential to mediate between government contractors and national government agencies. Capital cities are naturally the locations for such mediating organizations, and one can find a host of associations that represent national interests, such as chambers of commerce, labor unions, employers' associations, and industry associations (Gerhard, 2007). The latter not only focus on a national perspective, but also provide intermediary functions relevant to the context of public procurement and regional innovation. National industry associations, for example, stimulate regional linkages through conferences, meetings, exhibitions, and social gatherings (Smedlund, 2006). In bringing together actors that are relevant to public procurement efforts, these associations help exploit the resources that exist in a capital city in order to spur innovation activities (Tura & Harmaakorpi, 2005). The need to mediate on behalf of regional economic development and innovation results from the particular ways in which procurement is organized, as the aforementioned teamwork in projects intensifies the need for coordination among potential partner firms (Sedita & Apa, 2015). When searching for partner firms, government contractors face substantial transaction costs due to information asymmetries. Information asymmetries can relate, for example, to how partner firms balance their own interests and their commitment to the public procurement project over the course of time (Das & Teng, 1998). In the case of information technology (IT) services that are provided by KIBS firms, for instance, information asymmetries are particularly high, as these firms provide services that cannot fully be evaluated a priori (Aarikka-Stenroos & Jaakkola, 2012). National industry associations help government contractors reduce uncertainties by stimulating the formation of trusted relationships among their member firms (Glückler & Armbruster, 2003; Maennig & Ölschläger, 2011).

The third set of actors in a CC-RIS are local and regional economic development organizations. They have the potential to facilitate knowledge dynamics between national government agencies and government contractors. They support the latter by providing the "soft infrastructure of innovation" (Cooke, 2001, p. 946). They do so by initiating linkages between CC-RIS actors, fostering knowledge circulation, and shaping regional development strategies (Lagendijk & Cornford, 2000). Activities that stimulate and harness knowledge dynamics between government contractors and government agencies can create conflicts between regional and national interests (Howells, 2005). Development organizations act on behalf of regional interests, whereas government agencies act on behalf of national interests. The extent to which regional knowledge dynamics create benefits for the country as a whole influences the degree to which national government agencies are willing to engage in regional knowledge dynamics.

A fourth set of actors in CC-RIS are research organizations that support the innovation activities of government agencies and government contractors (Caniëls & van den Bosch, 2011). National-level research laboratories, think tanks, and universities, for example, generate and pool knowledge that is relevant to the context of public procurement. This includes technical or scientific knowledge, as well as know-how about developments in the marketplace (Broekel & Boschma, 2011). In the context of capital cities, iterative interactions facilitate spillovers between knowledge organizations and government contractors rather than a more linear technology transfer. In a capital city RIS, traditional boundaries blur and

> each actor should take the role of another, for example, higher education institutions (HEIs) play a role as source of firm formation, and industry plays a role as developer of training and research, while government supports these developments by adapting the regulatory system.
>
> (Caniëls & van den Bosch, 2011, p. 274)

Federal procurement as a driver of knowledge dynamics

Knowledge interactions within and between the two subsystems typically characterize a well-functioning RIS (Tödtling & Trippl, 2005). In the case of capital cities, the public-sector needs to influence these knowledge dynamics. Government agencies require specialized products and services, and they procure these from the private sector – some of these dynamics have been illustrated before and extend beyond IT and into development and foreign aid (Roberts, 2014). This public-procurement process is one of the main drivers of knowledge interactions in a CC-RIS. Capital city economies can benefit from a specific type of procurement, which is typically referred to as public procurement for innovation (PPI). PPI occurs when federal government agencies order goods or services, some of which may not yet exist or have not yet been developed (Edquist & Hommen, 2000, p. 5). PPI is by no means limited to capital city economies, as the public sector at all levels (local, state) and of all types (e.g. universities, military, etc.) engages in public procurement and can therefore stimulate innovation dynamics. Given that national government agencies and firms co-locate and their interactions can produce knowledge spillovers that are spatially sensitive, we consider PPI as an important driver for the knowledge dynamics within a CC-RIS.

The ways in which PPI contributes to the economic dynamics of a CC-RIS are twofold: First, PPI provides opportunities for innovation, entrepreneurship, and knowledge interaction. Linking PPI with knowledge-intensive entrepreneurship, Edquist, Zabala, and Timmermans (2012) emphasize that government agencies play an important role because they provide market and technical opportunities.

Market opportunities arise from public demand for new products and services. On the supply side, this requires that firms not only tap their internal research and development functions, but also take advantage of external knowledge. Doloreux (2002, p. 249) notes that "the ability to innovate is thought to be linked to the extent to which an actor learns through diffusing knowledge." Thus, the fulfillment of public procurement requires firms to become involved in interorganizational innovation processes, a key function of an RIS. PPI in this sense can function as a very specific driver of a CC-RIS, and these processes need to be considered when examining capital city economies. Second, PPI reduces risk in the innovation process (Rolfstam, 2008; Uyarra & Flanagan, 2010). As pointed out by Storper and Scott (1995), risk leads to a delay in transforming technology development into production, because economic actors tend to be risk-adverse. National government agencies help bridge this gap by taking the risk of being the first users – a role that is usually associated with high transaction costs since the product or service is not yet optimized (Edler & Georghiou, 2007). Moreover, national government organizations reduce risk by demanding a critical mass of the products or services, and, as a result, suppliers can take advantage of economies of scale (Edler et al., 2005). The strength of the PPI concept lies in focusing on demand and requirements as a crucial source of innovation. The empirical and theoretical significance of PPI has been recognized (Edquist & Zabala-Iturriagagoitia, 2012; Henkel & Hippel, 2005; Rolfstam, 2005), yet the approach has hitherto been largely ignored by innovation policy (Edler & Georghiou, 2007). Moreover, the RIS literature does not consider the ways in which public procurement influences innovation dynamics.

PPI directs our attention to public-sector needs and how those can influence innovation and knowledge dynamics. To understand public procurement in the CC-RIS, we also need to understand the ways in which procurement policies influence knowledge dynamics in the regional context. While being the driver for knowledge dynamics at the regional level, public procurement is regulated at the national level. These national-level procurement policies change the regulatory framework and also shape the behavior of government officials, thereby creating the conditions in which interactive learning takes place in CC-RIS (Gertler, 2002). This can happen in two ways: Public-procurement policies encourage either competition or cooperation (Roodhooft & Van den Abbeele, 2006). In competition-inspired policies, detailed requirements and specifications in requests for proposals lead to very similar proposals. Therefore, government contractors compete mainly on price as opposed to innovation. Stringent competition is also achieved through as few interactions as possible between government contractors and national government agencies in order not to favor individual government contractors. In cooperation-inspired policies, government agencies and government contractors develop a mutual understanding about the agency's need (Bovaird, 2006). In PPI studies, cooperation is seen as a necessary precondition for the development of innovation (Edquist, Vonortas, Zabala-Iturriagagoitia, & Edler, 2015). Obviously, there is tension between both goals since intensive interactions and trusting partnerships are favorable for innovation but provide a competitive advantage for the government contractors involved.

Innovation policies in federal procurement aim to widen the regular public-procurement process toward cooperation and alternative solutions (Edquist & Zabala-Iturriagagoitia, 2012). The regular procurement process typically follows the following five stages:

1   Federal agency defines technical requirements in detail.
2   Federal agency publishes request for proposals online.
3   Proposals are selected based on predefined criteria (with a strong focus on price and references).
4   A contract is awarded based on the proposal of the government contractor.
5   Development of the product or service.

While this process has been developed in the context of standardized products and services, it is not appropriate, for example, for complex IT government systems (Burnett, 2009). Originating from this regular process, there are many policies that focus on transforming this process into a more interactive, innovation-oriented one. Through the implementation of additional steps in the early phases, public demand and private supply are better coordinated. Moreover, public demand can be combined with other innovation policies (Edler & Georghiou, 2007). For example, a national government agency provides R & D funding to a government contractor and holds out the prospect of buying the result; this is known as precommercial procurement. It is also important to avoid over-detailed technical requirements as they constrain the possibilities for alternative solutions. Instead, outcome-based specifications enable the introduction of innovations (Timmermans & Zabala-Iturriagagoitia, 2013). Moreover, policies address the behavior of government officials since there are incentives for government officials to behave in ways that hamper innovation (Boyne, 2002). Too close relationships between government officials and government contractors may cause the unsuccessful contractors to file a bid protest, whereas arm's length relationships do not create any problems. This creates an incentive for government officials to behave in a rejecting and risk-averse manner.

Another set of policies aims to increase the participation of small and medium-sized enterprises (SMEs) in federal procurement. Strong participation of SMEs in federal procurement increases the number and variety of proposals and results in the development of more innovative solutions (Uyarra & Flanagan, 2010). Although SMEs are also often seen as drivers of disruptive technological changes (Acs, 2009), they face many barriers in public procurement, including the volume of contracts, the need to have a track record, and the costs of preparing proposals (Loader, 2013). Thus, any policy that aims to increase the participation of SMEs in procurement can be categorized as an innovation policy.

Spatial proximity and knowledge generation

Many relevant actors in public procurement are spatially concentrated in the capital city. As a result, public procurement can create regional knowledge dynamics.

Most importantly, government contractors benefit from spatial proximity to government agencies on the demand side. The development of government IT systems, for example, is a complex knowledge-intensive process that often results in the development of more or less intangible technologies such as, for example, software (Miles, 2012). For the development of such systems, government contractors need to mobilize and combine codified and tacit knowledge that is embodied in both the contractor and the client (Bettencourt, Ostrom, Brown, & Roundtree, 2002; Landry, Amara, & Doloreux, 2012). Spatial proximity facilitates the mobilization of tacit knowledge through trusted relationships derived from repeated face-to-face interactions (Jones, 2007). Moreover, face-to-face interactions enable government contractors to learn about the government client's preferences and expectations.

Aside from being close to government clients, government contractors benefit from spatial proximity to other CC-RIS actors (Landry et al., 2012). When a CC-RIS hosts many relevant public-procurement actors, it can provide opportunities for information and knowledge sharing. Spatial proximity facilitates the flow of information through frequent face-to-face encounters, both intended and unintended. In this context, the idea of local buzz (Bathelt, Malmberg, & Maskell, 2004) is well incorporated in the RIS approach (Doloreux & Parto, 2005; Trippl & Tödtling, 2011). Local buzz refers to regional circulation of "messages, information, news, rumours, gossip, and trade folklore" that actors automatically receive simply from being there (Bathelt & Gräf, 2008, p. 1947). In a well-functioning CC-RIS, local buzz happens when there is a constant information flow about procurement opportunities and developments.

It is crucial for government contractors to transform such information flows into procurement knowledge. Procurement knowledge refers to the various competencies to position a firm in the government marketplace. It requires absorptive capacity to tap into local information flows and filter economically-useful information (Sternberg 2007; Trippl, Tödtling, & Lengauer, 2009). Government contractors need to integrate various items of information and knowledge. This includes information about the unique regulatory procurement context and specific procedures such as procurement vehicles (Thai, 2001). In addition, knowledge about how procurement regulations unfold and shape procurement practices is necessary (Thai, 2009). Furthermore, client-specific information such as preferences, budgets, schedules, and procurement plans aid understanding of public-sector needs (Aarikka-Stenroos & Jaakkola, 2012). Finally, procurement knowledge includes project management competencies that are applicable in the specific context of national public procurement, which, in turn, is often associated with risk-averse clients, a culture of bureaucracy, and specific fiscal year-driven investment cycles (Boyne, 2002). In public procurement, the need to constantly gain and process procurement knowledge derives from the size of the contracts rather than the high dynamics of the market.

Innovation develops when procurement knowledge combines with technical knowledge (Sammarra & Biggiero, 2008). Tödtling and Grillitsch (2014) point out that most innovation studies provide a limited perspective on knowledge networks as they focus only on the generation and transfer of technical knowledge. Knowledge sources used by government contractors to acquire procurement knowledge differ in terms of geographical distribution from those that are used to acquire technical knowledge (Alberti & Pizzurno, 2015). Exchange of procurement knowledge, on the one hand, is facilitated through spatial proximity because of constant information updates attributable to the local buzz effect. The capital city context is important here. Technical knowledge, on the other hand, is exchanged with innovation partners who are located at greater geographical distances (Tödtling & Grillitsch, 2014) and not necessarily in the capital city.

Nevertheless, it is important to note that public procurement implies distinct mechanisms that decrease the importance of spatial proximity in the supply–demand relationship (Thai, 2009). First, spatial proximity does not play a role in reducing uncertainty about the quality of the outcome in public procurement. National government agencies select government contractors based on predefined criteria (Bovis, 2012). This represents a rationalized selection process that agencies need to be able to explain to unsuccessful bidders. A lack of transparency can result in litigation. In contrast, private market actors can try to reduce transaction costs through partner selections that are partially based on instinct, gut feelings, and trust (Scarso & Bolisani, 2012). In this case, face-to-face interactions constitute an important mechanism in convincing other parties (Maskell, Bathelt, & Malmberg, 2004). Second, national governments in the OECD context are required to publicize business opportunities. Every government contractor has open access to such information. In contrast, private market actors often communicate business opportunities in networks, and those networks are governed by trust (Glückler & Armbruster, 2003).

Development of a capital city regional innovation system

Thus far, we have focused on a well-functioning capital city regional innovation system (CC-RIS), in which frequent interactions between government agencies, government contractors, mediating organizations, etc. ideally yield knowledge dynamics and innovation. Public procurement can function as the driver of innovation dynamics in such a system. To function well, the CC-RIS ideally comprises a large network of actors that specifically work toward increasing knowledge dynamics and innovation. This requires a critical mass of organizations and individuals that are well connected. It also requires a healthy balance between the region's specialization in the public sector and a sufficient presence of the private sector that helps the region to diversify. However, given that capital city economies differ in terms of their development and actor composition, as well as in terms of system failures that they may exhibit in their RIS, we need to consider three types of such deficiencies: 1) organizational thinness, 2) fragmentation, and 3) lock-in (Tödtling & Trippl, 2005).

RIS can suffer from being organizationally thin, which means that they do not have a sufficient number of, or critical mass of, organizations that work toward improving innovation dynamics and economic development. Such a lack of relevant actors in the two subsystems of an RIS implies that the few that exist may not be capable of increasing a region's innovation potential. This deficiency is referred to as "organizational thinness" (Tödtling & Trippl, 2005). RIS may also exhibit a second deficiency when, for example, existing actors do not work well together and, as a result, there is a lack of knowledge transfer in a region (Blažek, Žížalová, Rumpel, & Skokan, 2011). Tödtling and Trippl (2005) refer to this as "fragmentation," and they state that in such a fragmented RIS, the central task of knowledge generation through intensive interaction does not work. Third, a lock-in of an RIS occurs when there is too narrow a focus on knowledge generation and exploitation and the innovation system is in danger of becoming "overembedded." In such a situation, CC-RIS actors tend to be strongly oriented toward activities that take place within a specific CC-RIS, and there is a danger that they may ignore relevant external developments. They become "overembedded" as the selection process of innovation partners is biased toward previously-successful partnerships (Woolthuis, Lankhuizen, & Gilsing, 2005).

CC-RIS can exhibit any of the three deficiencies, or even a combination of two or more. They may be organizationally thin when they function only as symbolic representations of the political power of a nation and when a well-functioning capital city-oriented private sector is missing. As a result, public procurement does not function as a driver for innovation dynamics. A fragmented CC-RIS may occur when existing actors – particularly public- and private-sector actors – do not work well together and there is no practice and culture of interaction through, for example, public procurement. Third, a CC-RIS may experience lock-in when activities are oriented too far toward one type of activity or one type of sector. In the context of a capital city, we refer to this situation as public-sector dependence.

RIS failures may lead to different stages of development of capital city econo-mies. Such economies may be weakly developed, moderately developed, or highly developed (Mayer, Sager, Kaufmann, & Warland, 2016). In a weakly-developed CC-RIS, all three deficiencies occur, while in a moderately-developed CC-RIS only one may exist. A highly-developed CC-RIS may only be in danger of experi-encing a lock-in in a previously-successful path of development. Table 2.1 outlines the various stages of development.

While the RIS perspective thus helps us understand the development of SCC economies, we lack a full explanation for how local or regional development strat-egies evolve in the first place. The RIS approach remains rather functionalist in this regard, expecting policymaking only in the event of system failure. However, SCCs do not follow this logic due to their basic reliance on the capital city func-tion and associated remuneration. Furthermore, the RIS concept covers only a limited range of possible policy choices that aim to increase the competitiveness of locations. Potential locational policies, such as image-building, attraction of firms, asking for public funds, or regional coordination are not covered by the RIS's take on policy intervention. In order to capture the multifaceted logic of SCC strategies, we propose an analytical framework of locational policies as outlined in the following sections. The proposed locational policies framework

Table 2.1 Capital city regional innovation system failures and stages of development

CC-RIS failures	Weakly-developed CC-RIS	Moderately-developed CC-RIS	Highly-developed CC-RIS
Organizational thinness	Yes. Capital city dominated by public-sector and important private-sector actors are missing	One of the two RIS failures is present	No. Public- and private-sector actors are present
Fragmentation	Yes. Public and private sector do not work well together		No. Well-functioning interactions between public- and private-sector actors
Lock-in	Yes. Lock-in in a weakly-developed CC-RIS may occur when the few actors that exist do not recognize new opportunities	Yes. Lock-in may occur when the existing actors engage in the same activities over time and no new actors are added	Yes. Lock-in may occur when a stable set of actors does not change and they engage in the same activities over time

ascribes an active role to local governments or regional cooperation organizations in their efforts to increase their economic competitiveness.

Locational policies

We define locational policies as policies formulated by local or regional policymakers that aim to enhance the competitiveness of a region.[1] Similarly, "the goal of such [locational] policies is clearly to position the city on the global scale of capital circulation by enhancing and presenting its attributes that are considered to be most competitive" (Van der Heiden, 2010, p. 10; based on Gordon, 1999; Ohmae, 2001; Brenner, 2004). Andrew and Doloreux (2012, pp. 1289–1290) point out that "developing strategies to build regional attractiveness and foster regional competitiveness are currently high on the political agenda of city-regions." They furthermore detect "a desire on the part of every local government to promote the comparative advantage of their city over other cities" (Andrew & Doloreux, 2012, p. 1289).

Locational policies as a concept emerged in the 1980s within the urban entrepreneurialism literature (Cochrane, 1987; Harvey, 1989). In this strand of literature, locational policies are problematized because they have emerged at the expense of territorial equalization polices (Begg, 1999). Thus, the concept of locational policies was merely a critique of emerging urban neoliberal strategies that consolidate economic competitiveness in urban centers at the expense of interregional and intraregional equalization of economic competitiveness. Locational policies have also been included in the neoclassic literature dealing with interurban competition. This strand of literature assumes that each city region has the potential to identify its own competitive niche (Porter, 1990, 1995). According to this perspective, locational policies should aim at enhancing the economic competiveness of the targeted locality by identifying, developing, and exploiting place-specific assets. This resembles the theory of comparative advantage, i.e. Ricardo's theorem (Ricardo, 1817), which suggests that regions should focus their production on domains in which they are comparatively most competitive. Pursuant to this logic, local governments should "adapt to this place-specific logic of competitiveness and push political institutions towards the place-specific economic assets of their respective city-regions" (Van der Heiden, 2010, p. 21).

As we seek to describe and explain the formulation of locational policies, we focus on their very purpose, which is to enhance the competitiveness of a region without engaging in the discussion of whether or not they are even desirable. Locational policies are empirical phenomena, and our primary aim is to describe and understand these formulated policies. In order to describe the phenomena of locational policies, we develop a systematic categorization of them. The challenge is to present a relatively-rich catalog of possible locational policies that integrates theories of urban studies, economic geography, and political science. Such an analytical framework is essential because it should do justice to the diverse strategies that cities formulate and simultaneously bring some order to the concept. Jonas and Ward (2007) highlight that local governments try to enhance the economic competiveness of their localities by formulating various policies such as job creation measures, supporting the growth of small companies, attracting outside investments, and organizing new urban governance arrangements. Furthermore, political initiatives have the potential to enhance the welfare of a region by coordinating actors, policies, and processes (Sager, 2005, 2006; Scharpf, 1997). Similarly, Young (2012) notes that the scope of policies that aim to develop the competiveness of a locality has expanded, making it difficult to empirically incorporate them in a study. More generally, Uyarra (2010) highlights the fact that such kinds of policies appear in complex bundles, do not occupy a narrow policy domain, and do not operate in isolation from each other as they are often mutually dependent.

In order to explain the phenomena of locational policies, we apply a neoinstitutional logic that emphasizes place-based resources and constraints in the formulation of policy choices. Some political scientists and economic geographers share similar intentions. Savitch and Kantor (2002) argue that urban development policies are formulated within complex sets of economic and political interactions that help us to explain these policies. Malecki (2007) proposes that the motivations to engage in interurban competition are similar in different places, but that the local economic development policy choices are shaped by place-based resources and constraints. Uyarra (2010, p. 132) analyzes economic development policies in RIS and concludes that these policies are not drafted "on a *tabula rasa*, but in a context of pre-existing policy mixes and institutional frameworks which have been shaped through successive policy changes." Van der Heiden (2010) examines urban foreign relations and finds that concrete forms of these endeavors are dependent on the respective location-specific needs and characteristics. Furthermore, Jessop and Sum (2000, p. 2291) propose that "the sort of strategies that are likely to be pursued will clearly depend on state institutional and/or territorial structures as well as on broader economic, political and sociocultural factors." Following this neoinstitutional literature, we assume that local conditions constrain or enable the formulation of locational policies in SCCs.

The phenomena of locational policies and their formulation process, i.e. locational politics, have been studied in cities and regions of global importance. For example, Brenner (1999) studies locational politics and locational policies following German reunification. Similarly, Jessop and Sum (2000) analyze policies and governance structures implemented by Hong Kong in its attempts to become an entrepreneurial city. Despite this, there is a lack of comparative studies of locational policies, arguably due to the absence of an analytical framework that would bring some order into what has hitherto been a rather fuzzy concept.

We propose a framework of locational policies comprising four categories (see Table 2.2). The categories of locational policies are distinguished by policy orientation and policy domain. With regard to the former, locational policies target institutions, groups, actors, or capital within the city or the region (inward orientation), or they may target these policies beyond the city region (outward orientation). The policy domain differentiates between the addressees of policies: Locational policies can address either individuals and corporate market actors (economic domain) or political entities at different levels (political domain).

Innovation policies

Innovation policies are an essential feature of the RIS concept. The overall aim of innovation policies is to improve the capabilities and performance of the

Table 2.2 Categorization of locational policies

Policy domain	Policy orientation	
	Inward	*Outward*
Economic	*Innovation policies*	*Attracting money*
	• Cluster policies • Stimulation of entrepreneurial ecosystem (e.g. incubators, public venture capital)	• Image-building • Attraction of firms and investments
Political	*Coordination*	*Asking for money*
	• Metropolitan government • Council of governments • Informal networks	• Compensation payments • Asking for public funds

region's firms, as well as the general business environment (Doloreux & Parto, 2005). Innovation policies aim to influence the economic performance of SCCs by fostering the transfer of ideas and knowledge between different actors of the RIS. As argued above, interactions between national government organizations and KIBS firms and the ensuing learning process are the drivers for innovation in an SCC-RIS. The transfer and sharing of knowledge between relevant industries, knowledge-generating institutions (e.g. universities, research institutes), and public actors in particular are fostered by innovation policies because these knowledge interactions are crucial in fostering innovation. These three types of actors are also known by the concept of the "triple helix" (Etzkowitz & Leydesdorff, 1995). Given the high density of public actors in CC-RIS, this specific type of triple helix actor is overrepresented in CC-RIS compared to other RIS within a country. As a consequence, innovation policies in SCCs should aim "to improve interactions between the knowledge infrastructures, firms, and institutions" (Doloreux, 2002, p. 248). Here, local governments and their formulated innovation policies may play a crucial role as they can act as "local brokers to 'connect and cluster' researchers, firms and talent" (Bradford & Wolfe, 2013, p. 11).

We can find evidence for different types of innovation policies in different regions, be they capital cities or other types of regional economies. To date, cluster strategies are probably the most frequently-implemented examples of innovation policies. The aim of cluster policies is to create spatially-concentrated networks of firms that produce similar or related products or conduct R & D in similar areas (Porter, 2000). The presence of a cluster, however, does not automatically stimulate economic development. "Many of the competitive advantages of clusters depend on the free flow of information, the discovery of value-adding exchanges or transactions, the willingness to align agendas and to work across organizations, and strong motivations for improvement" (Porter, 2000, p. 264). Local governments may stimulate the flow of information as well as exchanges and transactions between the different members of a cluster. Furthermore, cluster-oriented innovation policies may support and incentivize R & D, organize specific training, create cooperative networks, foster knowledge exchange between cluster entities, etc. (Cumbers & MacKinnon, 2004; Martin & Sunley, 2003). In SCCs, cluster policies should aim in particular to stimulate knowledge interactions between national governmental organizations and KIBS firms, because the former are crucial not just in their role as regulators, but also as buyers of product and service innovations. Innovation in these highly-regulated clusters (such as defense, education, health) thus depends on complex interaction patterns between public demand and private supply.

Further examples of innovation policies are initiatives that try to stimulate the regional entrepreneurial environment. Examples of this are the establishment of incubators or accelerators. Incubators offer an ideal environment for start-ups by providing office space at below-market-rates, consulting services in legal and administrative tasks, providing access to networks of investors, and by stimulating knowledge exchange with bigger firms and other start-ups. Similarly, so-called accelerators support young firms that have outgrown the start-up phase tailored to their level of development before they become fully independent. In this regard, accelerators usually act as early-stage investors that provide seed capital to growing firms. Another innovation policy that aims to support the growth of start-ups is the provision of public venture capital. When venture capital is lacking, different governmental entities may step in by providing public funds. An often-used practice to minimize risk in these kinds of innovation investments is for public funds to step in only if private investors are providing matching funds.

Innovation policies are also concerned with developing knowledge infrastructures in an RIS. The establishment of research universities enriched with science parks, technology transfer and commercialization programs, and university-based venture capital funds is helpful but not sufficient in promoting economic development. Generally, the research function of universities has been overstated by academics and practitioners, while the teaching function, i.e. the role in educating talent, has been underappreciated (Motoyama & Mayer, 2016). Universities should be considered as important underlying components of the regional knowledge-creation infrastructure and not as direct drivers of innovation (Mayer, 2007). The knowledge infrastructure in SCCs is not constituted by universities alone. National sector associations, chambers of commerce, and regional development agencies organize cumulative knowledge-sharing among different actors and coordinate collective actions (Maennig & Ölschläger, 2011). The establishment and fostering of such knowledge organization may help to stimulate knowledge flows in the complex economic environment of SCCs. Furthermore, innovation policies can be integrated into the public-procurement process. These kinds of policies focus on transforming a standardized and accountability-oriented process into a more interactive, innovation-oriented one. Innovation policies may also incentivize the participation of SMEs in the public-procurement process.

Attracting money

Locational policies designed to attract money target firms, new residents, and investments. We distinguish between strategies for image-building and attracting firms as two major manifestations of attracting money. Image-building is a specific tool of place marketing that is about creating and promoting a unique and positive image, which is conveyed to specific target groups such as tourists, prospective residents, talent, and investors. Attracting firms refers to strategies that aim to enlarge the tax base not through organic growth, but by attracting new firms.

Place marketing can be summarized as the application of marketing instruments to geographical locations (Eshuis, Braun, & Klijn, 2013). Braun (2003, p. 43) defines place marketing as "the coordinated use of marketing tools supported by a shared customer oriented philosophy, for creating, communicating, delivering, and exchanging urban offerings that have value for the city's customers and the city's community at large." In that sense, marketing is more about responsiveness to target groups than persuasion (Eshuis et al., 2013). Potential target groups are tourists, prospective residents, talent, and investors

(Eshuis et al., 2013; Harvey, 2012). Image-building strategies are a specific tool of place marketing and "include branding exercises, hosting cultural initiatives, tourism promotion, and even immigration campaigns" (Harvey, 2012, p. 4). Image-building is about creating and promoting a unique and positive image about a place. Nowadays, image-building is almost a necessity for public authorities in order to position their city in a global market by projecting specific images about the locality to the world (Eshuis et al., 2013; Harvey, 2012). Hannigan (2003, p. 353) links image-building to the "new entrepreneurial style of local economic development in which image promotion was privileged as being central by planners and politicians."

When formulating image-building strategies, it is essential to position the localities with attributes that are hard to imitate elsewhere in order to avoid a level playing field with cities that may have a more powerful image. Thus, image-building should be guided by considerations of locational substitutability. "The lower the locational substitutability of these place-bound assets, the harder they can be imitated by others and the stronger the region's position is in the (. . .) global economy" (Van der Heiden & Terhorst, 2007, p. 242). Image-building in SCCs may be pursued along two dimensions if these locational policies are guided by considerations of locational substitutability. First, the capital city status is probably the most obvious attribute to be exploited because it guarantees singularity at the national level. Depending on the target group of the image-building campaign, SCCs may, for example, link the capital city status to quality of life and to the presence of historical sites, monuments, and parks. Second, SCCs may also try to build an image as a specific sort of business town. Such an image-building strategy would not target visitors and tourists, but rather firms in highly-regulated and knowledge-intensive sectors that seek to tap into the specific CC-RIS. Hence, in image-building campaigns that target firms, SCCs could highlight their specific knowledge-intensive economy, the presence of national government organizations, and the highly-educated workforce.

Attracting firms, as another policy instrument of attracting money locational policies, refers to strategies designed to enlarge the tax base not by organic growth, but through the attraction of new firms. There is intense international competition in attracting firms. Organizations are established at the local or regional level with the purpose of attracting firms and mobile capital across the globe. Local governments may also commission the services of specialized brokers to this end. To initiate contacts with potential firms, local governments or their contractors may directly approach firms with inquiries or tailored propositions. Such contacts may be initiated at conferences or trade shows. Sometimes, brokers initially negotiate with site locators working on behalf of certain companies. Local governments and the actual firms potentially seeking to relocate may only come into play during the further steps of negotiations. Often, specific tax incentives, land deals, or reduced real estate costs are part of the "acquisitions package". But local governments cannot simply approach just any firm; instead, firms that fit existing clusters and industries are targeted with the intention of developing the cluster both qualitatively and quantitatively.

Similar to image-building, attracting firms strategies in SCCs can highlight the unique characteristics of a capital city economy for firms that operate in highly-regulated and knowledge-intensive markets, such as biotechnology, education, aerospace, and security. Such firms need spatial proximity to national government agencies in order to be close to the regulators or to further develop and stream-line their products. In turn, national government agencies need private expertise to develop and implement complex projects and services (Mayer, 2013). This mutual pull effect may be a decisive argument in the strategies of attracting firms to SCCs.

Coordination

Coordination is important for ensuring cooperation between decision-makers that may lead to policy coherence within a region. Such policy coordination addresses institutional collective action dilemmas that arise because decisions by one gov-ernment impact on other governments and their policies (Feiock, 2009, 2013). In our specific context, coordination aims to ensure regional cooperation and policy coherence in the formulation of locational policies at the regional level. Economic functions and regional linkages go far beyond the territorial boundaries of cities. Regional coordination is conditioned by the mismatch between functional regions and jurisdictional territories as reforms of the jurisdictional boundaries are not implemented at the same rate as the accelerating pace of urban sprawl (Kübler, 2012). According to Frederickson (1999), the interdependence of jurisdiction, organizations, and institutions is greatest in metropolitan areas and makes coordi-nation necessary and meaningful.

Coordination seems to be essential in SCCs because capitals are often situated in regions that are institutionally fragmented. There are two explanations for this: First, cities are chosen as capitals, often with the aim of uniting a country, and thus are located in areas of national tensions. A good example is the choice of Ottawa to bridge Anglophone and Francophone Canada. Second, specific governing structures (e.g. federal district) have been created for capitals that are relatively small-scale and thus cover only the core city of the capital region. For example, the metropolitan area of Washington, D.C. is highly fragmented as it incorporates the District of Columbia and three additional states (Virginia, Maryland, and West Virginia) that are, in turn, home to various independent local jurisdictions.

Feiock (2013) describes 12 different coordination structures to address collec-tive action dilemmas. He distinguishes between their integration mechanism and the scope of the policy fields these structures aim to coordinate. For example, mul-tiple local governments may be consolidated into a metropolitan general-purpose government. A less institutionalized and encompassing version is that of coun-cils of governments based on statutes, which incorporate only a small number of policy fields, such as public transportation, planning, and/or regional economic development. At the other end of the spectrum are informal networks that depend on the voluntary participation of their members. Such networks may enhance trust among members but do not feature any means of policy enforcement. Such looser forms of regional coordination often occur as alternatives to formal coordination bodies. Empirically, effective coordination is achieved not only through institutional consolidation or institutionalized coordination structures, but also through cooperative arrangements that stabilize networks of policy-relevant actors (Kübler & Heinelt, 2005; Sager, 2006).

Locational policies are a policy field in which regional coordination seems beneficial. Morgan (2014) points out that regional coordination agendas for the most part cover the policy fields of economic development, transportation, and spatial planning. In a comparative analysis, Kübler and Piliutyte (2007) suggest that there is likely to be a metropolitan area-wide commonality of interest regarding economic promotion. Feiock, Steinacker, and Park (2009, p. 256) point to great potential benefits of regional coordination in the policy field of economic development, but also add that "the transaction costs tend to be correspondingly high, making economic development one of the toughest cases for institutional collective action."

Local governments engage in interaction to capture spillover effects from growth if the gains of cooperation are likely to outweigh the transaction costs necessary to achieve it (Feiock et al., 2009; Kwon & Feiock, 2010; Ostrom, 1990). Thus, transaction costs and collective action problems, such as incentives to take a free ride or opportunistic defections from voluntary agreements, are barriers to coordination. Furthermore, the two-step logic of a firm's locational choice – the first step consisting of a regional choice and the second (and later) step involving the selection of a specific location within the chosen region (Cohen, 2000) – aggravates regional coordination. This reveals the double logic of competition: Competition within a region is a threat to economic competitiveness in the competition between regions.

The outcome of coordination can be assessed using Scharpf's (1994, p.27) welfare-theoretic concept: "[Coordination] is considered desirable whenever the level of aggregate welfare obtained through the unilateral choices of interdependent actors is lower than the level which could be obtained through choices that are jointly considered." A distinction between three types of manifestations of coordination helps us approach this category of locational policies. Positive coordination describes the proactive search for synergies higher than those achieved by individual action. The synergies of positive coordination should allow for compensating negatively-affected actors for their losses (Scharpf, 1994). Negative coordination means the mere avoidance of contradictory action and redundancies without actively generating synergies (Scharpf, 1994). Competition or beggar-my-neighbor policies would be the worst-case scenario of coordination (Keating, 1995). Competition or beggar-my-neighbor behavior can be seen as a failure of coordination.

Asking for money

Policies that involve asking for money are the other type of outward-oriented policies covered in the locational policies framework. In contrast to attracting-money strategies that target firms, residents, or investments, asking-for-money strategies target public funds from higher-level political entities (e.g. remuneration of capital city functions by national government). This locational policy aims to justify and increase monetary transfers. Important public funds are intergovernmental monetary transfers that may be unconditional or earmarked for a specific policy field or specific expenditure, such as economic development funds. Local governments also have the opportunity to apply for upper-tier public funds that are awarded competitively based on certain criteria, such as funds for the development of major infrastructure projects or for fostering specific industries. European cities can also attempt to tap into European Union (EU) funds. One such example is the European Regional Development Fund that supports modernization projects to increase regional competiveness. A newer EU funding instrument is the Smart Cities and Communities European Innovation Partnership, which supports technology-intense economic projects at the local level. National fiscal equalization schemes also belong in this category, but are, for the most part, based on non-negotiable allocation formulas.

The political science literature distinguishes between two types of compensation payments in the context of capital cities (Slack & Chattopadhyay, 2009; G. Young, 2008). First, some capital cities have negotiated compensation arrangements concerning specific additional expenses associated with capital city functions, such as additional policing due to a higher frequency of special events, preserving objects of national importance, hosting cultural events, and maintaining a high-quality infrastructure. In some capital cities, these additional services are rendered directly by national government organizations such as national planning committees or national security forces. Second, some capital cities receive compensation for lost revenue due to extraordinary constraints on their local tax autonomy. The most important compensation in this context is payment in lieu of taxes (PILTs). More specifically, payments in lieu of tax-exempted property are very important for local governments in capital cities because local governments are not permitted to levy taxes on land and buildings belonging to the national government or land and buildings of foreign governments (such as embassies and consulates). Even though this tax exemption holds for all local government in the country, this restriction affects capital cities in the most profound manner, given the high density of such tax-exempted properties. To compensate for these restrictions on the property tax base, some countries have established PILTs systems, while other nation states may compensate via lump sum payments.

Given that this locational policy targets public funds, local governments have to present political arguments, such as an emphasis of the capital city's importance for the nation and its political system. Cities are able to claim national importance in various ways. Larger cities can simply refer to their economic importance for the country as a whole, while smaller cities may highlight their role as regional centers for peripheral areas or as secondary centers in metropolitan areas (Kaufmann & Arnold, 2017). SCCs, for their part, are able to claim national importance by referring to their functional roles as political centers. They can base their claims on their special status in the national urban system as cities that should not only be measured by their economic successes, but also by their roles as places where political decisions are made and implemented, which may benefit the entire country.

Exclusive reliance on asking-for-money strategies would feature a preservative rather than a proactive development logic and could leave SCCs dependent on the nation state. Jessop and Sum (2000, p. 2293) assess such strategies as being unsustainable in the long term, stating that they "pose an awkward dilemma over the trade-off between maintaining local autonomy and accepting resources that come with restrictive strings attached." Consequently, attracting public funds or compensation-payment strategies should always be accompanied by other locational policies.

Linking the concept of RIS with locational policies

While the RIS approach allows us to capture knowledge-based development dynamics in SCCs, the locational policy approach allows for an analysis of the multiple policies that aim to develop the RIS and, more broadly, the economic competiveness of the region. However, thus far, the two approaches lack the conceptual linkage that helps us understand how RIS and locational policies interact in the context of a capital city.

CC-RIS differ in terms of their respective stage of development. Table 2.3 outlines these stages and combines RIS failures with possible locational policies. The two economic locational policies in particular – innovation policies and attracting money – are directly influenced by the RIS and its failures. As regards the two political locational policies – coordination and asking for money – we assume that political-institutional factors are more important for their formulation than the RIS, but the importance of these political locational policies increases or decreases depending on the different RIS stages. In the following, we present an analytical and dynamic framework that coherently links the RIS and locational policies literatures. The goal is to present an interdisciplinary framework within which to analyze the political economy of SCCs.

Weakly-developed CC-RIS face at least one but often multiple failures, such as organizational thinness, fragmentation, and lock-in. Regarding locational policies, weakly-developed CC-RIS benefit from innovation policies because these can stimulate interactive learning among the few actors and therefore contribute to knowledge spillovers and to increasing the connections between the actors. Attracting-money strategies are not persuasive in the context of weakly-developed CC-RIS. In the context of a weakly-developed CC-RIS, SCCs cannot compete with primary cities by referring only to a potential entrepreneurial and innovation environment that has not yet developed. It would simply not be persuasive and would result in the SCCs being outplayed by the mere economic power of other cities in the nation. Thus, for a less-developed SCC-RIS, the only outward-oriented locational policy left is to play the political card, i.e. to insist on its functional role as the one and only capital city. This strategy moves the focus away from its economic inferiority toward its political superiority. The asking-for-money positioning strategy can always be applied to upper-tier

Table 2.3 Combining RIS failures and locational policy frameworks

	RIS failures	Locational policies		Attracting money	Coordination	Asking for money
		Innovation policy				
Stages of RIS	*Weakly-developed CC-RIS*	At least one, but also all three failures (organizationally-thin, fragmented, locked-in) possible	Stimulating interactive learning, knowledge spillovers	Not persuasive, not many strategies	Favorable	Possible and essential
	Moderately- developed CC-RIS	Organizationally-thin OR fragmented; Lock-in present because of public-sector dependence	Increasing knowledge diffusion	Partly persuasive, mid-range strategies	Important	Possible and important
	Highly-developed CC-RIS	Possibility of a lock-in due to public-sector dependence	Tapping into external knowledge, stimulating new industry specializations	Persuasive, aggressive, and highly-targeted strategies	Essential	Possible and favorable

Source: Extension of Mayer et al. (2016).

political entities. However, it leaves an SCC dependent on the nation state with barely any room for independent local value creation. Coordinating policies at the regional level are certainly favorable, but the first priority seems to be to strengthen economic competitiveness by multiple local efforts that do not necessarily have to be coordinated.

Moderately-developed CC-RIS can be either organizationally-thin or fragmented. They often experience lock-in because of public-sector dependence. Therefore, innovation policies increase knowledge diffusion and may help to move from moderate development to high development. The development of an RIS allows the formulation of mid-range attracting-money strategies that may be based on capital city-specific clusters (such as cyber security, medical technology, or sustainable energy) and which are competitive and persuasive in interurban competition. Accordingly, the SCCs can relax the focus on asking-for-money strategies. These types of SCCs can formulate two-dimensional positioning strategies that emphasize both their capital city function and their specific regional economy. Regional coordination becomes important because the region is a competitive, but not central, node in interurban competition.

In contrast to the previous two stages of RIS development, highly-developed CC-RIS are neither thin nor fragmented. They are, however, highly dependent on the public sector and are therefore in danger of lock-in. As a result, tapping into external knowledge sources and stimulating diversification and new specializations are crucial and should be at the core of innovation policies. The development of the RIS allows the drafting of aggressive and highly-targeted attracting-money strategies on the global level. Attracting-money strategies can be formulated on the basis of the whole RIS and the capital city function. These strategies can target national firms that seek spatial proximity to national government organizations or firms from emerging markets or global investors that want to tap into the dynamic RIS. Asking for money is still possible, but the focus is likely to rest on economic-positioning strategies given the greater potential benefits these strategies hold. Regional coordination is essential because the whole region competes at the global level, necessitating regional policy coherence.

We ascribe innovation policies a crucial role in this framework. Innovation policies are sustainable locational policies options as they directly address the failures, needs, and problems arising from the SCC-RIS. Different innovation policies can launch, initiate, and stimulate the development process of an RIS. Innovation policies should be tailored to the various RIS stages. Whereas in stage I, stimulation of interactive learning is fruitful, stage III innovation policies should try to spur new industry specializations and the tapping into external knowledge. In that way, innovation policies can overcome the structural restraints of less-developed RIS and enable the formulation of aggressive and targeted attracting-money strategies. Thus, innovation policies have the potential to lay the foundation to move an SCC from nation state dependency toward more local autonomy.

The aim of coordination is, on the one hand, to generate synergistic effects of locational policies and, on the other hand, to prevent harmful kinds of competition within a region. Coordination seeks to ensure coherent policy-making and policy implementation within a region, because regional institutional fragmentation is an obstacle to creating these synergistic effects. The more advanced the RIS, the more complex the interaction within the political economy of a region, making coordination even more vital.

Outward-oriented locational policies, i.e. attracting money and asking for money, can be conceptualized as positioning strategies. In the context of SCCs, positioning strategies typically have two types of addressees: KIBS firms/residents and upper-level political entities. This implies two poles of money-accumulation strategies: taxes and transfer payments, to which corresponds the proposed dualism of attracting money and asking for money. When dealing with KIBS firms and/or residents, SCCs should use mainly economic arguments, whereas they should play the political card where vertically-upper-tier political entities are concerned. It is important to grasp that these two strategies are not a mutually-exclusive dichotomy. Quite the opposite – the most promising approach would be to combine these two strategies, since this would allow SCCs to target both sources of capital.

Note

1 We presented different versions of the locational policies framework in two other publications: A brief version is outlined in Mayer et al. (2016), while a more extensive version covering six categories of locational policies is postulated in Kaufmann and Arnold (2017).

References

Aarikka-Stenroos, L., & Jaakkola, E. (2012). Value co-creation in knowledge intensive business services: A dyadic perspective on the joint problem solving process. *Industrial Marketing Management, 41*(1), 15–26.

Acs, Z. J. (2009). Knowledge spillover theory of entrepreneurship. *Small Business Economics, 32* (1), 15–30. https://doi.org/10.1007/s11187-008-9157-3

Alberti, F. G., & Pizzurno, E. (2015). Knowledge exchanges in innovation networks: evidences from an Italian aerospace cluster. *Competitiveness Review, 25*(3), 258–287. https://doi.org/10.1108/CR-01-2015-0004

Andrew, C., & Doloreux, D. (2012). Economic development, social inclusion and urban governance: The case of the city-region of Ottawa in Canada. *International Journal of Urban and Regional Research, 36*(6), 1288–1305. https://doi.org/10.1111/j.1468-2427.2011.01025.x

Asheim, B., Smith, H. L., & Oughton, C. (2011). Regional innovation systems: Theory, empirics and policy. *Regional Studies, 45*(7), 875–891.

Aslesen, H. W., & Jakobsen, S.-E. (2007). The role of proximity and knowledge interaction between head offices and KIBS. *Tijdschrift Voor Economische En Sociale Geografie, 98*(2), 188–201.

Bathelt, H., & Gräf, A. (2008). Internal and external dynamics of the Munich film and TV industry cluster, and limitations to future growth. *Environment and Planning A, 40*(8), 1944–1965.

Bathelt, H., Malmberg, A., & Maskell, P. (2004). Clusters and knowledge: local buzz, global pipelines and the process of knowledge creation. *Progress in Human Geography, 28*(1), 31–56. https://doi.org/10.1191/0309132504ph469oa

Begg, I. (1999). Cities and competitiveness. *Urban Studies, 36*(5/6), 795.

Bettencourt, L. A., Ostrom, A. L., Brown, S. W., & Roundtree, R. I. (2002). Client co-production in knowledge-intensive business services. *California Management Review, 44*(4), 100–128.

Blažek, J., Žížalová, P., Rumpel, P., & Skokan, K. (2011). Where does the knowledge for knowledge-intensive industries come from? The case of biotech in Prague and ICT in Ostrava. *European Planning Studies, 19*(7), 1277–1303.

Bovaird, T. (2006). Developing new forms of partnership with the "market"in the procurement of public services. *Public Administration, 84*(1), 81–102.

Bovis, C. (2012). *EU Public Procurement Law*. Cheltenham: Elgar European Law.

Boyne. (2002). Public and private management: What's the difference? *Journal of Management Studies, 39*(1), 97–122.

Bradford, N., & Wolfe, D. (2013). Governing regional economic development: Innovation challenges and policy learning in Canada. *Cambridge Journal of Regions, Economy and Society. 6*(2), 331–347.

Braun, D. (2003). Dezentraler und unitarischer Föderalismus. Die Schweiz und Deutschland im Vergleich. *Swiss Political Science Review, 9*(1), 57–89.

Brenner, N. (1999). Globalisation as reterritorialisation: The re-scaling of urban governance in the European Union. *Urban Studies, 36*(3), 431–451.

Brenner, N. (2004). *New State Space: Urban Governance and the Rescaling of Statehood*. Oxford: Oxford University Press.

Broekel, T., & Boschma, R. (2011). Aviation, Space or eerospace? Exploring the knowledge networks of two industries in The Netherlands. *European Planning Studies, 19*(7), 1205–1227. https://doi.org/10.1080/09654313.2011.573133

Burnett, M. (2009). Using competitive dialogue in EU public procurement – Early trends and future developments. *EIPAScope*, (2), 17–23.

Caniëls, M. C. J., & Van den Bosch, H. (2011). The role of higher education institutions in building regional innovation systems. *Papers in Regional Science, 90*(2), 271–286.

Cochrane, A. (1987). *Developing Local Economic Strategies*. Milton Keynes: Open University Press.

Cohen, N. (2000). Business Location Decision-Making and the Cities: Bringing Companies Back. Working paper published by The Brookings Institution Center on Urban and Metropolitan Policy.

Cooke, P. (2001). Regional innovation systems, clusters, and the knowledge economy. *Industrial and Corporate Change, 10*(4), 945–974.

Cowell, M., & Mayer, H. (2014). Anchor institutions and disenfranchised communities: Lessons for DHS and St. Elizabeths. In K. Patterson & R. Silverman (Eds.), *Schools and Urban Revitalization: Rethinking Institutions and Community Development* (pp. 86–107). New York and London: Routledge.

Cumbers, A., & MacKinnon, D. (2004). Introduction: Clusters in urban and regional development. *Urban Studies, 41*(5–6), 959–969.

Das, T. K., & Teng, B. S. (1998). Between trust and control: Developing confidence in partner cooperation in alliances. *Academy of Management Review, 23*(3), 491–512.

Doloreux, D. (2002). What we should know about regional systems of innovation. *Technology in Society, 24*(3), 243–263. https://doi.org/10.1016/S0160-791X(02)00007-6

Doloreux, D., & Parto, S. (2005). Regional innovation systems: Current discourse and unresolved issues. *Technology in Society, 27*(2), 133–153.

Edler, J., & Georghiou, L. (2007). Public procurement and innovation—Resurrecting the demand side. *Research Policy, 36*(7), 949–963. https://doi.org/10.1016/j.respol.2007.03.003

Edler, J., Ruhland, S., Hafner, S., Rigby, J., Georghiou, L., Hommen, L., ..., Papadakou, M. (2005). Innovation and Public Procurement – Review of Issues at Stake. In *Study for the European Commission (No. ENTR/03/24)*. Karlsruhe: Fraunhofer-Institut für System und Innovationsforschung.

Edquist, C., & Hommen, L. (2000). Public Technology Procurement and Innovation Theory. In H. L. Charles Edquist & L. Tsipouri (Eds.), *Public Technology Procurement and Innovation* (p. 322). Boston, Dordrecht, and London: Kluwer Academic Publishers.

Edquist, C., Vonortas, N. S., Zabala-Iturriagagoitia, J. M., & Edler, J. (2015). *Public Procurement for Innovation*. Cheltenham: Edward Elgar.

Edquist, C., & Zabala-Iturriagagoitia, J. M. (2012). Public procurement for innovation as mission-oriented innovation policy. *Research Policy, 41*(10), 1757–1769. https://doi.org/10.1016/j.respol.2012.04.022

Edquist, C., Zabala, J. M., & Timmermans, B. A. (2012). Conceptual framework for analyzing the relations between demand and public innovative procurement and between knowledge intensive entrepreneurship and innovation. Working paper published by Circle at Lund University, Number 01.

Eshuis, J., Braun, E., & Klijn, E.-H. (2013). Place marketing as governance strategy: An assessment of obstacles in place marketing and their effects on attracting target groups. *Public Administration Review, 73*(3), 507–516.

Etzkowitz, H., & Leydesdorff, L. (1995). The Triple Helix—University-industry-government relations: A laboratory for knowledge based economic development. *EASST Review, 14*(1), 14–19.

Feiock, R. C. (2009). Metropolitan governance and institutional collective action. *Urban Affairs Review, 45*(3), 357–77.

Feiock, R. C. (2013). The institutional collective action framework. *Policy Studies Journal, 41*(3), 397–425.

Feiock, R. C., Steinacker, A., & Park, H. J. (2009). Institutional collective action and economic development joint ventures. *Public Administration Review, 69*(2), 256–270.

Feldman, M. (2001). The entrepreneurial event revisited: Firm formation in a regional context. *Industrial and Corporate Change, 10*(4), 861–891.

Feldman, M., Francis, J., & Bercovitz, J. (2005). Creating a cluster while building a firm: Entrepreneurs and the formation of industrial clusters. *Regional Studies, 39*(1), 129–141.

Frederickson, H. G. (1999). The repositioning of American public administration. *PS: Political Science and Politics, 32*(4), 701–711.

Gerhard, U. (2007). *Global City Washington, D.C.: Eine politische Stadtgeographie*. Bielefeld: transcript Verlag.

Gertler, M. (2002). Technology, culture and social learning: Regional and national institutions of governance. In M. Gertler, & D. A. Wolfe, *Innovation and Social Learning: Institutional Adaption in an Era of Technological Change*. New York: Palgrave Macmillan, pp. 111–134.

Glückler, J., & Armbruster, T. (2003). Bridging uncertainty in management consulting: The mechanisms of trust and networked reputation. *Organization Studies, 24*(2), 269–297.

Gordon, D. L. A. (2013). Ottawa: Lumber Town to Federal Capital. In H. Meyer (Ed.) *Im Herzen der Macht? Hauptstädte und ihre Funktion*. Universität Bern: Geographisches Institut, pp. 237–265.

Gordon, I. (1999). Internationalisation and urban competition. *Urban Studies, 36*(5–6), 1001–1016.

Hannigan, J. (2003). Introduction. *International Journal of Urban and Regional Research, 27*(2), 352–360.

Harvey, D. (1989). From managerialism to entrepreneurialism: The transformation in urban governance in late capitalism. *Geografiska Annaler. Series B. Human Geography, 71*(1), 3–17.

Harvey, J. (2012). Introduction. In J. Harvey & R. Young (Eds.), *Image-Building in Canadian Municpalities* (pp. 3–26). Montreal, Quebec and Kingston, Ontario: McGill-Queen's University Press.

Henkel, J., & Von Hippel, E. (2005). Welfare implications of user innovation. *Journal of Technology Transfer, 30*(1/2), 73–87.

Howells, J. (2005). Innovation and regional economic development: A matter of perspective? *Research Policy, 34*(8), 1220–1234. https://doi.org/10.1016/j.respol.2005.03.014

Ibert, O. (2004). Projects and firms as discordant complements: Organisational learning in the Munich software ecology. *Research Policy, 33*(10), 1529–1546. https://doi.org/10.1016/j.respol.2004.08.010

Jessop, B., & Sum, N.-L. (2000). An entrepreneurial city in action: Hong-Kong's emerging strategies in and for (inter) urban competition. *Urban Studies, 37*(12), 2287–2313.

Jonas, A., & Ward, K. (2007). Introduction to a debate on city-regions: New geographies of governance, democracy and social reproduction. *International Journal of Urban and Regional Research, 31*(1), 169–178.

Jones, A. (2007). More than "managing across borders?" The complex role of face-to-face interaction in globalizing law firms. *Journal of Economic Geography, 7*(3), 223–246.

Kaufmann, D., & Arnold, T. (2017). Strategies of cities in globalized interurban competition: The locational policies framework. *Urban Studies* Early online.

Keating, M. (1995). Size, Efficency and Democracy: Consolidation, Fragmentation and Public Choice. In D. Judge, G. Stoker, & H. Wolman (Eds.), *Theories of Urban Politics* (pp. 117–134). London: SAGE Publications Ltd.

Kübler, D. (2012). Governing the metropolis: Towards kinder, gentler democracies. *European Political Science, 11*(3), 430–445.

Kübler, D., & Heinelt, H. (2005). Metropolitan Governance, Democracy and the Dynamics of Place. In H. Heinelt & D. Kübler (Eds.), *Metropolitan Governance. Capacity, Democracy and the Dynamics of Place* (pp. 8–28). London and New York: Routledge.

Kübler, D., & Piliutyte, J. (2007). Intergovernmental relations and international urban strategies: Constraints and opportunities in multilevel polities. *Environment and Planning C: Government and Policy, 25*(3), 357.

Kwon, S.-W., & Feiock, R. C. (2010). Overcoming the barriers to cooperation: Intergovernmental service agreements. *Public Administration Review, 70*(6), 876–884.

Lagendijk, A., & Cornford, J. (2000). Regional institutions and knowledge-tracking new forms of regional development policy. *Geoforum, 31*, 209–218. https://doi.org/10.1016/S0016-7185(99)00031-7

Landry, R., Amara, N., & Doloreux, D. (2012). Knowledge-exchange strategies between KIBS firms and their clients. *The Service Industries Journal, 32*(2), 291–320.

Loader, K. (2013). Is public procurement a successful small business support policy? A review of the evidence. *Environment and Planning C: Government and Policy*, *31*(1), 39–55. https://doi.org/10.1068/c1213b

Maennig, W., & Ölschläger, M. (2011). Innovative milieux and regional competitiveness: The role of associations and chambers of commerce and industry in Germany. *Regional Studies*, *45*(4), 441–452.

Malecki, E. (2007). Cities and regions competing in the global economy: Knowledge and local development policies. *Environment and Planning C*, *25*(5), 638–654.

Markusen, A. (1996). Sticky places in slippery space: A typology of industrial districts. *Economic Geography*, *72*(3), 214–293.

Markusen, A., Hall, P., Campbell, S., & Deitrick, S. (1991). *The Rise of the Gunbelt: The Military Remapping of Industrial America*. New York: Oxford University Press.

Martin, R., & Sunley, P. (2003). Deconstructing clusters: Chaotic concept or policy panacea? *Journal of Economic Geography*, *3*(1), 5–35.

Maskell, P., Bathelt, H., & Malmberg, A. (2004). Temporary clusters and knowledge creation: The effects of international trade fairs, conventions and other professional gatherings. *Spaces*, *4*, 1–34.

Mayer, H. (2007). What is the role of the university in creating a high-technology region? *Journal of Urban Technology*, *14*(3), 33–58.

Mayer, H. (2013). Was produzieren Hauptstädte? Zur ökonomischen Rolle und Funktion von Hauptstädten. In H. Mayer, F. Sager, A. Minta, & S. M. Zwahlen (Eds.), *Im Herzen der Macht? Hauptstädte und ihre Funktion* (Vol. 58, pp. 125–150). Bern: Haupt Verlag AG.

Mayer, H., Sager, F., Kaufmann, D., & Warland, M. (2016). Capital city dynamics: Linking regional innovation systems, locational policies and policy regimes. *Cities*, *50*, 206–215.

Miles, I. (2005). Knowledge intensive business services: Prospects and policies. *Foresight*, *7*(6), 39–63.

Miles, I. (2012). KIBS and knowledge dynamics in client-supplier interaction. In E. Di Maria, R. Grandinetti, & D. B. Barbara (Eds.), *Exploring Knowledge-Intensive Business Services: Knowledge Management Strategies* (pp. 13–34). London: Palgrave Macmillan.

Morgan, K. (2014). The Rise of Metropolis: Urban Governance in the Age of the City-Region. In N. Bradford & A. Bramwell (Eds.), *Governing Urban Economies: Innovation and Inclusion in Canadian City-Regions* (pp. 297–318). Toronto: University of Toronto Press.

Motoyama, Y., & Mayer, H. (2016). Revisiting the roles of the university in regional economic development: A triangulation of data. *Growth & Change*. https://doi.org/10.1111/grow.12186

Muller, E., & Doloreux, D. (2009). What we should know about knowledge-intensive business services. *Technology in Society*, *31*(1), 64–72. https://doi.org/10.1016/j.techsoc.2008.10.001

Ohmae, K. (2001). How to Invite Prosperity from the Global Economy Into a Region. In A. Scott (Ed.), *Global-City Regions: Trends, Theory, Policy* (pp. 33–43). Oxford: Oxford University Press.

Ostrom, E. (1990). *Governing the Commons: The Evolution of Institutions for Collective Action*. Cambridge: Cambridge University Press.

Porter, M. (1990). *The Competitive Advantage*. New York: Free Press.

Porter, M. (1995). The competitive advantage of the inner city. *Harvard Business Review*, *74*, 55–71.

Porter, M. (2000). Location, competition, and economic development: Local clusters in a global economy. *Economic Development Quarterly, 14*(1), 15–34.

Ricardo, D. (1817). *The Principles of Political Economy and Taxation*. London: John Murray.

Roberts, S. M. (2014). Development capital: USAID and the rise of development contractors. *Annals of the Association of American Geographers, 104*(5), 1030–1051.

Rolfstam, M. (2005). Public technology procurement as a demand-side innovation policy instrument: An overview of recent literature and events. Lund: University of Lund.

Rolfstam, M. (2008). *Public Procurement of Innovation*. Lund: Media-Tryck.

Roodhooft, F., & Van den Abbeele, A. (2006). Public procurement of consulting services. *International Journal of Public Sector Management, 19*(5), 490–512. https://doi.org/10.1108/09513550610677799

Sager, F. (2005). Metropolitan institutions and policy coordination: The integration of land use and transport policies in Swiss urban areas. *Governance, 18*(2), 227–256.

Sager, F. (2006). Policy coordination in the European metropolis: A meta-analysis. *West European Politics, 29*(3), 433–460.

Sammarra, A., & Biggiero, L. (2008). Heterogeneity and specificity of inter-firm knowledge flows in innovation networks. *Journal of Management Studies, 45*(4).

Savitch, H., & Kantor, P. (2002). *Cities in the International Marketplace: The Political Economy of Urban Development in North America and Western Europe*. Princeton: Princeton University Press.

Scarso, E., & Bolisani, E. (2012). Trust in knowledge exchanges between service providers and clients: A multiple case study of KIBS. *Knowledge Management Research & Practice, 10*(1), 16–26.

Scharpf, F. (1994). Games real actors could play: Positive and negative coordination in embedded negotiations. *Journal of Theoretical Politics, 6*(1), 27–53.

Scharpf, F. (1997). *Games Real Actors Play: Actor-Centered Institutionalism in Policy Research*. Boulder: Westview Press.

Sedita, S. R., & Apa, R. (2015). The impact of inter-organizational relationships on contractors' success in winning public procurement projects: The case of the construction industry in the Veneto region. *International Journal of Project Management, 33*(7), 1548–1562.

Slack, E., & Chattopadhyay, R. (2009). *Finance and Governance of Capital Cities in Federal Systems*. Montreal, Quebec and Kingston, Ontario: McGill-Queen's University Press.

Smedlund, A. (2006). The roles of intermediaries in a regional knowledge system. *Journal of Intellectual Capital, 7*(2), 204–220. https://doi.org/10.1108/14691930610661863

Sternberg, R. (2007). Entrepreneurship, proximity and regional innovation systems. *Tijdschrift Voor Economische En Sociale Geografie, 98*(5), 652–666.

Storper, M., & Scott, A. J. (1995). The wealth of regions: market forces and policy imperatives in a local and global context. *Futures, 27*(5), 505–526.

Thai, K. (2001). Public procurement re-examined. *Journal of Public Procurement, 1*(1), 9–50.

Thai, K. (2009). *International Handbook of Public Procurement*. Boca Raton: Auerbach Publications.

Timmermans, B., & Zabala-Iturriagagoitia, J. M. (2013). Coordinated unbundling: A way to stimulate entrepreneurship through public procurement for innovation. *Science and Public Policy, 40*(5), 674–685. https://doi.org/10.1093/scipol/sct023

Tödtling, F., & Grillitsch, M. (2014). Types of innovation, competencies of firms, and external knowledge sourcing: Findings from selected sectors and regions of Europe. *Journal of the Knowledge Economy, 5*(2), 330–356.

Tödtling, F., & Trippl, M. (2005). One size fits all?: Towards a differentiated regional innovation policy approach. *Research Policy, 34*(8), 1203–1219.

Trippl, M., & Tödtling, F. (2011). Regionale Innovationssysteme und Wissenstransfer im Spanungsfeld unterschiedlicher Näheformen. In O. Ibert & H. J. Kujath (Eds.), *Räume der Wissensarbeit* (pp. 155–169). Wiesbaden: VS Verlag für Sozialwissenschaften.

Trippl, M., Tödtling, F., & Lengauer, L. (2009). Knowledge sourcing beyond buzz and pipelines: Evidence from the Vienna software sector. *Economic Geography, 85*(4), 443–462.

Tura, T., & Harmaakorpi, V. (2005). Social capital in building regional innovative capability. *Regional Studies, 39*(8), 1111–1125. https://doi.org/10.1080/00343400500328255

Uyarra, E. (2010). What is evolutionary about regional systems of innovation? Implications for regional policy. *Journal of Evolutionary Economics, 20*(1), 115–137.

Uyarra, E., & Flanagan, K. (2010). Understanding the innovation impacts of public procurement. *European Planning Studies, 18*(123–143).

Van der Heiden, N. (2010). *Urban Foreign Policy and Domestic Dilemmas: Insights from Swiss and EU City-regions*. Colchester: European Consortium for Political Research.

Van der Heiden, N., & Terhorst, P. (2007). Varieties of glocalisation: The international economic strategies of Amsterdam, Manchester, and Zurich compared. *Environment and Planning C: Government and Policy, 25*(3), 341.

Wood, P. (2006). Urban development and knowledge-intensive business services: Too many unanswered questions? *Growth and Change, 37*(3), 335–361. https://doi.org/10.1111/j.1468-2257.2006.00327.x

Woolthuis, R. K., Lankhuizen, M., & Gilsing, V. (2005). A system failure framework for innovation policy design. *Technovation, 25*(6), 609–619. https://doi.org/10.1016/j.technovation.2003.11.002

Young, G. (2008). The fiscal relationships between capital cities and their national governments. In *Building the Best Capital City in the World* (pp. 68–79). Washington, D.C.: DC Appleseed Center for Law & Justice.

Young, R. (2012). Introduction: Multilevel Governance and Its Central Research Questions in Canadian Cities. In M. Horak & R. Young (Eds.), *Sites of Governance: Multilevel Governance and Policy Making in Canada's Big Cities* (Vol. 3, pp. 3–25). Montreal, Quebec and Kingston, Ontario: McGill-Queen's University Press.

3 Setting the scene

The history, the political-institutional setting, and the economy of secondary capital cities (SCCs) are all shaped by the capital city function. More precisely, constitutional and state-theoretical ideas are mirrored in the selection of capital cities, as well as in the degree of local autonomy granted. The specific capital city economy is to a large extent influenced by the development of the national administration and the expansion of state activities. Given the importance of the capital city function, traditional capital city research often examines capitals from a nation-state perspective. In this book, we take a different approach: While we begin with a discussion of the traditional capital city literature that adopts a nation-state centered perspective, we study capital cities as actors embedded within the political-institutional setting of a nation state, but not necessarily determined by these settings. The story of SCCs is thus an interplay between national state influence and local agency.

Insights from traditional capital city research

Selection as capital cities

There are a wide variety of reasons why secondary cities were chosen as the capitals of their respective nations. Generally, federalist countries are more likely to select secondary cities as their capitals in order to balance power relations in the national urban system and to separate economic and political power (Elazar, 1987; Gottmann, 1977; Harris, 1995; Nagel et al., 2013; Slack & Chattopadhyay, 2009). Numerous national idiosyncrasies can explain why cities of secondary economic importance were chosen as capitals. At the time they were selected to serve as capital cities, the four cities we analyze in this book differed in terms of physical development, as well as economic and political importance. On the one hand, Bern and The Hague are purposely-selected capitals that carried certain functions in the national urban system prior to their selection as capital cities. Ottawa and Washington, D.C., meanwhile, are purpose-built capitals. Whereas the former two cities were already developed at the time they were selected as capitals, the latter two capitals were built from scratch.

Bern and The Hague were important economic or political centers prior to the establishment of the Swiss and Dutch nation states. At its pinnacle

(1500–1800), Bern was the largest European city state north of the Alps, and, as such, the city has a long tradition as an influential patrician-governed city state (Gerber, 2015). This glorious era of Bern as a city state came to an end in 1798 with its occupation by the French Revolutionary Army. The Hague never played the role of an economic or military center. Instead, since the Early Middle Ages, The Hague served as a neutral meeting place, a site for negotiations, and a venue for arbitration for the powerful Dutch city states of the late Middle Ages, namely Amsterdam, Delft, Dordrecht, Gouda, Haarlem, and Leyden (Van Krieken & McKay, 2005). As a result, the selection of The Hague as the capital appears to have been a straightforward decision by Prince Maurice in 1585. Since then, The Hague has for the majority of the time functioned as the political seat of various Dutch and occupying governments. Bern was chosen as the location for the Swiss capital city after a short and relatively bloodless Swiss civil war in 1847. The newly-established Swiss Confederation was in search of a permanent capital city to replace a system of rotating locations for political gatherings. Given the immediate provision of suitable infrastructure at the time, only the three cities of Bern, Lucerne, and Zurich were options. Bern was chosen for pragmatic reasons in 1848 since Lucerne – a conservative, Catholic stronghold – was still skeptical of the new federal state and Zurich was

Figure 3.1 The picturesque historic old town of Bern is a UNESCO World Heritage Site and represents Bern's former wealth and power (Source: Heike Mayer).

already economically too powerful (Kübler, 2009; Stadler, 1971). The choice of Bern as capital city was furthermore an inclusionary gesture on account of Bern's central geographic location and particularly because of its proximity to the French-speaking parts of Switzerland (Stadler, 1971).

Ottawa and Washington, D.C. differ from Bern and The Hague. While Ottawa was heavily developed to become Canada's capital, Washington, D.C. as the capital of the United States was built from scratch. Ottawa was a lumber town with only about 12,000 inhabitants when it became the capital of the Province of Canada in 1859 (Andrew & Doloreux, 2012). Queen Victoria chose Ottawa as the location of the capital city because the Canadian legislators were unable to reach a consensus. The choice for Ottawa was reputedly made for political and military reasons, but in its essence represented a compromise (Andrew, 2013). For political reasons: Ottawa was located between the primarily French-speaking Canada East and the primarily English-speaking Canada West. Furthermore, some of the national legislators argued that a capital city should be free from regional influence, which is why there was a reluctance to locate the capital in a large commercial center (Knight, 1977). For military reasons: Ottawa lies several days' march away from the US border, yet was still connected via the Rideau Canal to the border town of Kingston (Tassonyi, 2009).

The establishment of Washington, D.C. as the US capital under federal rule is a product of the US Constitution, which entered into force in 1789. Former president James Madison explained that, in order to ensure independence from any city, state, or commercial interest, the US capital should be under the exclusive authority of Congress (Hamilton, Madison, & Jay, 1982). Madison's

Figure 3.2 View from the Washington Monument, looking down the National Mall, with the United States Capitol in the background (Source: Heike Mayer).

main fear was any encroachment upon the federal government by an individual state. While the US Constitution does not specify a location for the Federal District, the choice of location is illuminating. Gilliland (2013) argues that the decision to move the US capital southwestward was a compromise between the Northern States that succeeded in having their war debts nationalized and the debt-free Southerners who wanted to liberate the capital from the influence of Pennsylvanian Northerners. President George Washington ultimately had the right to decide the exact location of the new federal capital and chose an area close to his own home in Mount Vernon, Virginia (Gilliland, 2013; Hazelton Jr, 1914). As a result, Washington, D.C. was founded in 1791 and inaugurated as the US capital in 1800.

The distinction between purposely-selected capitals and purpose-built capitals is relevant beyond the purpose of mere classification. This distinction becomes apparent in the degree of local autonomy that capital cities enjoy. The influence of the nation state on its capital city is more intense in purpose-built capitals than in purposely-selected capital cities. The two cities of Bern and The Hague exercised important functions in the national urban system at the time they were chosen to be the national capital. As a result, it seems unlikely that they would have accepted cutbacks in their local autonomy brought along by capital city status. In contrast, in the case of Ottawa and Washington, D.C., the idea was to reach a compromise or to isolate the capital from commercial influence. This argument served as legitimation to implement central government control mechanisms over these capitals, representing the constraints on local autonomy in purpose-built capital cities.

Local autonomy of capital cities

Washington, D.C. in particular faces many local autonomy constraints. D.C. residents have been allowed to participate in presidential elections since 1961, but they have no representation in the legislative branch of the US (Ghandi, Yilmaz, Zahradnik, & Edwards, 2009). They are represented only by a nonvoting delegate in the US House of Representatives, who may vote in committees but has no right to vote on the floor of the House. The current governing system of the US capital is described as "Home Rule under Congressional supervision" (Nagel, 2013). Congress can influence local policymaking in the District by either blocking spending on particular budgetary items or directly vetoing District laws (Nagel, 2013). Congress has used this power extensively (Fauntroy, 2003, 2009; Nagel, 2013). Experts and local policymakers currently assess Congressional oversight as highly controversial, based on D.C. local government plans to implement societally-contested policies such as legalizing abortion and marihuana consumption, establishing a needle exchange program, and tightening firearms regulations (Washington, D.C. interviews, 1, 39, 42, 43, & 44). The Republican majority in Congress exercised its "authority over locally generated funds as a means to enact its own legislative provision through so-called 'social riders' (. . .). These 'social riders' specifically impact district policy, but actually reflect broader political debates" (Ghandi et al., 2009, p. 279). Thus, the deep partisan divide in the US has a profound impact on local policymaking in Washington, D.C. Furthermore, the US federal level can intervene in local matters via the National Capital Planning Commission (NCPC), which represents federal interests in respect of federal land and buildings in the entire Washington, D.C. region (Ghandi et al., 2009).

In addition to these political autonomy constraints, D.C. also deals with limitations in its fiscal autonomy. The Home Rule Act of 1973 prohibits D.C. from levying the 'Commuter Tax' on the income of nonresidents that work in the District. US states normally tax nonresidents (Nagel, 2013). This tax restriction harms the District financially because nonresidents earn about two thirds of the income in the capital. Thus, a large proportion of personal income tax revenue is lost to Maryland and Virginia (Ghandi et al., 2009). Yilmaz (2009) calculated that taxing the nonresidential workforce would account for an additional USD 2.26 billion revenue in 2005. Furthermore, federal property is tax exempt in the entire country. Unsurprisingly, this tax exemption has the greatest negative financial consequences for the Washington, D.C. region (Washington, D.C. interviews, 34 & 39). Federally-owned properties and other tax-exempt property such as embassies make up 41% of the District's property tax base (O'Cleireacain, 1997). Yilmaz (2009) calculated that this specific tax loss accounted for about USD 540 million in 2005. The constrained tax autonomy creates a structural income deficit, which is seen as one of the reasons for D.C.'s high tax rates (O'Cleireacain, 1997). The federal level acknowledges these tax constraints and the unique fiscal situation of the District in The Home Rule Act of 1973 and the Revitalization Act of 1997. Both acts account for these limitations by establishing federal compensation payments (Ghandi et al., 2009).

Ottawa is also a purpose-built capital, but faces fewer local autonomy constraints than Washington, D.C. In general, municipalities are not recognized in the Constitution of Canada. Reference to municipalities is made only as "creatures of the provinces" (Tassonyi, 2009). Consequently, the City of Ottawa operates under the statutory framework of the Province of Ontario. The federal level has a foothold in the capital city via its federal land use agency for the capital city region: The National Capital Commission (NCC). The NCC exerts direct control with respect to planning, zoning, and developing land owned by the federal government. "This means that neither the provincial nor the local authority has any rights of taxation, legislation, or regulation over such property, except what the national authority chooses to give it" (Taylor, 2011, p. 28). The NCC is the single-largest property owner in Ottawa and directly controls approximately ten percent of all land, including prominent spots, for example along the banks of the Ottawa River (Champagne, 2011). This strong position of the NCC puts Ottawa's city hall in an ambivalent position: On the one hand, local officials feel they are dictated to by the federal government in some instances (Andrew & Doloreux, 2014). On the other hand, city hall depends on federal expenditure to sustain the budget (Andrew & Chiasson, 2012).

Figure 3.3 Centre Block of the Parliament of Canada, with the Peace Tower on
        Parliament Hill in Ottawa (Source: Martin Warland).

The two purposely-selected capitals do not face any local autonomy constraints ensuing from their capital city status. The law treats Bern like any other
Swiss municipality. Theoretically, this means that the City of Bern, like any
other Swiss municipality, has to transit its contacts to the federal level via cantonal authorities. In practical terms, however, local Bernese policymakers have
better access to their federal counterparts on account of their spatial proximity.
In addition, the federal level coordinates with the Bernese local government rather
pragmatically (Kübler, 2009). Similarly, The Hague does not face constraints on
its local autonomy.

   All capital cities face constraints stemming from their local property tax
base because a large proportion of their land and buildings belong to national
and foreign governments or international bodies and these properties are tax
exempt. These constraints are not limited to capital cities, since all jurisdictions that host governmental organizations face such constraints. Examples
include cities that feature military bases or large governmental research organizations (public universities, laboratories, etc.). In the case of capital cities,
however, government organizations have a greater propensity to cluster within
the vicinity of the capital. Furthermore, the presence of these agencies as well

as foreign embassies decreases the supply of land and real estate, which may lead to increased property prices in capital cities.

This brief discussion of the determinants of why these secondary cities were selected as capitals and the local autonomy constraints following from this selection resembles traditional capital city research in political science and public administration (Harris, 1995; Nagel et al., 2013; Rossman, 2017; Slack & Chattopadhyay, 2009). This strand of literature follows the work of the Canadian political scientist Donald Rowat (1968, 1973) who compared the central–local relationship in 17 federal capitals. This type of capital city research conceptualizes capital cities as objects of the nation state and does not tell us much about how their political economies function, what kind of economic interactions are prevalent in capital city regions, or what kind of policies are formulated by local actors.

Profiles of the four capital city regions

To gain a comprehensive understanding of the four capital cities, we present the geographical location, the political-institutional setting in the region and the population dynamics before turning to look intensively at the economic characteristics of the four secondary capital cities.

Bern

Bern is located between the three largest metropolitan regions in Switzerland (Zurich, Lausanne-Geneva, and Basel) in a region that is known as the Swiss Plateau. The Bern metropolitan area connects to a vast agricultural and mountainous hinterland (e.g. regions like the Emmental or the Bernese Oberland). As a result, Bern's more centrally-located jurisdictions are distinctively urban, but become increasingly rural with increased distance from the city center. The Bern metropolitan area is institutionally fragmented because it is home to 29 municipalities with rather small areas (see Figure 3.4).

The City of Bern has around 130,000 residents and is the fifth-largest city in Switzerland based on population, behind Zurich, Geneva, Basel, and Lausanne. The population of the City of Bern shrank significantly from 145,000 in 1980 to 122,000 in 2006 (see Table 3.1). This decline can be explained by the tendency of the population (particularly families) to move out of the city to smaller jurisdictions in the surrounding suburbs. To some extent, Bern has experienced the same declining population trends as other Swiss cities since the 1950s, which was further accentuated by the establishment of public-transport systems in the 1980s. However, this trend was more pronounced and prolonged in the case of Bern (Kaufmann, Warland, Mayer, & Sager, 2016). Recent data about population dynamics in Bern show a turnaround, and they illustrate that the city is benefitting from a trend toward reurbanization, meaning Bern's population is

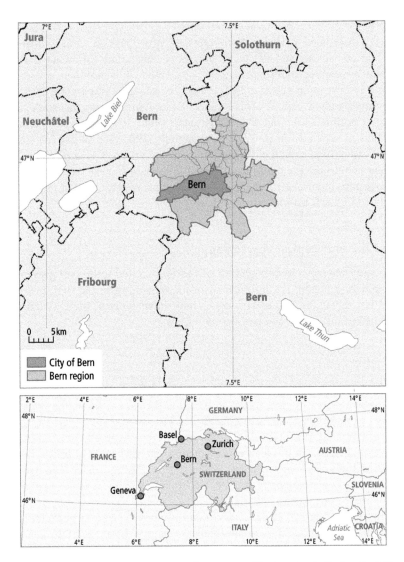

Figure 3.4 Map of the Bern metropolitan area and its location in Switzerland (Source: Alexander Hermann).

likely to grow in the future. The larger metropolitan area is home to 314,223 inhabitants. It ranks fourth among urban agglomerations in Switzerland, yet is significantly smaller when compared to metropolitan areas like Zurich, Geneva, and Basel. The agglomeration of Bern ranks third last out of 56 Swiss agglomerations with respect to population growth between 1980 and 2010 (Hermann, 2013).

Table 3.1 Population dynamics in the four capital city regions.

City	1980	1990	2000	2010	2015	Change (%) 1980–2015
Bern	145,285	134,629	122,484	123,841	131,554	−10.42
Bern metropolitan area	300,008	297,800	288,611	295,772	314,223	+4.52
Ottawa	557,829	687,825	786,975	911,985	957,148	+71.58
Ottawa-Gatineau metropolitan area	—	—	1,110,344	1,250,553	1,332,001	+19.97 (2001–2015)
The Hague	456,886	441,506	441,094	488,553	514,861	+12.69
The Hague metropolitan area	681,045	691,872	715,300	802,746	838,015	+23.05
Washington, D.C.	638,333	606,900	572,086	601,723	672,228	+5.04
Washington, D.C. metropolitan area	—	4,122,914	4,796,183	5,582,170	6,097,684	+32.39 (1990–2015)

Sources: Bern: Swiss Federal Statistical Office (2015a): Municipalities Statistics 1981–2014; Ottawa: Statistics Canada (2016a); The Hague: Statistics Netherlands (2014); Washington, D.C.: United States Census Bureau (2015).

Notes: Bern: The earliest data for Bern are for 1981, not 1980. The data for the Bern metropolitan area are aggregated based on municipality data referring to MS region 11. Ottawa: These population data consist of estimates based on population censuses. Earliest data at the regional level are from 2001. The Hague: The Municipality of The Hague is also known as *'s-Gravenhage*. We used the COROP region (*Agglomeratie 's-Gravenhage*) (=NUTS NL332). Washington, D.C.: These population data represent estimates based on population censuses. We used the Washington-Arlington-Alexandria (DC-VA-MD-WV) Metro Area. FIPS MSA Code 8840.

Ottawa

Ottawa is located in eastern Canada in the southeast of the Province of Ontario. It lies on the southern bank of the Ottawa River, which marks the border between the provinces of Ontario and Quebec for most of its length. Following municipal amalgamations of the large city of Ottawa and smaller municipalities in 2001–2002, the City of Ottawa covers a relatively large territory of approximately 2,796 square kilometers. In consequence, the metropolitan area now consists of a small urban core and more than 80% rural areas (Tassonyi, 2009). On the other side of the Ottawa River, the City of Gatineau has also grown as a result of municipal amalgamation. The Ottawa-Gatineau metropolitan area is dominated by the eponymous two cities that belong to different provinces. The provincial border between Ontario and Quebec cuts through the very center of the metropolitan area (see Figure 3.5). Thus, Ottawa is directly located at a symbolically and politically charged border (Veronis, 2013).

Ottawa is the fourth-largest city in Canada, ranked behind Toronto, Montreal, and Vancouver. The city has not experienced any decline due to suburbanization trends. In fact, the reverse is true, and the city has grown steadily since 1980.

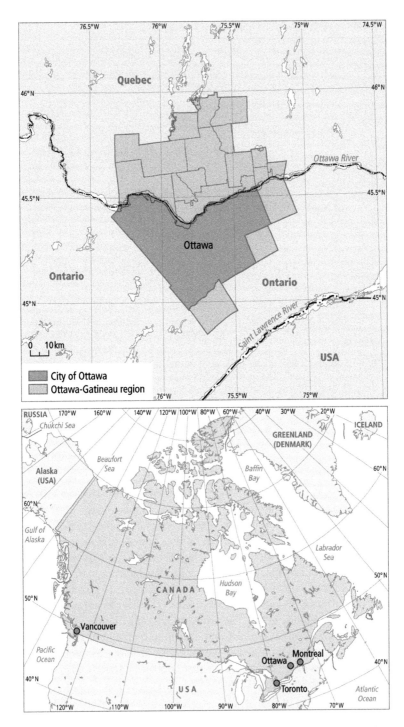

Figure 3.5 Map of the Ottawa-Gatineau metropolitan area and its location in Canada (Source: Alexander Hermann).

In 2015, around 957,000 people lived in the Canadian capital (see Table 3.1). The population censuses of 2006 and 2011 (Statistics Canada, 2016a) show that the City of Ottawa and the metropolitan area have grown at a fast pace. The fact that the City of Ottawa has the fourth-largest immigration rate following Toronto, Vancouver, and Calgary is partly responsible for this growth (Andrew & Doloreux, 2012). With a total of 883,391 inhabitants in 2011, Ottawa is 3.3 times bigger in population terms than Gatineau, which counted 265,349 inhabitants in 2011. A rather diverse population lives in the Ottawa-Gatineau metropolitan area: Half of the inhabitants grew up speaking English, almost a third of the population's mother tongue is French, while the rest speak a nonofficial language (Statistics Canada, 2011). This population diversity can be explained by the Ontario–Quebec border location, but is also due to immigration.

The Hague

The Hague is located in the so-called Randstad, a polycentric urban region located in the western part of the Netherlands. The name Randstad comes from the Dutch word *rand*, meaning rim, and refers to the horseshoe-shaped encircling of a green open area known as the Green Heart (Meijers, 2005). Beside Amsterdam, Rotterdam, and Utrecht, The Hague counts as one of the four urban centers in the Randstad. The latter can be further divided into a North Wing and a South Wing. The North Wing includes Amsterdam, Utrecht, and surrounding cities. The South Wing is the part of the Randstad that belongs to the province of South Holland (*Zuid Holland*) and includes Rotterdam, The Hague, and surrounding cities such as Delft and Leiden. The Randstad is institutionally fragmented due to the fact that many administrative boundaries cut through this functional urban area. The larger region of The Hague (*Agglomeratie 's-Gravenhage*), as defined by Statistics Netherlands (2014), consists of six municipalities (see Figure 3.6). The urban agglomerations within the Randstad are well connected. For example, the neighboring City of Rotterdam is only about 20 kilometers away and function-ally well connected to The Hague (Meijers, Hollander, & Hoogerbrugge, 2012).

Similar to Bern, The Hague has experienced fluctuating population dynamics over the past 55 years. In 1960, The Hague counted around 600,000 inhabitants. In the following years, the population steadily dropped until it stagnated at around 450,000 inhabitants between 1986 and 2003. Today, around 515,000 people live in The Hague (see Table 3.1). The population decrease in the 1970s and 1980s can be explained by the relocation of Dutch middle-class families to neighbor-ing towns, such as the newly-created satellite town of Zoetermeer (Meijers, Hoogerbrugge, Louw, Priemus, & Spaans, 2014). While the greater The Hague metropolitan area grew steadily over the last 35 years, the city only began to reurbanize in the first decade of the 21st century.

Washington, D.C.

The District of Columbia was originally a rotated rectangle carved out of the states of Maryland and Virginia. In 1846, the US Congress retroceded the entire

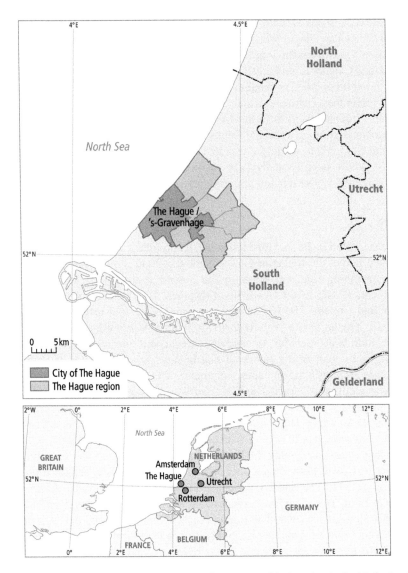

Figure 3.6 Map of The Hague metropolitan area and its location in the Netherlands (Source: Alexander Hermann).

district territory southwest of the Potomac River to the Commonwealth of Virginia, which explains its current shape (Richards, 2004). The Washington, D.C. metropolitan area covers 23 counties and independent cities and spans three states (Maryland, Virginia, and West Virginia) as well as the District at its very core (see Figure 3.7). An expert and a local policymaker add that the federal level

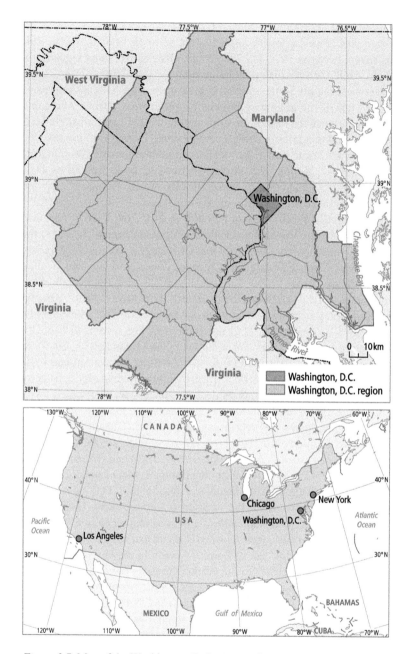

Figure 3.7 Map of the Washington, D.C. metropolitan area and its location in the United States (Source: Alexander Hermann).

as an additional political layer contributes further to the complexity of governing the metropolitan area (Washington, D.C. interviews, 37 & 44).

Washington, D.C. faced a decline in population between 1950 and 2006. This decline was severe between 1970 and 2000 as the District lost about a quarter of its population, while the suburban population doubled (O'Cleireacain & Rivlin, 2001). Leavers were mainly white middle-class families, with African Americans accounting for 70% of the remaining population (Sturtevant, 2014). According to the interviewees, since the turn of the millennium, the D.C. administration has made population growth a priority and has implemented measures to improve the school system, combat crime, and make location-based investments (Washington, D.C. interviews, 1, 37, & 46). This strategy proved to be successful as D.C. achieved a remarkable turnaround in population dynamics. Between 2000 and 2010, the District showed a population increase of nearly 30,000 people (5.2% growth) (Sturtevant, 2014). With about 672,000 in 2015, the District accounts for more than 10% of the population in the metropolitan region. In 2015, the Washington, D.C. metropolitan area was the sixth-largest metropolitan region in the US after New York, Los Angeles, Chicago, Dallas, and Houston (United States Census Bureau, 2015).

The demographics of the District are diverse and in some ways divided: "Despite the current population growth and the families that moved into D.C., there are two Washington, D.C.'s" (Washington, D.C. interview, 19). The income distribution peaks at the highest-income earners and at the very poor (Ghandi et al., 2009). In fact, the median income is USD 101,000 for D.C.'s white population and USD 39,000 for D.C. African Americans (Ruble, 2016). Income disparity constantly challenges the District's policymaking as decision-makers are confronted "with balancing the needs of its residents for services such as education, healthcare, transportation, housing, parks and recreation, and others" (Ghandi et al., 2009, p. 265). The District's poverty rate (19%) remains persistently high and was even higher for specific groups such as African Americans (26%) and Hispanics (22%) compared to Whites (7%) in 2012 (Ghandi, Spaulding, & McDonald, 2016).

The profiles of Bern, Ottawa, The Hague, and Washington, D.C. do not allow for any broad generalizations about the location of capital cities. However, as the four cases show, there is a tendency to establish capital cities in regions that bridge subnational political cleavages. One could argue that capital cities serve as symbols of national unity. In the case of Bern, for example, the city was chosen as the capital because of its proximity to the French-speaking parts of Switzerland. Similarly, Ottawa is located at the border between French-speaking and English-speaking Canada. Washington, D.C. was established between Northern and Southern states – a political compromise. The Hague was not chosen because of its symbolic location, but rather because of its symbolic legacy as a place of arbitration and neutrality. In all four capital cities, the population dynamics have developed somewhat differently over the last 35 years (see Table 3.1). Bern is the only capital city with fewer inhabitants in 2015 than in 1980. Ottawa is the only capital that has grown consistently since 1980. Bern, The Hague, and Washington, D.C. all experienced suburbanization of middle-class families. This trend ceased in the first decade of the 21st century, and since then all capital cities have seen population growth. It seems that the population dynamics in the four capital cities developed to a large extent exogenously from the capital city function. These population patterns are relatively comparable to the general suburbanization and reurbanization trends of cities in most Western democracies.

The economies of the four capital city regions

The economies of the four SCCs are deeply rooted in their function as capital cities. The most important shared characteristic is clearly the concentration of employment in the public sector. Of the four cities, the relative importance of this sector is the highest in Washington, D.C. At all levels of government, public administration accounts for 21.5% of Washington, D.C.'s workforce (Bureau of Labor Statistics, 2016). Very similar to the share in Washington, D.C., public administration accounts for 21% of the regional workforce in Ottawa (Statistics Canada, 2012). Of 315,455 Canadian federal employees, 135,865 are located in Ottawa (Statistics Canada, 2011). While in Canada, the provincial government is located in Toronto, the municipal government adds additional employees that total 148,500 jobs in public administration in Ottawa (Statistics Canada, 2012). Although public administration is also the key driver of the economy in The Hague, the share of the regional workforce is lower, at 14% (Uitvoeringsinstituut Werknemersverzekeringen, 2014). The central government accounts for the lion's share of the 58,700 jobs in public administration. This number used to be significantly lower in the 1970s and 1980s, when the central government relocated some of its agencies to Rijswijk, Voorburg as well as to more peripheral regions of the country (Meijers et al., 2014). This decentralization of national government agencies was inspired by the goal of ensuring equal economic development in all parts of the country. However, only a decade later, increasing international competition between cities caused a change in the distribution strategy of government agencies in favor of consolidating economic development in the cities of the Randstad. To strengthen The Hague, some of the agencies were relocated there in the late 1980s. In Bern, public administration, defense, and social security account for only 11.4% of the workforce (Swiss Federal Statistical Office, 2013). While part of the explanation for this low share lies in the idea of a lean federal government and relative autonomous cantonal and local governments, the shape of the statistical region also contributes to this low share. Despite the fact that the boundaries are defined in terms of functional integration, the economic structure of the agglomeration is characterized by heterogeneity. For example, the percentage of people who are employed in the service sector declines rapidly with distance from the center (Kaufmann et al., 2016). Thus, if we look only at the City of Bern, the share of people that work in public administration, defense, and social security increases to 17.3% (City of Bern, 2014b).

Hosting the national government not only creates employment in the public sector, but also influences the capital city's private sector in a number of ways. Many government employees live in the capital city region and spend part of

Figure 3.8 The Dutch government shapes The Hague's cityscape: The Binnenhof
          complex of buildings with the Prime Minister's office is seen at the front.
          At the back, from left to right: The Ministry of Education, Culture and
          Science, the Ministry of Health, Welfare and Sport, the Ministry of Security
          and Justice, and the Ministry of the Interior and Kingdom Relations
          (Source: Martin Warland).

their income on local goods and services. As such, national government has a
pronounced effect on the local resident-serving economy. In addition, public
procurement and tourism are important factors that induce further spending in
local economies. For example, a study that analyzed direct, indirect, and induced
effects of the Swiss federal government in 2004 revealed that the City of Bern,
as the core of the capital city region, benefited from CHF 555.7 million capital
city-related investments that induced an additional CHF 375 million added value
in the city (Ecoplan, 2004).

Tourism plays a crucial economic role in capital cities, often because of
the capital's iconic architecture (Maitland, 2009). This effect is evident in the
case of Washington, D.C., which had 20.2 million visitors in 2014, who spent
a total of USD 6.81 billion, and supported 74,570 jobs (Destination DC, 2015).
Although impossible to categorize and quantify, much of this tourism is linked
to Washington, D.C.'s capital city status. People from the USA and around the
world come to Washington, D.C. to experience its symbolic architecture. The
White House symbolizes US political and military power and the National Mall
represents many aspects of US heritage and culture unlike any other place.

In contrast to Washington, D.C., tourism does not drive the regional economy to a similar extent in Bern, The Hague, and Ottawa. International tourists neglect these cities to a large extent when compared with the prime cities of their nations. This becomes particularly obvious when comparing tourism in The Hague with tourism in Amsterdam. Amsterdam is not only the primary economic center, but also the cultural hub of the Netherlands. While The Hague accounted for 293,000 arrivals in 2011, Amsterdam accounted for 4.3 million overnight stays in the same year (Gastvrij Nederland, 2012). One can observe a similar pattern when comparing Bern to Zurich (Schweizer Tourismusverband, 2016) or Ottawa to Toronto (City of Ottawa, 2015; City of Toronto, 2016).

While the national parliaments are among the main tourist attractions in each of the three cities, there are also many government-related business trips on account of the presence of government agencies, private-sector firms, and other types of institutions. Meetings between politicians and interest groups take place in the capital city and attract visitors. This explains why the three cities show an above-average share of domestic visitors as opposed to international visitors (City of Ottawa, 2015). For example, 42% of the City of Bern's visitors are from Switzerland, a proportion half as large as the city of Zurich (21%) (Schweizer Tourismusverband, 2016).

The most important driver of the regional economy in the four cities is, however, the procurement activities of national government agencies. All four capital cities are the most important locations in their respective countries for national-level public-procurement activities. Firms that are located in Washington, D.C., for example, won USD 71.1 billion, or 16% of US federal

Figure 3.9 Swiss parliament building in Bern (Source: Frederike Asael).

procurement spending in 2015 (Fuller, 2016). These procurement activities generate direct effects, as well as indirect and induced effects. In 2002, a study on behalf of the National Capital City Region Commission revealed that any dollar spent on federal procurement in the Washington, D.C. region creates a benefit of USD 1.80 (Fuller, 2002).

The four capital city economies tend to be relatively immune to fluctuations and crises because their regional economies are anchored in the public sector. This is reflected in an unemployment rate ranging from 2.9 to 4.6% between 2004 and 2013 in the City of Bern (City of Bern, 2014a). As in Bern, Ottawa benefits from low unemployment rates: The rate of unemployment here increased from 4.3% in 2008 to 6.3% in 2013 – a moderate change compared to other Canadian cities (CBC, 2014). Thus, Ottawa struggles less during national economic downturns, but also benefits less from national economic growth. The US government follows an anti-cyclical employment approach in this regard. When private-sector employment in Washington, D.C. declined by 181,300 jobs during the Great Recession, the federal government tried to compensate to some extent and created 49,000 new federal government jobs in the region (Fuller, 2015). When the regional economy recovered, federal government downsized by cutting 23,800 jobs (Fuller, 2015). The Hague is an ambivalent case in this regard. With its large proportion of public-sector jobs, the region for a long time appeared to be immune to recession. Nevertheless, the financial crisis of 2008 had a strong impact on the regional economy. In the city of The Hague, the unemployment rate increased from 4.3% in 2008 to 11.1% in 2011 (Meijers et al., 2014). Unlike the US government, the Dutch government did not compensate for this job loss in the private sector. While the central government accounted for 123,355 employees in 2008 across the Netherlands, this number gradually decreased to 116,413 by 2013 (Ministry of the Interior and Kingdom Relations, 2016).

Features of the knowledge-based capital city economy

A prominent perspective on the regional economy of capital cities entails looking at direct, indirect, and induced income and employment effects that are generated through hosting the national government. However, this is hardly the most appropriate approach. What tends to be overlooked by this perspective is that the overall shift in the economy toward knowledge, information, and services has transformed the capital city economy. The four cities we examined also have distinct characteristics in terms of the knowledge-based economy.

Highly-regulated clusters in a knowledge-based economy

The four regions are very much alike in terms of the clustering of knowledge-based firms in highly-regulated sectors. These highly-regulated sectors benefit from the presence of and spatial proximity to the national government. Ottawa's knowledge-based economy is specialized in aerospace, security and defense, software, communications technologies, cleantech and life science, as well as digital media, film, and TV (Invest Ottawa, 2017). Together, these clusters account for more than 1,900 firms, or 75,000 employees. Ottawa's knowledge economy features many leading global defense firms, such as General Dynamics with 660 local employees, Lockheed Martin with 250 local employees, and Thales with 180 local employees (Ottawa Business Journal, 2014).

Clusters in Bern also reflect the region's advantage in hosting the federal government. Knowledge-based firms here specialize in information and communications technology (ICT), consulting, energy, and medicine (Wirtschaftsraum Bern, 2015). The ICT and consulting clusters are closely connected to federal government agencies, whereas the energy and medical clusters are primarily linked to agencies at the cantonal level of government. The economic structure is strongly characterized by microenterprises, with less than ten full-time equivalent employees, accounting for 85% of all firms (Swiss Federal Statistical Office, 2015b).

The Hague's knowledge-based economy is specialized in ICT, accounting for 14,000 jobs (City of The Hague, 2014c); as well as in security, accounting for 10,000 jobs (City of The Hague, 2014d); in finance, accounting for 13,000 jobs (City of The Hague, 2014b); in oil and gas, accounting for 12,000 jobs (City of The Hague, 2014a); and in international organizations, accounting for 19,500 jobs (Decisio & City of The Hague, 2014). The ICT cluster and security cluster in particular cannot fully be explained by the presence of the national government, but need to be considered in the context of The Hague's role as a location for international organizations. The Hague is one of the main centers of the United Nations, alongside New York, Geneva, and Vienna. Approximately 370 international organizations are at the core of this cluster, including large EU organizations, nongovernmental organizations, and embassies, as well as their affiliated organizations (Decisio & City of The Hague, 2015). The most prominent examples include the International Court of Justice, the International Criminal Court, and the European Patent Office. The cluster of firms in finance has no relation to international organizations, but is strongly linked to the national government. Large national finance firms co-locate with national government agencies as they are sensitive to changes in the regulatory framework. Firms in this cluster focus on long-term activities such as pension funds, insurance, and asset management, as opposed to short-term trading transactions. Therefore, The Hague's financial activities are sometimes referred to as "slow finance" (The Hague interview, 8). The cluster of oil and gas firms is a product of history. Linkages to the Dutch government have historically been important for these firms because the Dutch government administered colonies that owned large oil fields. For example, Royal Dutch Shell, the anchor organization of this cluster, is located in The Hague because the first oil extractions in the former Dutch colony of Indonesia needed authorization and support from the colonial administration. Nowadays, linkages between firms in this cluster and national government agencies are relatively unimportant.

Similarly, in Washington, D.C., there are several clusters of knowledge-based firms that are linked to the federal government (Fuller, 2015). These clusters

Table 3.2 Overview of clusters in the four secondary capital cities.

Bern	Ottawa	The Hague	Washington, D.C.
ICT	Software	ICT	ICT
Consulting	Communications technologies	International	Business and
Energy	Aerospace, security, and	organizations	financial services
Medical	defense	Security	Security
cluster	Life sciences	Business services	Advocacy
	Digital media, film, and TV	Energy	Biological and
	Cleantech		health technology

operate in highly-regulated sectors. The largest cluster in the region is the ICT cluster, with around 205,000 jobs. Early developments of this cluster were closely related to the development of the Internet (Ceruzzi, 2008). In cooperation with the Defense Advanced Research Projects Agency (DARPA), firms in Washington, D.C. invented the underlying technologies. These firms grew substantially, and the region's ICT cluster became the largest agglomeration of telecommunication providers in North America (Metropolitan Washington Council of Governments, 2012). Another important cluster is business and financial services, which accounts for 190,000 regional jobs (Fuller, 2015). Between 2005 and 2015, the cluster experienced substantial growth of 39%. Washington, D.C. also offers advantages for knowledge-based firms in the security sector. Since the region is home to the National Security Agency, the Department of Defense, and the Department of Homeland Security, security firms cluster in Washington, D.C. and account for 124,000 jobs. As major threats take the form of cyber-attacks, many of these firms specialize in cyber intelligence and network protection. A more traditional, but also knowledge-based cluster, is advocacy, which accounts for 116,000 jobs. The share of advocacy organizations, such as lobbying firms and national sector associations, is more than three times higher than the figure nationwide. Finally, knowledge-based firms also cluster in biological and health technology, which accounts for 55,400 jobs. As a result of the extensive research resources of the National Institutes of Health (NIH), the region is also a competitive location for firms in biotechnology (Mayer, 2007).

Underlying trends: Increased tertiarization

In all four SCCs, the knowledge-based economy is highly specialized in the knowledge-intensive business service (KIBS) sector. Table 3.3 shows the ratio between employment in the KIBS sector and employment in the high- and medium-tech manufacturing sector for the four regions compared to other cities. If we compare the four case study regions to the three largest regions in each of the countries concerned, it becomes apparent that the KIBS sector has a unique importance in SCCs. This is particularly pronounced in Washington, D.C. While there are about six jobs in the KIBS sector for every job in the high- and medium-tech manufacturing sector in New York, this ratio is about four

Table 3.3 Number of employees in knowledge-intensive sector for selected regions in Switzerland, Canada, USA, and the Netherlands, 2012.

Category of city	Name of city	Knowledge-intensive business service	High- and medium-tech manufacturing	Ratio
Switzerland				
Capital city	Bern	30,877	8,429	3.66
Largest city	Zurich	112,074	33,402	3.35
Second-largest city	Geneva	37,972	20,133	1.88
Third-largest city	Basel	36,321	41,948	0.87
Canada				
Capital city	Ottawa	93,271	9,2411	10.09
Largest city	Toronto	251,752	106,032	2.37
Second-largest city	Montreal	426,115	120,909	3.52
Third-largest city	Vancouver	166,795	30,195	5.52
USA				
Capital city	Washington, D.C.	517,949	21,353	24.26
Largest city	New York	710,316	123,111	5.77
Second-largest city	Los Angeles	633,648	195,111	3.25
Third-largest city	Chicago	322,567	125,272	2.58
The Netherlands				
Capital city	The Hague	50,098	3,642	13.76
Largest city	Groot-Rijnmond	56,645	15,401	3.68
Second-largest city	Groot-Amsterdam	123,606	9,665	12.79
Third-largest city	Utrecht	109,193	9,312	11.73

Sources: SFSO 2013 (Switzerland); Statistics Canada 2013 (Canada); US Census Bureau 2016 (USA); LISA (The Netherlands).

Note: Data for Canada refers to 2011. Moreover, numbers of employees were estimated based on mean value formation of employment size categories. Firms with 500 or more employees were excluded since it was not possible to make any reliable estimates for this category on account of undefined limits ("500 or more").

times higher in Washington, D.C. Similarly, Ottawa stands out in the national comparison because its economic structure reveals a strong specialization of knowledge-based firms in the service sector. In Switzerland and the Netherlands, the differences between SCCs and major regions is not as pronounced. In our comparison, Bern leads in terms of KIBS specialization, but is closely followed by Zurich. Similarly, The Hague shows the highest degree of specialization of knowledge-based employment in KIBS but is closely followed by Amsterdam.

A closer look at the composition of the KIBS sector reveals that IT is the most important subsector in Washington, D.C. and Ottawa, and the second most important subsector in The Hague and Bern (see Table 3.4). Firms in

Table 3.4 Composition of KIBS sector, 2012.

North American Industry Classification System (NAICS)	Washington, D.C.		New York	
	Employees	%	Employees	%
Computer systems design and related services	184,170	35.6	127,972	18.0
Management, scientific, and technical consulting services	103,758	20.0	80,986	11.4
Architectural, engineering, and related services	73,328	14.2	68,609	9.7
Legal services	49,001	9.5	130,981	18.4
Scientific research and development services	44,994	8.7	45,889	6.5
Accounting, tax preparation, bookkeeping, and payroll services	30,017	5.8	117,570	16.6
Other professional, scientific, and technical services	16,282	3.1	41,423	5.8
Advertising, public relations, and related services	13,745	2.7	82,692	11.6
Specialized design services	2,654	0.5	14,194	2.0
Total	517,949	100	710,316	100

NAICS	Ottawa		Toronto	
	Employees	%	Employees	%
Computer systems design and related services	19,676	33.1	74,698.5	27.6
Architectural, engineering, and related services	10,459.5	17.6	36,924	13.6
Scientific research and development services	7,948.5	13.4	11,259.5	4.2
Management, scientific, and technical consulting services	6,524.5	11.0	37,247	13.7
Legal services	4,455.5	7.5	28,960	10.7
Other professional, scientific, and technical services	4,172	7.0	23,994.5	8.9
Accounting, tax preparation, bookkeeping, and payroll services	3,675.5	6.2	24,363.5	9.0
Advertising, public relations, and related services	1,641	2.8	26,123	9.6
Specialized design services	851	1.4	7,396	2.7
Total	59,403.5	100	270,966	100

General Classification of Economic Activities (NOGA)	Bern		Zurich	
	Employees	%	Employees	%
Architectural and engineering activities; technical testing and analysis	8,455	27.4	25,526	22.8
Computer programming, consultancy, and related activities	8,022	26.0	24,152	21.6
Activities of head offices; management consultancy activities	5,610	18.2	27,984	25.0
Legal and accounting activities	4,778	15.5	18,993	16.9
Advertising and market research	1,856	6.0	8,288	7.4
Scientific research and development	1,142	3.7	3,410	3.0
Information service activities	1,014	3.3	3,721	3.3
Total	30,877	100	112,074	100

Standard Industrial Classifications (SBI)	The Hague		Amsterdam	
	Employees	%	Employees	%
Legal and accounting activities	14,320	28.6	28,564	23.1
Computer programming, consultancy, and related activities	9,703	19.4	18,939	15.3
Activities of head offices; management consultancy activities	8,984	17.9	35,711	28.9
Architectural and engineering activities; technical testing and analysis	8,233	16.4	13,409	10.8
Scientific research and development	4,591	9.2	5,108	4.1
Advertising and market research	3,217	6.4	18,170	14.7
Information service activities	1,050	2.1	3,705	3.0
Total	50,098	100	123,606	100

Sources: SFSO 2013 (Switzerland); Statistics Canada 2013 (Canada); US Census Bureau 2016 (USA); LISA (The Netherlands).

Note: Data for Canada refers to 2011.

this KIBS subsector help their clients deal with complex information system environments and digitalization processes. Major activities include system integration, software development, network security, and pervasive computing. Due to the fast-changing nature of this subsector, firms are constantly involved in knowledge creation and knowledge processing (Strambach, 2008). Since the IT subsector is an important factor in virtually all sectors of modern economies, the regional economies under study are well equipped for future challenges as they provide a strong innovation capacity in IT KIBS.

KIBS firms in public procurement

Two major factors explain the relative importance of the KIBS sector in the four capital cities and, in particular, the importance of KIBS firms in the IT cluster. First, due to their status as capital cities, the four cities have never developed a strong manufacturing base (Andrew & Doloreux, 2012). In part, the cities were chosen as the seat of government precisely because of the lack of industrial importance, in order to separate and balance economic and political power (Gottmann, 1977; Nagel et al., 2013). Second, national government agencies increasingly rely on knowledge inputs from KIBS firms. The shift in the demand structure of national government agencies from industrial goods to complex services is well documented in the case of the US defense industry (Markusen, Hall, Campbell, & Deitrick, 1991) and more recently in the field of foreign aid (Roberts, 2014). Markusen et al. (1991) describe how "the tertiarization of the defense industry" increased the importance of interaction between supplying firms and demanding agencies. Firms that work on government contracts benefit in several ways from spatial proximity to federal agencies on the demand side, a process that we will discuss in the next chapter. This shift in the demand structure caused a transformation of Washington, D.C.'s economy from traditional services to complex services such as system integration. Because of the aforementioned lack of any strong manufacturing base in Washington, D.C., the region was able to easily adapt to this transformation. In this regard, Fuller (2015, p. 11) argues that Washington, D.C. "always possessed the fundamental ingredients of the future economy for which the nation's other major metropolitan area economies are striving."

US federal procurement might be an extreme case demonstrating the shift toward KIBS due to its intensity and pace. Nevertheless, the general trend in public demand toward complex services is the same in nearly all industrialized countries (Dunleavy & Carrera, 2013). This enhances the capital cities' competitive advantage in hosting firms that rely on close collaborations with government agencies. For example, if we look at Canada, KIBS firms that are involved in public procurement are disproportionally concentrated in Ottawa. The region's share of total federal procurement between 2009 and 2014 was 19.34%, or CAD 16.90 billion (Figure 3.10). This share is significantly higher if we look only at federal spending for KIBS as opposed to federal procurement spending for all goods and services. Of a total of 12.56%, or CAD 10.99 billion, spent by federal agencies on KIBS between 2009 and 2014, Ottawa won 36.61%, or CAD 4.02 billion.

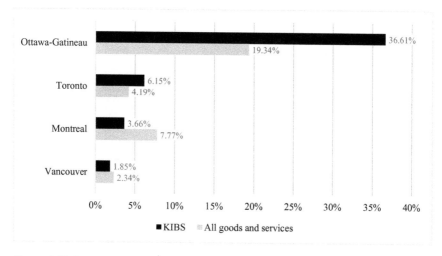

Figure 3.10 Percentage of public procurement of KIBS compared to all goods and services, Canada (Source: Public Works and Government Services Canada (PWGSC), 2009–2014).

The data show that while economic impact analyses look only at the amount of public-procurement spending that goes to firms located in capital cities, it is important to note that it is knowledge-intensive firms in particular that co-locate with national government agencies on the demand side. In this regard, the four SCCs may benefit from any further increase in the demand for IT systems (Dunleavy, Margetts, Bastow, & Tinkler, 2008). One major underlying force is that national government agencies tend to use new technologies to perform traditional public services more efficiently and effectively. Citizens and businesses increasingly interact digitally with government agencies. To give but one example, in many countries, income tax returns can now be filed electronically, via online applications. As a result of the overall trend toward IT, public procurement of government IT systems typically accounts for 1 to 1.5% of GDP (Dunleavy et al., 2008).

Table 3.5 shows the volume of public procurement, at all levels of government, for the countries of the four case studies. The US clearly stands out in terms of total public-procurement spending. The US public-sector purchases more goods and services than any other public sector in the world (Congressional Research Service, 2015). US federal procurement spending not only stands out in terms of its absolute size, but is also the only case in our sample in which procurement spending is rapidly declining. After a period of immense growth between 1992 and 2009, particularly in the wake of the terrorist attacks on September 11th, 2001, federal procurement spending has been in decline since 2010 (Gordon, 2012). Meanwhile, the Netherlands stands out in terms of size of public procurement as a share of total government expenditure. The Netherlands spent more

Table 3.5 Public-procurement spending in Switzerland, the Netherlands, Canada, and USA, 2014.

Country	Total public-procurement spending (in USD million)	Public-procurement spending per capita (in USD)	Public procurement as share of total government expenditure (in %)	Public procurement as percentage of GDP (in %)
Switzerland	5,507	692.36	25	8.4
The Netherlands	14,245	847.70	44.4	20.8
Canada	13,805	390.87	32.8	13.3
USA	445,752*	1,408.55*	26.1	10.1

Sources: USAspendig.gov (USA); PIANOo, 2011 (The Netherlands); SFDF 2015 (Switzerland); PWGSC 2015 (Canada); OECD 2015.

Notes: Data for the Netherlands refer to 2010.

*Data account only for procurement spending at the federal level of government.

than 44% of total government expenditure on public procurement – more than any other OECD country (OECD, 2015). In all four countries, governments significantly stimulate the private market through public procurement.

Knowledge infrastructure

Knowledge organizations (e.g. universities, research laboratories, etc.) are considered an important element in regional innovation systems (RIS) (Doloreux & Parto, 2005). The emergence of Ottawa's technology cluster is an excellent example of the role that national-level research organizations potentially play for regional innovation and economic development. In 1916, the Canadian government founded the National Research Council (NRC) as a general-purpose scientific organization. The foundation was inspired by other national laboratories that were established about the same time, such as Australia's Advisory Council of Science and Industry or the United Kingdom's Department of Scientific and Industrial Research (Phillipson, 1991). In the 1950s, the NRC began to flourish. It grew into a large organization during World War II and was equipped with an adequate budget, political support, and the clear task to train more researchers. The NRC attracted scientists and engineers from all parts of Canada and from around the world. Scholarships and grants were awarded to young researchers who moved to Ottawa. Moreover, federal research laboratories that were operated by the NRC began to spin off firms such as Computing Devices (now General Dynamics Canada), Northern Radio, and Mechron (Doyletech, 2008). The 1960s were marked by the development of key technologies that took place in the sphere of the NRC (Bathelt, 1991). Computing Devices, for example, developed military technologies such as aircraft navigation systems. Joint research with the NRC and public-procurement contracts triggered the growth of Computing Devices and led to a second generation of spin-offs. One of these firms was Leigh Instruments, which contracted with the NRC to manufacture and market the crash position indicator, a precursor of the modern black box flight recorder. NRC spin-offs like Leigh Instruments created "the core of the local telecommunication industries," which began to prosper (Spigel, 2011, p. 55). During the 1980s and 1990s, Ottawa's high-tech cluster experienced rapid growth. Public R & D investments were increasingly matched by private investments. The endowment with federal research laboratories, and in particular the NRC Division of Radio and Electrical Engineering, contributed to Northern Electric's decision to locate its R & D activities in Ottawa (Marsh, 2000). Northern Electric was originally a subsidiary of the US firm Western Electric but became an independent firm under the brand Bell Northern Research, which was later acquired by Nortel. Nortel had a significant impact on Ottawa's cluster development through its function as an incubator of start-ups. According to a genealogy of high-technology firms (Doyletech, 2008), 329 high-tech firms in Ottawa trace themselves back to Nortel, either through transfer of technology or key people. Nortel was a pivotal factor for the creation of an entrepreneurial environment in which firms focused almost entirely on private-sector clients. However, federal research laboratories remained important in providing research that is relevant in the field of telecommunications. In the mid-1990s, Ottawa secured 30% of Canada's federally-funded research activities, which increased to CAD 5 billion per year (Mallett, 2004). By 2000, the cluster reached its peak. What emerged from military-related technologies had become "Silicon Valley North," a global knowledge hub for microelectronics, telecommunications, and software (Shavinina, 2004). Although the bursting of the Internet bubble in 2001 and the financial crisis in 2008 hit the region hard, the number of ICT workers has been on the rise since 2009. In 2014, it reached a total of 68,300 workers in this sector, which comes close to the maximum of 72,700 back in 2000 (Ottawa Business Journal, 2014). Thus, while the later development of the Ottawa high-tech cluster was the result of many regional and extra-regional factors (Spigel, 2011), it was the public research infrastructure that triggered cluster development in the first place.

The federal government also drives much of the research in Washington, D.C. There are a total of 103 federal laboratories, including the prestigious Naval Research Laboratory. Moreover, 13 out of 42 federally-funded R & D centers are located within the region (Fuller, 2015). One important field of research is health, on account of the fact that the NIH has substantial research resources at its disposal in the region. Moreover, much of the federally-funded research takes place within the field of defense. In this regard, DARPA has gained global recognition as a driver for R & D projects that often result in radical innovations. In addition to federally-funded research, R & D activities at colleges and universities accounted for more than USD 3 billion in 2010 (Metropolitan Washington Council of Governments, 2012). Important universities include the "three Georges" – Georgetown University, George Washington University, and George Mason University.

In The Hague, the Netherlands Organization of Applied Scientific Research (TNO) is an important capital city-specific element of the knowledge infrastructure. TNO is devoted to providing technical expertise in defense and security, as well as other government-dominated industries such as urban development, energy, and health. In 2015, revenue totaled EUR 416 million, of which approximately 40% was from direct government funding (TNO, 2015). Partnering with the Ministry of Defense, TNO conducts a great deal of research in the field of defense. When looking at the wider research infrastructure of The Hague, it becomes apparent that the City of The Hague itself does not have a university, giving it the unofficial and unflattering title of "the largest European city without its own university." Nevertheless, the region also encompasses the cities of Leiden and Delft, both of which are home to universities.

In our case study sample, Bern is an exception as regards federally-shaped knowledge infrastructure. Some of the organizations that one would expect to find in the capital city are decentralized and spread across the country (Kübler, 2009). In 1854, politicians decided that Zurich should host the Swiss Federal Institute of Technology (ETH). It was a conscious decision to balance power relationships in the newly-founded federation (Von Bergen & Steiner, 2012). Bern had already been selected as the seat of the government, so that hosting the ETH should have satisfied Zurich's political class. The decision had far-reaching consequences as the ETH Zurich became a world-class university with strong spillover effects. For example, since 1973, ETH Zurich has served as a seedbed for 315 spin-offs (Pinter, 2015), and these firms created more jobs than the average start-up in Switzerland (Oskarsson & Schläpfer, 2008). The status of Bern as a capital city without major federal research organizations did not alter, even when a second ETH was designated. In 1969, the University of Lausanne was restructured, and the former École polytechnique de l'Université de Lausanne became the ETH Lausanne (École polytechnique fédérale de Lausanne—EPFL) (Jorio, 2012). Despite the lack of federally-funded research, Bern has abundant sources of knowledge and talent. The University of Bern and the Bern University of Applied Sciences are the two most important educational organizations.

Because of the broad research infrastructure and the concentration of KIBS firms, the four cases are characterized by a highly-educated workforce. For example, Ottawa is the region of Canada with the highest proportion of the workforce with a doctorate degree (1.67%), the highest proportion of master's degrees (7.64%), and the second-highest proportion of the workforce with a post-secondary degree (61.63%) (Statistics Canada, 2016b). The same pattern can be found in Washington, D.C., where 47% of the workforce holds a bachelor's degree and 23% an advanced degree (Metropolitan Washington Council of Governments, 2012), making Washington, D.C. the most educated metropolitan area in the country (Marchio & Berube, 2015).

In summary, the four cities are similar in terms of their preconditions for innovations. They all feature highly-developed knowledge-based economies characterized by a large pool of qualified labor. More specifically, the four cities feature knowledge-based economies that are specialized in KIBS. Comparing the four cases, respectively, to the largest regions in their respective countries reveals that the relative importance of KIBS is greater in the four cities under study. The growing demand among national governmental agencies for complex IT solutions explains this economic pattern. There is a disproportionately-high concentration of KIBS firms that provide complex IT services to national governmental agencies in the four capital cities examined. The following chapter will analyze how these firms benefit from being located in the capital cities. We investigate the unique type of RIS that occur in government-anchored capital cities, but we will also provide explanations as to why these similar preconditions for innovation translate into different dynamics in the four cities.

References

Andrew, C. (2013). The Case of Ottawa. In Klaus-Jürgen Nagel (Ed.), *The Problem of the Capital City: New Research on Federal Capitals and Their Territory* (pp. 83–102). Barcelona: Generalitat de Catalunya: Institut d'Estudis Autonomics.

Andrew, C., & Chiasson, G. (2012). La ville d'Ottawa: Représentation symbolique et image publique. In R. Clement (Ed.), *Villes et langues: Governance et politiques*. Ottawa: Invenire Books.

Andrew, C., & Doloreux, D. (2012). Economic development, social inclusion and urban governance: The case of the city-region of Ottawa in Canada. *International Journal of Urban and Regional Research*, *36*(6), 1288–1305. https://doi.org/10.1111/j.1468-2427.2011.01025.x

Andrew, C., & Doloreux, D. (2014). Linking Innovation and Inclusion: The Governance Question in Ottawa. In N. Bradford & A. Bramwell (Eds.), *Governing Urban Economies: Innovation and Inclusion in Canadian City-Regions* (pp. 137–160). Toronto: University of Toronto Press.

Bathelt, H. (1991). *Schlüsseltechnologie-Industrien. Standortverahlten und Einfluss auf den regionalen Strukturwandel in den USA und in Kanada*. Berlin and Heidelberg: Springer Verlag.

Bureau of Labor Statistics. (2016). *Washington Area Employment – July 2016*. Retrieved from www.bls.gov/regions/mid-atlantic/news-release/areaemployment_washingtondc.htm

CBC. (2014). *Ottawa's Economy 5 Years After the Market Crash*. Retrieved from www.cbc.ca/news/canada/ottawa/ottawa-s-economy-5-years-after-the-market-crash-1.2555310

Ceruzzi, P. E. (2008). *Internet Alley: High Technology in Tysons Corner, 1945–2005*. Cambridge, MA: The MIT Press.

Champagne, E. (2011). Transportation Failure in the Federal Capital Region. In R. Chattopadhyay & G. Paquet (Eds.), *The Unimagined Canadian Capital: Challenges for the Federal Capital Region* (pp. 27–34). Ottawa: Invenire Books.

City of Bern. (2014a). *Arbeitslosigkeit in der Stadt Bern 2004 bis 2013: Entwicklung, Verteilung und kleinräumige Betrachtung*.

City of Bern. (2014b). *Jahrbuch 2014 (Berichtsjahr 2013)*.

City of Ottawa. (2015). *Tourism Edition: Visitor Profile 2012*. Retrieved from http://ottawa.ca/en/business/-business-resources/economic-development-initiatives/tourism-edition-visitor-profile

City of The Hague. (2014a). Factsheet: Energy: Oil & Gas.

City of The Hague. (2014b). Factsheet: Finance.

City of The Hague. (2014c). Factsheet: ICT & Telecom.

City of The Hague. (2014d). Factsheet: The Hague Security Delta.

City of Toronto. (2016). *Key Industry Sectors – Tourism, 2015*.

Congressional Research Service. (2015). *The Federal Acquisition Regulation (FAR): Answers to Frequently Asked Questions*.

Decisio, & City of The Hague. (2015). The Hague: International City of Peace and Justice. Study on behalf of the City of The Hague.

Destination DC. (2015). *Visitor Statistics*. Retrieved from http://destinationdc.dmplocal. com/dsc/collateral/2014_Washington_DC_Visitor_Statistics.pdf

Doloreux, D., & Parto, S. (2005). Regional innovation systems: Current discourse and unresolved issues. *Technology in Society, 27*(2), 133–153.Doyletech Corporation. (2008). The Family Tree of Ottawa-Gatineau High Technology Companies. Poster. Ottawa.

Dunleavy, P., & Carrera, L. (2013). *Growing the Productivity of Government Services*. Cheltenham: Edward Elgar.

Dunleavy, P., Margetts, H., Bastow, S., & Tinkler, J. (2008). *Digital Era Governance: IT Corporations, the State, and e-Government*. Oxford: Oxford University Press.

Ecoplan. (2004). Bern als Bundesstadt: Positive und negative Effekte. Report. Retrieved from www.bk.admin.ch/themen/gesetz/07212/07416/index.html?lang=de

Elazar, D. J. (1987). *Exploring Federalism*. Tuscaloosa: The University of Alabama Press.

Fauntroy, M. (2003). District of Columbia voting representation in Congress: Background, issues and opinions. In D. Martin (Ed.), *District of Columbia: Current Issues* (pp. 23–42). Waltham, MA: Nova Biomedical.

Fauntroy, M. (2009). Home Rule for the District of Columbia. In R. Walters & T.-M. Travis (Eds.), *Democratic Destiny and the District of Columbia: Federal Politics and Public Policy*. Lanham, MD: Lexington Books.

Fuller, S. (2002). The Impact of Federal Procurement on the National Capital Region. www.ncpc.gov/DocumentDepot/Publications/FedProcurementReport.pdf.

Fuller, S. (2015). The Roadmap for the Washington Region's Future Economy. Analysis prepared for the 2030 Group.

Fuller, S. (2016). The Roadmap for the Washington Region's Future Economy. Analysis presented at the 24th Annual Economic Conference (January 14, 2016).

Gastvrij Nederland. (2012). *Key Figures 2012 – Leisure and Tourism Economy*.

Gerber, R. (2015). Bern – eine Zunftstadt? Die Ratensetzung von 1384 und deren Folgen für die Stadt am Ende des Mittelalters. *Schweizerische Zeitschrift für Geschichte, 65*(2), 164–192.

Ghandi, N., Spaulding, J., & McDonald, G. (2016). Budget Growth, Spending, and Inequality in DC, 2002–2013. In D. Hyra & S. Prince (Eds.), *Capital Dilemma: Growth and Inequality in Washington, D.C.* (pp. 159–179). New York and London: Routledge.

Ghandi, N., Yilmaz, Y., Zahradnik, R., & Edwards, M. (2009). Washington, District of Columbia, United States of America. In E. Slack & R. Chattopadhyay (Eds.), *Finance and Governance of Capital Cities in Federal Systems* (pp. 263–291). Montreal, Quebec and Kingston, Ontario: McGill-Queen's University Press.

Gilliland, A. (2013). Choosing the Federal Capital: A Comparative Study of the United States, Canada and Australia. In K.-J. Nagel (Ed.), *The Problem of the Capital City: New Research on Federal Capitals and Their Territory* (pp. 25–60). Barcelona: Generaltat de Catalunya, Institut d'Estudis Autonomics.

Gordon, D. I. (2012). Reflections on the federal procurement landscape. *The Government Contractor, 54*(7).

Gottmann, J. (1977). The role of capital cities. *Ekistics: The Problem and Science of Human Settlements, 44*(264), 240–243.

Hamilton, A., Madison, J., & Jay, J. (1982). *The Federalist Papers*. New York: Bantam.

Harris, C. W. (1995). *Congress and the Governance of the Nation's Capital: The Conflict of Federal and Local Interests*. Washington, D.C.: Georgetown University Press.

Hazelton Jr, G. C. (1914). *The National Capitol: Its Architecture, Art, and History*. New York: JF Taylor & Company.

Hermann, M. (2013). Dynamische Stadt, bremsendes Land? Berns Realität ist komplexer. Retrieved from www.forum.unibe.ch/de/Veranstaltungen/StadtLand/Folien/Folien_Hermann.pdf

Invest Ottawa. (2017). Ottawa, Canada. Why Would You Want to Live Anywhere Else? Retrieved from www.investottawa.ca/why-ottawa/

Jorio, M. (Ed.). (2012). *Historisches Lexikon der Schweiz*. Basel: Stiftung Historisches Lexikon der Schweiz.

Kaufmann, D., Warland, M., Mayer, H., & Sager, F. (2016). Bern's positioning strategies: Escaping the fate of a secondary capital city? *Cities, 53*, 120–129. https://doi.org/10.1016/j.cities.2016.02.005

Knight, D. (1977). *Choosing Canada's Capital: Jealousy and Friction in the 19. Century*. Toronto: McClelland & Stewart.

Kübler, D. (2009). Bern, Switzerland. In E. Slack & R. Chattopadhyay (Eds.), *Finance and Governance of Capital Cities in Federal Systems* (pp. 238–262). Montreal, Quebec and Kingston, Ontario: McGill-Queen's University Press.

Maitland, R. (2009). Introduction: National Capitals and City Tourism. In R. Maitland & B. W. Ritchie (Eds.), *City Tourism – National Capital Perspectives*. London: MPG Books Group.

Mallett, J. G. (2004). Silicon Valley North: The Formation of the Ottawa Innovation Cluster. In L. Shavinina (Ed.), *Silicon Valley North – A High-Tech Cluster of Innovation and Entrepreneurship* (pp. 3–20). Amsterdam: Elsevier.

Marchio, N., & Berube, A. (2015). *Benchmarking Greater Washington's Global Reach – The National Capital Region in the World Economy*. Washington, D.C.: The Brookings Institution.

Markusen, A., Hall, P., Campbell, S., & Deitrick, S. (1991). *The Rise of the Gunbelt: The Military Remapping of Industrial America*. Oxford: Oxford University Press.

Marsh, J. H. (2000). *The Canadian Encyclopedia*. Toronto: McClelland & Stewart

Mayer, H. (2007). Biotech industry clusters in the United States: The case of Washington D.C. and Kansas City. *Geographische Rundschau International Edition, 3*(1), 10–16.

Meijers, E. (2005). Polycentric urban regions and the quest for synergy: Is a network of cities more than the sum of the parts? *Urban Studies, 42*(4), 765–781.

Meijers, E., Hollander, K., & Hoogerbrugge, M. (2012). *Case Study Metropolitan Region Rotterdam-The Hague*. The Hague: European Metropolitan Network Institute.

Meijers, E., Hoogerbrugge, M., Louw, E., Priemus, H., & Spaans, M. (2014). City profile: The Hague. *Cities, 41*, 92–100.

Metropolitan Washington Council of Governments. (2012). *Economy Forward*. Retrieved from www.mwcog.org/uploads/pub-documents/ov5dxfc-20120912132659.pdf

Ministry of the Interior and Kingdom Relations. (2016). *The Dutch Public Sector*.

Nagel, K.-J. (2013). Representation for the taxed? Projects to end the asymmetry of Washington DC and why (most of them) have failed. In K.-J. Nagel (Ed.), *The Problem of the Capital City: New Research on Federal Capitals and Their Territory* (pp. 61–82). Barcelona: Generaltat de Catalunya, Institut d'Estudis Autonomics.

Nagel, K.-J., Andrew, C., Gilliland, A., Obydenkova, A., Van Wynsberghe, C., & Zimmermann, H. (2013). *The Problem of the Capital City: New Research on Federal*

Capitals and Their Territory. Barcelona: Generaltat de Catalunya, Institut d'Estudis Autonomics.

Ottawa Business Journal. (2014). Employment and Investment in Ottawa's Tech Sector. *Ottawa Technology* (supplement), Fall issue.

O'Cleireacain, C. (1997). *The Orphaned Capital: Adopting the Right Revenues for the District of Columbia*. Washington, D.C.: The Brookings Institution Press.

O'Cleireacain, C., & Rivlin, A. (2001). Envisioning a Future Washington. Retrieved from www.brookings.edu/~/media/research/files/reports/2001/6/cities%20ocleireacain/dcfuture.pdf

OECD. (2015). *Government at a Glance*. Paris: OECD Publishing.

Oskarsson, I., & Schläpfer, A. (2008). *The Performance of Spin-Off Companies at the Swiss Federal Institute of Technology Zurich*. (I. Oskarsson, A. Schläpfer, M. Kraak, & G. Scheller, Eds.). Zurich: ETH transfer.

Ottawa Business Journal. (2014). Ottawa technology by the numbers. *Ottawa Technology*, Fall 2014.

Phillipson, D. (1991). The National Research Council of Canada: Its Historiography, its Chronology, its Bibliography. *Scientia Canadensis: Canadian Journal of the History of Science, Technology and Medicine*, *15*(2), 177–193.

Pinter, V. (2015). *Overview and Analysis of the Performance of Spin-Offs at the Swiss Federal Institute of Technology Zurich and Their Effect on the Swiss Economy*. (M. Hölling, M. Kraak, & D. Wensauer, Eds.). Zurich: ETH transfer.

Richards, M. D. (2004). The debates over the retrocession of the District of Columbia, 1801–2004. *Washington History*, *16*(1), 55–82.

Roberts, S. M. (2014). Development capital: USAID and the rise of development contractors. *Annals of the Association of American Geographers*, *104*(5), 1030–1051.

Rowat, D. (1968). The problems of governing federal capitals. *Canadian Journal of Political Science*, *1*(3), 345–356.

Rowat, D. (1973). *The Government of Federal Capitals*. Toronto: University of Toronto Press.

Rossman, V. (2017). *Capital Cities: Varieties and Patterns of Development and Relocation*. London and New York: Routledge.

Ruble, B. (2016). Conclusion: Contesting Change and Legacy: Lessons from the DC Story. In D. Hyra & S. Prince (Eds.), *Capital Dilemma: Growth and Inequality in Washington, D.C.* (pp. 331–340). New York and London: Routledge.

Schweizer Tourismusverband. (2016). Schweizer Tourismus in Zahlen 2015, Struktur und Branchendaten.

Shavinina, L. (2004). *Silicon Valley North – A High Tech Cluster of Innovation and Entrepreneurship*. London: Elsevier.

Slack, E., & Chattopadhyay, R. (2009). *Finance and Governance of Capital Cities in Federal Systems*. Montreal, Quebec and Kingston, Ontario: McGill-Queen's University Press.

Spigel, B. (2011). Series of Unfortunate Events: The Growth, Decline, and Rebirth of Ottawa's Entrepreneurial Institutions. In G. Libecap & S. Hoskinson (Eds.), *Entrepreneurship and Global Competitiveness in Regional Economies: Determinants and Policy Implications* (pp. 47–72). Bingley, UK: Emerald Group Publishing Ltd.

Stadler, P. (1971). Die Hauptstadtfrage in der Schweiz: 1798–1848. *Schweizerische Zeitschrift für Geschichte*, *21*, 526–582.

Statistics Canada. (2011). *Census 2011*.

Statistics Canada. (2012). *Labour Force Survey Estimates (LFS), Employment by Census Metropolitan Area*, 2011.

Statistics Canada. (2016a). *Table 051-0056 – Estimates of Population by Census Metropolitan Area.*

Statistics Canada. (2016b). *Table 282-0131 – Labour Force Survey Estimates (LFS).*

Statistics Netherlands. (2014). *Population Dynamics: Birth, Death and Migration per Region.*

Strambach, S. (2008). Knowledge-intensive business services (KIBS) as drivers of multilevel knowledge dynamics. *International Journal of Services Technology and Management, 10*, 152. https://doi.org/10.1504/IJSTM.2008.022117

Sturtevant, L. (2014). The new District of Columbia: What population growth and demographic change mean for the city. *Journal of Urban Affairs, 36*(2), 276–299.

Swiss Federal Statistical Office. (2013). *Statistik der Unternehmensstruktur STATENT 2012.*

Swiss Federal Statistical Office. (2015a). *Bilanz der ständigen Wohnbevölkerung nach demographischen Komponenten, institutionellen Gliederungen, Staatsangehörigkeit und Geschlecht.*

Swiss Federal Statistical Office. (2015b). *Statistik der Unternehmensstruktur STATENT 2011–2013.*

Tassonyi, A. (2009). Ottawa, Canada. In E. Slack & R. Chattopadhyay (Eds.), *Finance and Governance of Capital Cities in Federal Systems* (pp. 55–78). Montreal, Quebec and Kingston, Ontario: McGill-Queen's University Press.

Taylor, J. (2011). The Crippling Influence of the National Authority. In R. Chattopadhyay & G. Paquet (Eds.), *The Unimagined Canadian Capital: Challenges for the Federal Capital Region* (pp. 27–34). Ottawa: Invenire Books.

TNO. (2015). *Annual Report 2015.* The Hague.

Uitvoeringsinstituut Werknemersverzekeringen. (2014). *Regio in Beeld, Haaglanden.*

United States Census Bureau. (2015). *2013 State & Local Government Database.* Retrieved from www.census.gov/govs/local/

Van Krieken, P., & McKay, D. (2005). *The Hague: Legal Capital of the World.* The Hague: T-M-C Asser Press.

Veronis, L. (2013). The border and immigrants in Ottawa-Gatineau: Governance practices and the (r) production of a dual Canadian citizenship. *Journal of Borderlands Studies, 28*(2), 257–271.

Von Bergen, S., & Steiner, J. (2012). *Wie viel Bern braucht die Schweiz?* Bern: Stämpfli Verlag AG.

Wirtschaftsraum Bern. (2015). Cluster. Retrieved from www.wirtschaftsraum.bern.ch/de/wirtschaftsraum/35/59/?oid=1912&lang=de [Accessed 23 October 2015].

Yilmaz, Y. (2009). The effect of federal preemption on the District of Columbia's tax revenue. *State Tax Notes, 5*, 31–37.

4   The economic geography of secondary capital cities

The economic geography of capital cities is unique in the sense that the public sector drives economic development dynamics through public procurement. If we want to analyze public procurement as a driver of knowledge dynamics in capital cities, we need to understand how national government agencies on the demand side influence the innovative activities of supplier firms. Building on the insight stated previously that the capital city is the center of public procurement activities, this section adopts a microperspective. We explain how public procurement manifests itself in the physical infrastructure of the four cities, why firms co-locate with national government agencies, and to what extent firms in capital cities engage in interactions with other actors.

Public procurement as a driver of secondary capital cities

Spatial expressions of public-procurement activities

Secondary capital cities (SCCs) not only represent themselves through symbolic architecture, but also through an economic structure, which has unique spatial expressions. Firms that work on government contracts are not only concentrated at the regional level, but are unevenly distributed within capital cities. The two North American cases in our sample are similar in the sense that geographic location patterns exist in the inner city and the suburbs. In Washington, D.C., many government contractors locate along Interstate 495, the beltway surrounding Washington, D.C. (Ceruzzi, 2008). When this pattern evolved in the 1970s, these firms were sometimes referred to as "beltway bandits," reflecting not only their location, but also their prosperous business (Markusen, Hall, Campbell, & Deitrick, 1991). The pattern of firms clustering in the region's suburbs is particularly pronounced in Tysons Corner, Fairfax County, Virginia. The firms create a physical infrastructure characterized by large office buildings that appear as islands in oversized parking spaces. The buildings often take the form of functional boxes with reflective glass facades and are designed in a way that makes it easy to restrict access to authorized people only. Although the term "inside the beltway" is often used to describe activities in the federal marketplace, location patterns of government contractors extend beyond the actual beltway. The corridor that connects Tysons Corner with Dulles Airport is an important location for IT firms, which flourished as a result of the development of the Internet (Ceruzzi, 2008). A somewhat more urbanized concentration of government contractors inside the beltway is found in the Rosslyn-Ballston Corridor in Arlington County. This concentration can be explained by the presence of important DoD and DHS agencies and close proximity to the District (Cowell & Mayer, 2014; Mayer & Zalneraitis, 2005). In the Maryland part of the metropolitan region, location patterns are anchored primarily by the National Institutes of Health (NIH) in Bethesda and the Food and Drug Administration (FDA) in Silver Spring. Thus, Maryland serves as a preferred location for

Figure 4.1 K Street is a preferred location for firms seeking proximity to Congress and the White House (Source: Ulrike Dietz).

government contractors specializing in health, IT, biotechnology, medical technologies, etc. The Maryland suburbs of Bethesda and Silver Spring are located just next to the northern part of the District of Columbia. In addition to the suburban location patterns, large contractors locate their divisions for government relations and public affairs in downtown Washington, D.C., preferably along K Street. K Street serves as a microconcentration of lobbying firms and interest groups that benefit from being within walking distance of Congress and the White House. Nevertheless, some interviewees indicated that K Street has lost some of its glamor and reputation, leading many firms to relocate.

Although the location patterns of contractors have unique prehistories in Ottawa and Washington, D.C. (Ceruzzi, 2008; Gordon, Donald, & Kozuskanich, 2000), Ottawa's location patterns to some extent mirror the situation in Washington, D.C. Most contractors are located either downtown next to Parliament Hill or in the suburbs. Firms in downtown Ottawa value the walking distance to government agencies as well as the urban atmosphere. Perhaps the most popular location for software firms contracting with government agencies is World Exchange Plaza, a 20-story office complex just next to Parliament Hill. Kanata serves as a suburban technology hub and is home to major contractors such as General Dynamics, Lockheed Martin, and Cisco Systems. Firms located in Ottawa city center are different than those located in the suburbs. Despite the fact that they both provide services classified as system development, system design, system integration, and programming services in the official procurement database, their core business is very different. Downtown contractors are primarily engaged in software development. Many of these firms operate at the interface of software engineering, technology consulting, and digital transformation. Meanwhile, contractors located in suburban Kanata are primarily engaged in system integration, as well

Figure 4.2 Arlington County, Virginia, is a preferred location for firms working on DoD and DHS contracts (Source: Heike Mayer).

as in the aerospace and defense sector. They combine technological components in integrated systems by ensuring interoperability between devices. These firms benefit from cheaper office space, inexpensive parking, and the fact that they can avoid downtown traffic jams, all while remaining accessible to their government clients who are just a 30-minute car journey away. The architecture of the buildings in Kanata echoes the esthetics found in Washington, D.C.: Reflective glass facade buildings surrounded by large parking spaces and landscaped park features. As in the case of Washington, D.C, large government contractors are located not just in the suburbs, but also downtown. For example, Lockheed Martin has a team of government affairs experts downtown, while the majority of their regional employees are located in Kanata.

Bern and The Hague differ from Ottawa and Washington, D.C. as far as the location patterns of firms are concerned. Due to their smaller size, the exact location within the capital city does not appear to play an important role. In Bern, IT consulting firms locate in the historic city center, a prestigious area that has the highest office rents within the region. Firms tend to use such locations to boost their reputation and to reflect their dominant market position. Small and medium-sized enterprises (SMEs) that are involved in public procurement are found not just in Bern's residential neighborhoods, but also in more peripheral areas. In The Hague, the central business district (CBD) functions as the preferred location for firms that work on procurement contracts. The Hague's CBD is a Z-shaped prime location in the heart of the city with excellent transport links.

Figure 4.3 Avoiding Ottawa's traffic jams: Firms in Kanata (Source: Martin Warland).

Firms here appreciate the proximity to national government agencies, as about one third of the CBD's tenants are from the public sector (CBRE, 2013). This development could potentially grow stronger in the near future since the government established The Hague Security Delta (HSD) within the CBD in 2012. HSD member organizations located within the CBD include large firms such as Siemens and Deloitte. Moreover, the location pattern of government contractors that cluster in the CBD follows a general trend in the Dutch office market. High-grade facilities in prime locations prosper, while secondary and tertiary locations increasingly suffer (CBRE, 2013). The relocation of AT&T or Deloitte from peripheral areas of The Hague to the CBD is illustrative of this trend.

Benefits of being located next to national government agencies

Given the concentration of firms contracting with government agencies in capital cities, the question is, of course, what underlying forces explain this geographical location pattern? The regions' competitive position for public-procurement activities might indicate some kind of access to government agencies that arise from co-location. So how exactly do these firms benefit from co-location with government agencies?

Taking the World Trade Organization (WTO)'s procurement regulations and principles into account, one could even argue that firms could be located anywhere in the country because the public-procurement process includes various mechanisms that *decrease* the importance of spatial proximity in the supply–demand relationship (Thai, 2009). First, spatial proximity does not play a role in reducing uncertainty about the quality of the outcome in public procurement. National government agencies select government contractors based on predefined criteria (Bovis, 2012). The selection process is highly rational because government agencies need to be able to provide explanations to unsuccessful bidders, and a lack of transparency can give rise to litigation. In contrast, private-market actors can try to reduce transaction costs through partner selections that are based partially on instinct, gut feelings, and trust (Scarso & Bolisani, 2012). In this context, face-to-face interactions are an important mechanism in convincing other parties (Maskell, Bathelt, & Malmberg, 2004). Second, national government agencies must publish business opportunities. Every government contractor has open access to such information, something that is quite different in the private marketplace where business opportunities are often communicated through networks that tend to be governed by trust (Glückler & Armbruster, 2003).

In fact, however, the regulated process rather *increases* the importance of spatial proximity because this is a crucial way for firms to gain a competitive advantage through informal knowledge-sharing. To outline this argument, a closer look at the public-procurement process is necessary. The stylized, regular, open public-procurement process can be divided into five stages:

1   The government agency defines technical requirements in detail.
2   The agency publishes a request for proposals online.

3   Proposals are selected based on predefined criteria (with a strong focus on price and references).
4   A contract is awarded based on the proposal of the government contractor.
5   Development of the product or service.

From the perspective of a supplying firm, the procurement process in principle starts when a government agency publishes the request for proposals. However, at this point, agencies have already set technical specifications. They have decided on the underlying technology, which is subsequently implemented in a rather linear way. This is why interviewees stated that it is crucial for them to have informal relations before the publication of a request for proposal. At this stage of the process, procurement officials are willing to meet with company representatives and discuss their issues. To avoid any false impression, we should mention that this is legal and practiced in all four case study regions.

The interaction between procurement officials and firms changes entirely once the request for proposals is published. At this point, government agencies "shut the door" (Bern interview, 25). Informal interactions between firms and agencies cease almost entirely, to avoid any legal issues. Technically, this stage is intended to provide the opportunity for interested firms to clarify any unresolved issues. However, this stage is relatively unimportant for knowledge exchange since all questions and answers will be made accessible to all competitors. As interviewees noted, some firms even ask irrelevant questions just to irritate their competitors.

Government contractors use spatial proximity to achieve a decisive time advantage in the procurement process. They constantly interact with government officials to find out about potential procurement projects as early as possible. Government contractors try to get as much face-to-face time as possible with government officials in order to establish trusted relationships and to gain unique insights into the demands of the agencies. While it is difficult to establish new relationships, ongoing procurement projects provide good opportunities to maintain close relationships since the firm concerned already has access to the agency. Government contractors tend to supplement formal meetings by adding informal meetings over lunch or coffee. These contractors gather intelligence about challenges the particular agency is facing; they want to know "what keeps the federal agency up at night" (Washington, D.C., interview 22). Government contractors collect all relevant information to gain an understanding of the agency's requirements, desires, preferences, and fears. As soon as the contractors become aware of procurement plans, they try to condition the government agency to look for a certain kind of solution. They advertise what a good solution might look like and try to influence the request for proposals in their favor. One interviewee explained:

If you are sitting there and wait for requests for proposals to suit your solution, then you are going to die. You have to be out there cultivating the need that creates the requirements.

(Ottawa interview, 30)

Some government agencies publish reports about their procurement activities, including information on where they have spent budgets and areas in which they are planning new expenditure. Government agencies also describe their technology platforms and plans for the migration of older technologies to newer ones. Most interviewees considered these reports to be important sources of knowledge. However, agencies generally publish reports only once a year, so that interviewees supplement the reports with one-on-one visits with the budget managers to find out whether the priorities are still the same or whether these have changed. When there are changes, firms that closely interact with government officials have more time to position themselves, and therefore gain a crucial competitive advantage.

It is striking how similar the responses of interviewees were across all four secondary capital cities. The majority of interviewees stated, in one way or another, that if they were to hear of a procurement opportunity through the official publication for the first time, they would not have a chance and, therefore, would not even bother to submit a proposal. Given that this holds true across the four regions, it indicates that informal and complex relationships between public and private sectors are a prominent feature of public procurement. One senior manager who is responsible for government affairs at his firm noted:

> *The official government answer is, "Well, we publish everything on the bulletin board, so if you're interested in bidding on something, just pull it down on the bulletin board and then just go ahead and bid it." The thing is, by the time it's published, it's too late. If you don't know what's happening and what's coming and you're not preparing for it ... it's just not enough time.*
> (Ottawa interview, 23)

In the same vein, another interviewee noted:

> *So I gather that intelligence, and from that, we effectively position ourselves and know who to talk to, what might be technology directions that we should start to recruit for immediately, and so have a good depth and story to tell when the bid comes out.*
> (Ottawa interview, 18)

In this regard, one of the few differences between the four cases concerns the volume of contracts. As the largest buyer of IT in the world (Congressional Research Service, 2015), the US government regularly awards contracts with two-digit million values. Of course, winning such large contracts requires different kinds of relationship-building and resources. In terms of resources, government contractors need to set up specialized teams that include members with backgrounds from multiple disciplines. Teams include "deal shapers" who are very familiar with how the client thinks, but they also require program managers, solution architects, computer programmers, technology consultants, lawyers, and business administrators. There is typically a counterpart for each of the team positions on the government client side.

The composition of teams points to the fact that firms not only position themselves through shaping the request for proposal, but also through providing innovative technical solutions. The example of a government contracting process in Washington, D.C. is both insightful and typical: Although no contract has yet been awarded, government contractors start to search for potential solutions. Solution architects spin ideas about possible software components, underlying technology, and how potential solutions could be integrated within existing government IT systems. At this stage, solution architects from prime contractors and subcontractors go back and forth between the purchasing agency and the proposing team. Simultaneously, deal shapers, lawyers, and business administrators work on smoothing the process for the agency to award a contract. This includes, for example, issues such as what procurement vehicles could be used. This stage of the process is characterized by intensive team interactions. Communication that aims to put every team member on the same level of information is conducted mainly by e-mailing and phoning. Discussions about how a change in the technical solution could potentially affect strategic and legal aspects take place in frequent face-to-face meetings.

In the four capital cities, interviewees explained the need for co-presence, which is a consequence of the high number of government actors involved on the client side. Since knowledge and decision-making power about fiscal budgets, IT infrastructure, legal aspects, priorities, and end-user preferences are distributed among many different actors, there is often a high number of stakeholders involved in public procurement. One could argue that this simply mirrors large firms with their separate legal, financial, and purchasing departments, but national government agencies seem to be more independent:

> *Departments are much more independent than the divisions of a firm (...). I believe that we are the only ones who have an overview of the whole project. Some are just focused on ensuring those matters are in order they are responsible for.*
>
> (Bern interview, 11)

As the decision-making process concerning new technical solutions involves several different units and agencies, one interviewee highlighted how many people's confidence he needs to win before a contract is awarded. He explained:

> *Toronto is just completely commercial and this is completely a public sector and there is a big difference. You need to go to all these associations. You need to do a lot more relationship-building. You need to understand the whole procurement process. It's not a matter of, "I got the best thing for the cheapest price," and you're going to buy it. That has nothing to do with it. You have to be able to play the game and understand the procurement vehicles. You have to do so much that's here ... Put it this way, when you go in Toronto, you're going to need one guy in the organization who has the*

ability to sign. You're here, you need a committee to sign and you need all the technical people who are doing the record numbers and all of the technical people who all say, "Yeah, we think this might be a good decision." So there's a need to be here.

(Ottawa interview, 30)

Due to the high number of stakeholders, firms need to establish and maintain trusted relationships with a large number of individuals in the public sector. This holds true for all four case studies. The stakeholders differ from project to project and depend on the selected procurement procedure, end-user departments, contract value, and security level.

Cooperation between government contractors?

So far, we have identified geographical concentration patterns of contractors that maintain formal and informal relationships with government agencies. A central element of a functional regional innovation system (RIS) is the dynamic interplay and interaction between firms. Horizontal linkages – for example, those between potential competitors – allow for the circulation of knowledge within the region and increase regional competitiveness (Doloreux & Parto, 2005).

Several factors that are specific to public procurement stimulate cooperation between government contractors. First, governments often require large firms and SMEs to partner in order to reduce the risk of unsuccessful project outcomes and to increase the participation of SMEs in public procurement. While the Canadian, Dutch, and Swiss legal framework does not allow for preferential treatment of SMEs, the US federal government strongly facilitates the participation of SMEs in procurement by reserving federal business opportunities for SMEs, so-called set-asides. The Small Business Act aims for at least 23% of the annual federal procurement budget to be spent on SMEs. In this regard, only contracts for which SMEs act as prime contractors are taken into account, so that the actual participation is much higher. One of the consequences is that there are many contracts where an SME acts as the prime contractor and a large defense firm serves as the subcontractor. This is also facilitated through the fact that large US government contractors operate SME subcontracting programs and organize networking events where SMEs can pitch their ideas and establish relationships with the firm.

Second, in all four cases, interviewees stated that procurement officials informally encourage (potential) suppliers to partner with large firms, especially SMEs, when the participation of SMEs is not explicitly stated in the request for proposals. Because of informal relationships, employees who write proposals have a good sense of unpublished information, which might provide an advantage. In order to increase the chances of being awarded, suppliers typically follow the recommendations of procurement officials.

Third, firms collaborate with other firms in order to share the costs of bidding. Competitive bidding is associated with gaining procurement knowledge, as well as uncertainty about the probability of winning, so that firms consider bidding as a costly and risky process, which they can often more efficiently manage with partners.

Fourth, firms partner with others when they lack project references. As government is seen as a risk-averse client, it is crucial for firms to provide references that the firm has delivered similar projects in order to win tenders. Many interviewees stated that if they themselves lack references and cannot find a partner firm with a solid record of accomplishment, they do not even bother to submit a proposal in the first place, since references have such a large impact in the evaluation of bids. The selection of partner firms, therefore, is a critical activity that affects a government contractor's business success (Sedita & Apa, 2015).

When we look at how these factors shape the capital city RIS in practice, we can observe unique processes of knowledge circulation. The parallelism of cooperation and competition, often labeled as coopetition (Brandenburger & Nalebuff, 1996), seems to be a pervasive phenomenon in public-procurement-driven economies. During project execution, firms share knowledge beyond the scope of a particular project and become important sources of knowledge. The management of relationships with partner firms is therefore a critical task for government contractors. Firms need to open up to partner firms and to share insights about their technical approaches and internal knowledge management. Nevertheless, they also need to protect their core competences to secure a competitive advantage (Jiang, Bao, Xie, & Gao, 2016). One interviewee claimed

> It has this weird ecosystem where you and I could be competing this morning on one opportunity. We could be teaming this afternoon on another opportunity. And tomorrow you might be trying to buy me.
>
> (Washington, D.C. interview, 15)

One interviewee in Washington, D.C. highlighted that there is no aggressive rivalry between two or three major firms. Instead, procurement activities create complex partnerships in which competition takes place in a more subtle and covert manner. As he explained:

> In this town, you have to learn to take "no" for an answer, … it is, of course, a competitive town, but somebody will be your opponent today, it's just as likely he could be your ally tomorrow.
>
> (Washington, D.C. interview, 13)

To the extent that public procurement is organized through partnerships, it increases the level of knowledge circulation in a capital city. Government contractors constantly acquire knowledge from partner firms when working collaboratively on procurement contracts. The organization of IT projects in teams, for example, creates opportunities for knowledge transfer, as one interviewee reveals in the following statement:

Most government projects are project-driven. And so a project will start up and grow and you have to hire and bring in talent. And then, when the project is finished, it shrinks down again. And that causes engineers to look for different work, so, a lot of the staff move from one company to another company. And a lot of the smaller companies are suppliers to many different bigger companies, so, it's a whole system of systems.

(Ottawa interview, 17)

Canadian and US federal agencies organize pre-bid conferences where interested government contractors come together in one place and can ask questions about upcoming procurement projects. During such conferences, government contractors observe which competitors are present, how competitors position themselves, and with whom they may collaborate. In addition, spatial proximity helps to collect information on competitors. For example, one interviewee described how two government contractors were battling to become the "top dog" in content management in Washington, D.C. This involved an important strategic decision on whether to build that capability as a prime contractor or to position themselves as subcontractors. The firm benefited from being located in Washington, D.C. as this allowed it to monitor competitors and to collect opinions and views that provided a sound basis for the decision not to compete but to position itself as a partner firm.

In this regard, the idea of local buzz (Bathelt, Malmberg, & Maskell, 2004) is well incorporated in RIS studies (Doloreux & Parto, 2005; Trippl & Tödtling, 2011). Local buzz refers to regional circulation of "messages, information, news, rumours, gossip, and trade folklore" that actors automatically receive just by virtue of being there (Bathelt & Gräf, 2008, p. 1947). As such, capital city RIS can circulate federal procurement-related information flows. For firms that are located in the four cities, it is easy to monitor competitors and to have an "ear to the wall to see what everybody is doing" (Washington, D.C. interview, 29).

Partnering as a driving force for cooperation between government contractors is the same in the four case study regions – although to differing degrees. Partnering activities seem to be particularly important in Ottawa and Washington, D.C., whereas they are less important in Bern and The Hague. The main reason might be that the Swiss and Dutch government policies do not foster delivering in project teams to the same extent as their Canadian and US counterparts. Firms in Bern and The Hague reported that they typically deliver a project as a single firm but also have experience in working in project teams. In Washington, D.C. and Ottawa, it is exactly the other way around, as they reported working on public-procurement projects mostly in teams.

Danger of lock-in

Since, as we have outlined, federal procurement is to a considerable degree a capital city business, it is important to note that this situation is not entirely positive for the four regions and carries the inherent danger of lock-in (Grabher, 1993).

Lock-in as a main deficiency of capital city RIS becomes apparent in all four cases. In Bern, interviewees frequently stated that the "usual suspects" win the lion's share of contracts (Bern interviews, 18, 21, & 31). Some firms in Bern stated that they do not even rotate their employees when working for public- and private-sector clients. If an employee previously worked on a government contract and the firm received positive feedback, the firm makes sure the same person will continue working on follow-up projects. Over time, the same individuals repeatedly work on projects relating to the public sector. Many interviewees indicated that they maintain very strong one-on-one relationships with government officials, which were developed through repeated interactions.

In Ottawa, there is evidence of the same pattern. One interviewee noted that that "it tends to be a very incestuous pool of people that just keep moving around and around and around" (Ottawa interview, 23). In the same vein, another interviewee claimed that "it is a very small town in terms of IT. Everyone knows everyone, and it's the same individuals who are always rotating through the different jobs" (Ottawa interview, 27). These statements indicate that firms are strongly oriented toward activities that take place within Ottawa, at the risk of ignoring relevant technological developments that take place elsewhere.

Washington, D.C. displays a similar lack of openness and flexibility, primarily as a result of the strong concentration of procurement activities in this city. In this regard, the term "bubble" was used by several interviewees, which may be indicative of overembeddedness. One interviewee stated that it is the "same set of players over and over again" (Washington, D.C. interview, 25). A Washington, D.C. government official talked about this tendency when he noted:

> *Even if you open up the competition to the entire world, you're probably only going to get three, four, five bids. The fact that in theory a company in Minnesota, Montana, or Switzerland could submit a bid is irrelevant. They are not going to. You're going to get bids from Northrop Grumman, BAE Systems, Lockheed Martin, and Raytheon.*
>
> (Washington, D.C. interview, 4)

In The Hague, interview patterns reveal a clear tendency of firms to seek partner firms at the regional level. This case also illustrates that the lack of extra-regional partners is not primarily a matter of spatial distance, but also of cognitive distance (the same could be said about Bern) (Boschma, 2005). A representative of a development consulting firm in Amsterdam noted that firms in Zuidas, the Netherlands' most rapidly-growing business center and accessible within only 45 minutes from The Hague, do not even bother to engage in the type of business that is done in The Hague because the two locations represent "two different worlds" (The Hague interview, 13).

Several factors explain why the circulation of knowledge is not only biased toward the capital city region, but also limited to a very stable set of actors. When firms work on government contracts, they are in a good position to diversify their business into the public sector and win additional federal contracts. Since they already have access to government agencies, they have a deeper understanding of public sector needs. From a national government agency perspective, there is good reason to continue to work with well-known firms because these firms have proven their capabilities in navigating a public-sector environment that is complex in terms of both bureaucratic specificities and its technical elements. When these firms chase government business opportunities that require suitable partner firms, the identification and selection of partner firms is biased toward previously-successful regional partnerships, and they are most likely to team up with a firm that they already know and where representatives from both firms frequently meet on different occasions.

Moreover, security clearance requirements have been stated as a factor that further increases the danger of lock-in. Firms need to have security clearance because much of the work they provide for national government agencies takes place in defense and security and involves sensitive data. Therefore, government contractors are required to be in possession of security clearance at the employee level. Partner firms have similar access to the data, and thus need to meet the same security requirements. As a result, when KIBS firms seek partner firms, they are restricted to those firms that meet the security requirements. Since acquiring security clearance is time- and cost-intensive, it is mainly those KIBS firms that hold the clearance that are frequently involved in federal procurement. Such firms, in turn, have strong incentives to be close to government agencies (Hyypiä & Kautonen, 2005). As a result, security requirements create a bias toward partner firms that are located in the capital city.

Firms that are new to the region may be an effective way to break the situation of lock-in and help an RIS to remain or become more innovative (Sternberg, 2007). However, public procurement creates many barriers for new firms. Firms need to invest in training the workforce to cope with the complexity of procurement processes and are likely to have some unsuccessful bids before winning their first federal procurement contract. Employees that are dedicated to writing government proposals are most likely to fail a couple of times before they submit successful proposals because this is an exceptionally-complicated process (Spigel, 2011). As we described earlier, IT solutions are complex and requests for proposals contain only part of the information. The following information is not included in the publications: Preferences of decision-makers or background information on previous experiences. In order to be successful, firms need to obtain this additional information. The information is channeled through trusted relationships, in addition to publicly-available information. Since a single procurement project typically involves several agencies and several units within these agencies, contractors need to invest a great deal of time in relationship-building. Thus, breaking into the public-sector marketplace entails considerable upfront costs that may exclude some firms from the procurement business.

Many contracting firms operate globally and, thus, have access to knowledge from anywhere. Indeed, while our interviews indicate that extra-firm linkages are highly localized, intra-firm linkages – particularly those of larger firms – are more global. Many government contractors are multibranch firms with offices in several capital cities around the world. They use intra-firm linkages to channel knowledge to its place of demand. The representatives of such multibranch firms that we talked to indicate that knowledge exchange in the public-sector division across countries is very important. In Bern, one interviewee, who works for a globally-active firm, explained:

> *The exchange in the public-sector division is much more intensive than the exchange within one location. This means that the topic is more important than the location.*

(Bern interview, 31)

The intra-firm knowledge transfer from one location to another should not be considered as a matter of identical replication, but rather as an important element of the firms' knowledge-creation process (Glückler, 2011). Firms need to customize the technology to the specific needs of the client, and they need to ensure interoperability with existing technologies if the service was originally developed for another client in another country. Moreover, firms use intra-firm linkages to acquire knowledge about general trends in the public sector globally. They have experts who are explicitly dedicated to monitoring topics around the world and combine this knowledge with regional federal procurement knowledge. One interviewee explained how the process of knowledge generation is organized:

> *So, the way [name of the firm] works is we have our Health and Public Sector business that we house here locally. But we also have a number of global industry teams within it. So each of those operate globally, and their job really is to generate thought leadership that we can bring to our clients. And they're really the mechanism that glues our regional components together from a thought leadership perspective. I'll just use Public Safety as an example. There's a Public Safety leader; he's actually based in the UK. He's got a member of his team in the US; he's got a member of his team in the UK; he's got a member of his team in Australia; and a member of his team in Paris ... We'll, for the most part, if we see an opportunity within a particular client ... I'm chasing one now in the Public Safety domain. I've had that Public Safety lead and members of that team in here probably ten times in the last year. They come in to help support our client meetings and all the rest.*

(Ottawa interview, 20)

Intra-firm linkages are not restricted to a firm's public-sector division. Many large government contractors have a specialized division for government clients, whereas the rest of the firm is often focused on private-sector clients. One interviewee from a multinational government contractor used the metaphor of a "spear" to describe the relationship between various firm divisions: The government division is the spearhead, which is shaped and pointed to do business with the national government. However, once the firm has acquired a contract, it reaches back to the entire intra-firm network to leverage additional capabilities and talent.

Nevertheless, based on the qualitative material that underpins this book, it remains difficult to assess the extent to which these global intra-firm linkages are able to compensate for the lack of overall openness of the four regions. The way interviewees stressed the importance of the regional level when tapping into knowledge sources suggests that lock-in remains a considerable deficiency of the four regions. It seems fair to say that a more permeable membrane between actors inside and outside the capital cities would stimulate knowledge dynamics and increase regional innovative capability.

Interestingly, none of the four regions has addressed this issue and implemented policies that help to overcome the danger of lock-in. One explanation for the lack of such policies might be that there is no common interest in overcoming this RIS failure in the four cities. While the region as a whole would benefit from an RIS that is more open to new patterns and actors, there are also many firms that would not benefit from such a change. Firms that are working on procurement contracts have already overcome entry barriers to access the federal marketplace. They committed to procurement, so that many of them do not want the government to open up the marketplace to more firms unless those firms are willing to invest to the same extent as they already have. These firms do not want the government to reduce the complexity of procurement procedures in order to remove some of the barriers. They are the same barriers to procurement, which, on the one hand, increase the danger of a regional lock-in, but, on the other hand, also generate a competitive advantage for many of the experienced firms.

Another explanation for the lack of policies to ameliorate lock-in and overcome barriers might be that the lock-in simply does not seem to be too devastating to some of the firms. Some interviewees noted that even if the region is too focused on local activities and becomes self-producing over time, the capital city will remain the most important location for national procurement activities. The scenario in which another region surpasses the capital city in terms of procurement-driven technologies, services, products, etc. seemed highly unlikely to all of the interviewees. This points to a major difference between capital cities and the types of regions that have been discussed in the RIS literature. In traditional industrial regions, as have often been discussed in the RIS literature (Tödtling & Trippl, 2005), firms export their technologies and compete on a global scale. If firms are too strongly oriented toward activities that take place within these regions, other regions take over the role as innovation hubs for new technologies. Interviewees take the view that public procurement will always be a capital city-centric business, regardless of how innovative other regions might be.

Bridging the public–private sector gap

A key theme in almost all of the interviews was the differing rationales between the public and private sectors. Public demand, on the one hand, is often associated with constraining procurement procedures, a culture of bureaucracy, arm's length relationships, nonprofit incentives and risk-averse government officials (Roodhooft & Van den Abbeele, 2006). Interviewees stated that government officials are rather reluctant to share knowledge with supplying firms. They are afraid of favoring individual firms, exceeding their competences, and violating rules by disclosing information. Private supply, in the form of IT government contractors, on the other hand, is usually associated with rapidly-changing technologies, collaborative strategic relationships, and risk-taking entrepreneurs (Trippl, Tödtling, & Lengauer, 2009). The need to mediate knowledge between both sectors and to overcome differences is particularly relevant in the case of knowledge-intensive services. While the development of standardized goods and services requires little interaction between public and private organizations, the development of knowledge-intensive services requires in-depth interaction. Supplying firms depend on resources that are held by the client in order to generate innovations (Bettencourt, Ostrom, Brown, & Roundtree, 2002). For example, supplying firms need to closely interact with government agencies in order to learn what their preferences are. The willingness of agencies to share information and to coproduce the services therefore becomes critically important to the success of procurement projects. Organizations that are positioned at the public–private interface – so called intermediaries – are an important element of RIS because they increase regional innovativeness by fostering knowledge dynamics. The new structure of public demand toward knowledge and technology services, as described in Chapter 3, further increases the importance of bridging knowledge between public- and private-sector actors.

Semipublic organizations as intermediaries

Washington, D.C. and The Hague are both examples of capital cities in which semipublic organizations actively leverage procurement for innovation. While regional economic development agencies in all four cities promote the presence of federal agencies through websites and brochures, it is only in Washington, D.C. and The Hague that there are any strategies to utilize public procurement in terms of innovation. As we will show, the methods used to do this are very different in the two cities.

Displaying a strong awareness of the need to foster public–private knowledge dynamics in order to exploit the presence of government agencies for economic development, The Hague established the HSD. The HSD is a semipublic cluster organization in the field of security that stimulates knowledge dynamics by coordinating public demand and private supply. For example, the HSD coordinated the National Innovation Agenda for Security 2015. This initiative aims to align R & D projects of firms with the requirements of federal agencies. The HSD invited all relevant stakeholders to identify and discuss the main challenges and developments in security that they projected would be important over the next couple of years. At the federal level, the Ministry of Security and Justice and the Ministry of Defense have been involved in the process. As a result, 16 key innovation focus areas were identified in the report. The agenda intends to give firms some reliability for investments in R & D in these areas. As a result of the Agenda, firms also have a better idea about how much and what federal agencies are going to purchase in the future. Thus, the HSD allows firms to match their innovation activities to the future demand of federal agencies.

Regional public and semipublic development organizations also facilitate knowledge dynamics between national government agencies and government contractors in Washington, D.C. These efforts differ markedly from those in The Hague: Whereas one single organization predominantly orchestrates innovation linkages in The Hague, a great many semipublic organizations focus on such linkages in Washington, D.C. This not only reflects differences in the sheer size of the regions, but also points to the various small-scale concentrations of contractors in Washington, D.C. The latter is home to 23 counties, each of which specializes in slightly different industries. As a result, the activities of the counties' development organizations are tailored to the unique type of government contractors they host. Arlington County, for example, is dominated by contractors specializing in homeland security (Cowell & Mayer, 2014). The county's development agency, Arlington Economic Development, therefore fosters its business community by facilitating networking and matchmaking between government contractors and federal agencies in the field of security, such as DARPA or DHS. A good example in this regard is the county's Tandem National Security Innovations (TandemNSI) program. The program provides a platform for innovative firms to showcase their solutions for imminent national security challenges. Having strong linkages with the relevant federal agencies, TandemNSI brings innovative firms together with government officials, allowing them to connect personally. Moreover, federal agencies visit TandemNSI events in Arlington to present security challenges they are facing and to establish relationships with firms that may have potential solutions.

As TandemNSI shows, US government officials are willing to become involved in activities initiated by the region's economic development agencies. As the case of Washington, D.C. shows, national government officials do not hesitate to engage with regional organizations that focus on the capital city's advancement as a regional innovation system. This is a very different behavior on the part of the procurement officials than those described in the other three cases. Interviewees in Ottawa and Bern stressed difficulties in convincing national government officials to engage with the local contractor community. Being afraid of favoring the capital city region over other regions, government officials refrain from even participating in regional initiatives.

As a result, activities by Ottawa's regional economic development agency (Invest Ottawa) are weakly linked to government contractors. The organization focuses on providing start-ups with support services, branding the city as an entrepreneurial location, and attracting international investments rather than playing an important role for the contractor community. One of the few attempts by Invest Ottawa to stimulate knowledge dynamics in the government contractor community is through an online database that lists public-procurement business opportunities. In cooperation with the Economic Development and Innovation Department at the City of Ottawa, Invest Ottawa collects federal business opportunities from various state and national procurement databases in Canada and the US. Designed to grow the regional economy, Invest Ottawa's database shows only procurement opportunities that match their regional clusters, such as software development, wireless technologies, and security networks.

As in Ottawa, interviewees in Bern argued that national government officials who work with public procurement would simply not be willing to engage with the region's development organizations to avoid giving the impression of regional preference. Since regional organizations in the case of Bern do not have strong linkages with federal agencies, they cannot leverage such linkages, and, therefore, tend to be unable to effectively bring together the relevant public and private actors. For example, Capital Region Switzerland (CRS, Hauptstadtregion Schweiz) is dedicated to highlighting and enhancing the region's role as Switzerland's political center. CRS was founded in 2010 in direct response to an external shock: In the revision of the federal spatial concept, the Swiss Federal Office for Spatial Development designated Zurich, Basel, and Geneva/ Lausanne as economic engines, whereas Bern was neglected. Covering a rather large perimeter, policymakers at the municipal and cantonal levels of government formed CRS to emphasize that the status of the greater region as a regular urban agglomeration is not consistent with the important political functions that the region provides. While it has enjoyed some political success (Kaufmann, 2016), CRS has not yet occupied a relevant position in stimulating communication between government contractors and national agencies. In the same vein, regional development organizations and cluster managers advertise the seat of the federal government as a regional advantage, but they do not provide significant bridging functions in this regard.

Having addressed the tension between regional and national interests in Bern and Ottawa, we now turn to The Hague, an example of how this tension was successfully overcome. Although government officials have been characterized as being careful to not give preference to the capital city region and local firms, the HSD was able to convince several national government agencies to engage with regional initiatives. It is clear to the actors involved that economic development of the capital city region in itself does not constitute the sole reason for the involvement of government agencies. Instead, in every project, the HSD needs to explicitly outline how projects help national government agencies to accomplish their own mission and help to create a more innovative, effective, or efficient public sector. As we can see, the extent to which regional knowledge dynamics create benefits for the country as a whole influences the degree to which national government agencies are willing to engage in regional knowledge dynamics.

National sector associations as intermediaries

National sector associations are important intermediaries in capital cities. Many interviewees stated that procurement officials tend to be more willing to engage with national sector associations rather than with regional development agencies. Sector associations provide the benefit of representing firms regardless of their location and are therefore perceived to be neutral with regard to regional interests.

In Washington, D.C., sector associations have played an important role as intermediaries since the 1970s, when the region benefited from increased government outsourcing of tertiary activities that were not linked to manufacturing. In 1972, the Professional Service Council (PSC) was established in Washington, D.C. as one of the first associations that focused on bridging the gap between firms that work on federal procurement contracts and federal agencies. Early on, PSC received a great deal of attention in the contractor community and "served as a focal point for common benefit" (Feldman, 2001, p. 882). PSC grew to about 390 members, all of which are active in public procurement and many of which are located in the capital city region. One key theme of PSC is to address issues in which procurement practices do not keep pace with changes in the demand structure. While the demand structure experienced a shift from buying products to acquiring services and, as a result, necessitating different practices and capabilities (Gordon, 2012), the training and practices of government officials involved in procurement did not change. PSC addresses the resulting problems from the suppliers' perspective and discusses them with procurement officials. This includes close collaboration with the General Service Administration (GSA), an independent agency that advises other federal agencies on how to purchase products and services. In order to gain attention and strength, PSC coordinates some of its activities with the Acquisition Reform Working Group (ARWG). ARWG is a group of eight national sector associations that all deal exclusively with federal procurement in the Washington, D.C. context.

When it comes to high-volume procurement contracts, US federal agencies also use large national sector associations to tap market knowledge and to learn about what industry can actually provide before entering the tendering process. Government officials present how they plan to procure a specific service in front of member firms of the respective association. They also present timelines and answer questions about public procurement. During the following ten days, member firms discuss feasibility, advantages, and disadvantages of how the federal agency plans to procure. After obtaining the views of the member firms, the association develops a set of recommendations for the purchasing agency. Some weeks later, the government officials come back to the association's office and respond to the recommendations.

Another pioneer association is the American Council for Technology and Industry Advisory Council (ACT-IAC), which was established in the 1970s. What distinguishes ACT-IAC from other associations is the fact that it is organized as a public–private partnership. In addition to the 7,000 members in the private sector, 3,000 government officials are also ACT-IAC members. Therefore, it is perceived as a neutral ground where government officials and contractors can interact. When the Office of Management and Budget asked ACT-IAC to provide recommendations on how to better manage the modernization of federal financial systems in 2011, the association set up a working group that addressed this issue from several perspectives. The main challenge was to develop a framework that helps federal agencies to make better decisions when they need to decide either to improve existing government IT systems or to create new systems. After months of discussions and analysis, ACT-IAC developed a framework that outlined the exact ways in which incremental or radical improvements of government IT elements increases the complexity of the entire system. In response to this project, ACT-IAC established the Institute for Innovation, which integrates knowledge from both the private and public sectors. Moreover, established in 2014, the institute's annual innovation award receives a lot of attention in the federal marketplace and provides a platform for innovative firms to showcase their technologies to interested federal agencies.

In Washington, D.C., sector associations were set up in the 1970s, around the same time government agencies began to outsource activities. In the intervening period, the landscape of sector associations has become increasingly diversified. Many associations focus on particular subgroups of the contractor community. For example, the Washington, D.C.-based Government Technology & Services Coalition (GTSC) is an important support organization for SMEs in public procurement. GTSC facilitates knowledge exchange between SMEs and government agencies in terms of improving the procurement process toward innovation. They do so by organizing workshops where SMEs present challenges and problems in the current procurement processes to officials of the Department of Homeland Security's Procurement Office. Moreover, SMEs explain how they organize their search for new solutions, innovative partners, and new technologies. These workshops deepen the procurement officials' understanding of how SMEs operate and how procurement practices influence SMEs' innovation activities, while providing ideas of how to improve the process. The dialogue with procurement officials also increases acceptance of certain procurement practices among SMEs.

Sector associations in Ottawa play a more traditional role and are involved mainly in lobbying and building relationships in the public-procurement marketplace. However, the importance of these traditional functions should not be downplayed as far as fostering knowledge exchange between public and private actors is concerned. The Canadian Association of Defence and Security Industries and the Aerospace Industries Association of Canada are the two most important sector associations for firms working with the national government in Canada. They frequently invite government officials to their meetings to discuss how certain procurement practices affect the development and delivery of IT services. For the firms involved, addressing issues through a sector association provides the advantage of highlighting problems in how the government interfaces with supplying firms while keeping their names clean. Some firms stated that they are otherwise rather reluctant to address certain issues directly with their public-sector clients because they are concerned about ruining their name. Moreover, national associations are more effective than an individual firm in advocating changes in procurement practices, e.g. a limitation of liability clause, as the industry speaks with one voice. However, two interviewees of large system integrators stated that they often disagree with what the national associations are trying to push for, since they primarily represent the interests of SMEs as their largest group of members, as opposed to large system integrators. In addition to membership of various associations, large system integrators typically have their own lobbyists to advocate on their behalf. Moreover, sector association meetings with government officials give firms a sense of what services and technologies might interest agencies in the future. One interviewee noted that

> *Whenever there are big procurements coming up or big initiatives that the government is looking at, it's a group of vendors that get together ... So we'll sit down and talk to the government about how do they plan to procure. So when they're looking at Cloud, what are they thinking? Is this reasonable for them? What horizon are they looking at? Should we invest this year? Should we invest next year? So we meet probably on a quarterly basis to sit down and have those far-reaching conversations. And then, we also on a monthly basis, we need to talk about more the status of procurements. So when the government is issuing large procurements, then we'll sit down with them on a monthly basis. And their director general of procurement comes in and says, "Okay, so this big procurement is progressing here. It should come out in July. This one's here. It should come out here," so that we can start to plan, and prepare, and partner, and figure out what we're gonna do.*
>
> (Ottawa interview, 23)

Bern and The Hague differ from Washington, D.C. and Ottawa as regards the role and relevance of national associations. The associations are relatively unimportant in fostering knowledge exchanges in the field of federal procurement in Bern and The Hague. In Bern, there are only a few organizations that facilitate knowledge interactions between federal agencies and the contractor community. Some government contractors considered that swissICT contributes to a federal procurement agenda that makes innovation possible. The organization advocates for the use of agile software development in public procurement. Reports and blogs illustrate the advantages and disadvantages of certain procurement practices. swissICT's role can be described as providing knowledge inputs and promoting the issue of innovation in public procurement more than fostering personal relationships. While headquartered in Zurich, SwissICT's federal procurement-related activities are mostly virtual, but when they take place physically, they occur in Bern.

One of the few events in Bern where national sector associations bridge knowledge between public and private actors in the context of public procurement is the Conference for IT Procurement (IT-Beschaffungskonferenz). Relevant actors in the field of IT federal procurement come together to discuss how public-procurement practices encourage innovation. The annual conference is co-organized by two sector associations in cooperation with the region's main university, the federal IT steering unit, and a public-sector organization that coordinates IT projects between different cantonal and federal levels of government. The conference provides an opportunity to establish new contacts, share experiences, and exchange best practices. In The Hague, none of the firm representatives interviewed for this project stressed the importance of national sector associations when talking about bridging the public–private sector gap. Thus, associations appear not to be relevant in the Dutch capital city.

In sum, the examples illustrate that development organizations and sector associations can function as important intermediaries by coordinating public-sector procurement activities with private market knowledge. More specifically, intermediaries provide a platform for national government agencies to present current challenges. Firms can present possible solutions and are given a voice in addressing obstacles in federal procurement from a supplier's perspective. They also function as networking arenas where firms can seek potential partners and can help match firms' innovation agendas with national government procurement agendas. Thus, intermediaries provide critical functions that help connect public- and private-sector actors.

Public-procurement policies and programs

Public-procurement policies can either foster or hamper innovation activities and can therefore explain knowledge dynamics in capital cities. The procurement framework differs across the four countries that provide the national context for our case studies. Washington, D.C. clearly benefits the most from public-procurement policies directed toward innovation. Despite the myth of noninterventionist policies in the US (Mazzucato, 2013), there are several instruments and policies that stimulate knowledge exchange between the public and private actors. The Small Business Innovation Research (SBIR) program is a prime example of how R & D funding and public demand are combined as a powerful instrument that catalyzes innovation activities in small firms (see for example Feldman, Francis, & Bercovitz, 2005; Keller & Block, 2013). The program finances innovative technical solutions developed by SMEs that seem promising in meeting a federal agency's need. If federal agencies have a budget in excess of USD 100 million, they are required to spend a

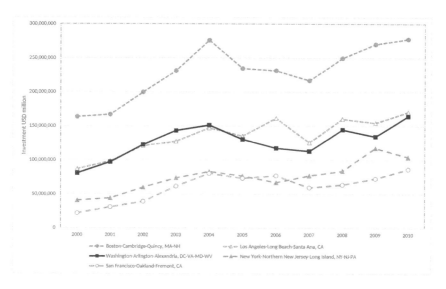

Figure 4.4 SBIR awards by MSAs, 2000–2010 (Source: SBIR).

certain percentage of their budget on SBIR contracts. The 11 federal agencies that take part in the SBIR program award approximately 160,000 R & D contracts to innovative SMEs per year. While the metropolitan areas of Boston and Los Angeles win most of the SBIR contracts, Washington, D.C. disproportionally benefits from the SBIR program (see also Figure 4.4). Former public-sector employees who turn to entrepreneurship are very familiar with federal needs and therefore have a competitive advantage in winning contracts (Feldman et al., 2005). Moreover, firms that frequently interact with federal agencies in Washington, D.C. are far more likely to hear about the program and to speak with someone who has personal experience of SBIR.

Emphasizing the relatively strong link between public procurement and innovation in Washington, D.C, it is important to note that federal agencies differ. Cyber security and health IT are characterized by risk-taking with innovation-oriented agencies such as the Defense Advanced Research Projects Agency (DARPA), the Department of Homeland Security (DHS), the National Institutes of Health (NIH), and the National Telecommunications and Information Administration (NTIA). Describing different government clients, one interviewee noted that "there are pockets of the federal government that are leading-edge technologies and there are pockets of the federal government that are 20 years' laggards" (Washington, D.C. interview, 15). Thus, the US federal government is by no means uniform in terms of public procurement, and the commitment to innovation differs radically across agencies (Vonortas, 2015).

In comparison with the US, the Netherlands and Canada have only recently identified public procurement as a tool to stimulate innovation. The Hague and Ottawa are just starting to benefit from procurement policies that explicitly target innovation. The Dutch government shows awareness of the potential to stimulate innovation through public procurement. This becomes apparent when looking at the main procurement agency, which is known as the Professional and Innovative Tendering Network for Government Contracting Authorities (PIANOo). About half of PIANOo's workforce is dedicated to finding ways in which procurement regulations and practices can facilitate innovative solutions. PIANOo accelerates the use of outcome-based specifications and interactive behavior of government officials. However, Dutch public procurement is highly decentralized, and every national agency is responsible for its own purchases. Thus, PIANOo's capability to leverage purchasing power is limited to providing consultancy to national government agencies.

Inspired by the way the US government uses programs to leverage procurement, the Dutch government created its own SBIR program in 2005. From 2005 to 2012, seven federal agencies used SBIR and awarded 650 contracts (Ministry of Economic Affairs, 2014). Based on an agency's needs, firms can propose a solution. While the needs may be well defined, there are no technical specifications, and firms can submit any solution regardless of underlying technologies. Based on predefined criteria, a small group of firms are awarded a contract to conduct a feasibility study for their innovative solutions. During the next step, the most promising solutions are awarded a contract. As soon as a prototype exists, national government agencies have the opportunity to procure the outcome of this process and become the first user of that technology. As an early adopter of that technology, federal agencies encourage other users to follow. Finally, firms can start to commercialize their product with other clients in the public and private sectors. To ensure compliance with the regulatory framework, Dutch SBIR is limited neither to SMEs nor to national firms, which differs from the situation in the US.

The Canadian government also utilizes federal procurement as a vehicle to stimulate innovation. An important program in this regard is the Build in Canada Innovation Program (BCIP), which encourages federal agencies to become first purchasers of private-sector innovations. Starting as a pilot in 2010, Canada's federal procurement arm Public Works and Government Services Canada (PWGSC) released the program to close the gap between precommercial innovations and the market place. National agencies take the risk of being the first user and provide detailed feedback to enable government contractors to further improve the service or product. In five years, Canadian agencies have awarded 183 contracts to innovative projects (Public Services and Procurement Canada, 2016).

The interaction between supply and demand was further improved through the implementation of "smart procurement." The procedure was developed for major transformations, such as when the federal government changes their e-mail system. It includes many steps in the early phases before the request for proposals is published to ensure that government contractors have sufficient intelligence about what exactly is needed and that government officials have intelligence about which solutions are feasible. Additional steps include, for example, industry days, informal discussions, focus groups, one-on-one consultations, and requests for information.

In 2006, the Canadian government established the Office of Small and Medium Enterprises (OSME) to promote participation of SMEs in procurement. OSME informs SMEs about procurement regulations and procedures and puts them in touch with purchasing agencies. As part of the central procurement agency, OSME also directly addresses procurement practices that discriminate against SMEs. Nevertheless, since SMEs are defined as firms with up to 500 employees, criticism has been leveled at the scheme, saying that the range of represented firms is too wide and leads to conflicting interests in federal procurement.

At the other end of the spectrum is Bern, where development is rather hampered by reluctant federal procurement policies. Federal procurement is not considered as a policy instrument that spurs innovations in Switzerland (Hotz-Hart & Rohner, 2014). There are no formal mechanisms to stimulate knowledge-sharing between public and private actors or that reward government officials for taking risks. One exception is the implementation of the competitive dialogue procedure in the Swiss federal procurement framework in 2010. Originally created by EU Public Procurement Directives in 2004, the competitive dialogue procedure is explicitly designed for demanding innovative IT systems. Compared to regular procurement procedures, the competitive dialogue procedure is more flexible in the ways in which it allows federal agencies and (potential) supplying government contractors to interact. As an outcome-based procedure, it specifies the need without limiting innovative solutions through detailed technical specifications.

Overall, the four examples show that capital cities are located within very different procurement frameworks. The framework can be shaped toward innovation and support the development of a more vibrant capital city economy, as in the case of Washington, D.C., or the framework can be characterized by the absence of procurement innovation policies, as in the case of Bern. One of the reasons for the differences in federal procurement frameworks can be found in the capabilities of intermediaries. Intermediaries can leverage synergies and bundle forces. They get involved in policy formulation and lobby for better use of innovation-targeted instruments instead of the regular, constrained federal procurement procedures. Thus, intermediary organizations in capital cities can positively influence procurement frameworks toward knowledge generation and innovation.

Regional innovation systems of secondary capital cities – a holistic perspective

So far, we have analyzed public procurement as a driver of knowledge dynamics. We described how a community of contractors unfolds based on location and how partnering is an important mechanism that supports the spatial concentration of contractors. Next, we compared how regional intermediaries connect public demand and private supply. What constitutes an RIS, however, goes beyond the linkages between national government agencies and supplying firms. A capital city RIS also includes actors and mechanisms that are not directly attributable to public procurement. Linkages between various regional actors stimulate innovation activities (Tödtling & Trippl, 2011). Therefore, a more systemic perspective, which captures the wider political economy of capital cities, is required.

Presence or absence of linkages

Turning to regional linkages across various actors, Bern and Ottawa appear to suffer from fragmentation. This means that economic actors in these capital cities are not well connected and experience fragmentation of knowledge flows and links. Both regions feature innovative actors and elements, but linkages between them are either missing or weak. Starting with Bern, formerly state-owned firms constitute one type of innovation actor. Formerly state-owned firms seem to be of greater importance as anchor organizations in Bern than in the other three regions. The national train company Schweizerische Bundesbahnen (SBB, Swiss Federal Railways) is headquartered in Bern. Moreover, in 1998, the federally-owned postal and telecommunications organization PTT (Post-, Telefon- und Telegrafenbetrieb) was split and privatized into two firms. The resulting Schweizerische Post (Swiss Post) and Swisscom, the leading telecommunications firm in Switzerland, both remained in Bern. Both firms have in recent years expanded their presence by building or renovating offices in strategic locations. In addition, their business models have changed drastically over the past decade. In light of digitalization,

Figure 4.5 Formerly state-owned firms located in Bern (Source: Martin Warland).

the traditional infrastructure services have been supplemented with a variety of new products and services. Swiss Post, for example, entered a new segment by developing an e-health platform that enables the exchange of electronic patient files among doctors and nurses. Given the increased complexity of the products and services these firms offer, they rely on external sources of knowledge, including suppliers, competitors, and research organizations. For example, two Chinese telecommunication firms, ZTE Corporation and Huawei, recently located branch offices in Bern specifically to be in close proximity to Swisscom.

In Bern, however, these state-owned firms, together with a group of regional suppliers, appear as isolated innovation islands within the region. One of the explanations for weak knowledge transmission to other regional actors might be found in the legal status of these firms. Despite privatization, the Swiss government still holds shares in these firms, and, thus, all three formerly state-owned firms remain subject to public scrutiny. Consequently, Swisscom, SBB, and Swiss Post are rather reserved as regards their engagement in Bern's economic development efforts, fearing conflicts with their national mandates.

Another dimension of fragmentation in the case of Bern relates to the linkages between knowledge organizations and firms. Research cooperation between these two groups of actors seemed to be barely existent. For particular public-procurement projects, interviewees in Bern reported neither an example where the supplying firm cooperated with a university nor an example where the supplying firm commercialized research outcomes. Nevertheless, knowledge organizations seem to be important in providing education. Many firms in IT find it difficult to recruit new, sufficiently-qualified employees, and they stressed the importance of university programs that address this issue.

The weak transmission of knowledge from research organizations to firms was also apparent in Ottawa. Despite Ottawa's strong endowment with federal research laboratories and university institutes, research is sparsely translated into commercialization. This result is surprising given the specialization of some of the research organizations in IT, which corresponds well with the regional economic structure, rooted in IT services. Carleton University places a great deal of emphasis on creating knowledge in the fields of software engineering, network security, and pervasive computing. Carleton Computer Security Lab, for example, conducts research about security issues in networked information systems and illustrates that the knowledge support subsystem can be considered to correspond to the needs of IT firms, which work on government contracts. Overall, interviewees did not regard the knowledge subsystem as particularly relevant as far as partnerships for innovation are concerned. Regional policymakers show awareness of the absence of linkages between national research laboratories and regional firms in the case of Ottawa. Here, one of the policy goals is to better take advantage of research laboratories in terms of commercialization, but this has not yet led to powerful instruments or initiatives.

One of the possible explanations for the absence of linkages between regional firms and knowledge organizations in Ottawa is the unique character of public-procurement projects. Interviews indicate that many of the Canadian procurement projects are not very sophisticated in terms of technical knowledge. As the complexity of projects arises from bureaucratic environments, rather than from technical requirements, firms that work on government contracts do not rely heavily on cutting-edge research provided by federal research laboratories. Nevertheless, as in Bern, Ottawa's two regional universities are important in providing human capital. Some firms stated that part of their workforce graduated from regional universities and students often stay in the region because of its high quality of life.

The case of Washington, D.C. provides a strong contrast to Bern and Ottawa in terms of regional knowledge transmission. Knowledge organizations are well matched to the needs of regional firms, and one can observe a high degree of cooperation between different regional actors. The Basic Research Innovation and Collaboration Center (BRICC) is a good example of how joint innovation projects are fostered. BRICC is a nonprofit corporation that is part of the Virginia Tech Research Center in Arlington. As part of a Partnership Intermediary Agreement (PIA) with the Air Force Office of Scientific Research, their explicit task is to transfer knowledge between higher education institutions, firms, and federal agencies. Specifically, BRICC takes on three roles: It identifies technologies in the contractor community that could be useful for federal agencies, it identifies technologies in government agencies that could be useful for government contractors, and it facilitates joint research projects. Thus, a major challenge for BRICC is how to identify technologies that could unleash innovation through application in new contexts. To address this question, BRICC started a series of events where program managers from DARPA, NIH, the National Science Foundation (NSF), the Air Force, and many more agencies share experiences. Thus, BRICC serves as a platform to enhance knowledge-sharing within the Washington, D.C. region.

Another example of cooperation in the Washington, D.C. region is the Mason Enterprise Center (MEC), which brings together different regional competences to promote economic development. Affiliated with George Mason University, MEC offers technology transfer support and entrepreneurship services with the goal of transmitting ideas from the university to the market. While such services can nowadays be regarded as standard for larger universities, MEC provides a capital city-specific approach by focusing their regional activities around federal agencies. Therefore, the Small Business Administration co-finances MEC. MEC hires public-procurement specialists who raise awareness of business opportunities among SMEs and advise SMEs on how to access government agencies, major system integrators, nonprofit organizations, universities, and community colleges. In addition to informal relationships with several federal agencies, MEC has established formal relationships with DoD and the Defense Logistics Agency. As part of these partnerships, MEC initiated more than 40 projects in which DoD, SMEs, and major system integrators work together while drawing on resources available at George Mason University.

Our results indicate that the Washington, D.C. capital city RIS benefits from such cooperation arrangements. Innovation activities are organized around the

Figure 4.6 Maintaining strong partnerships with federal agencies: George Mason University (Source: Martin Warland).

needs of national government agencies and combine the knowledge of various actors. A potential explanatory factor for this kind of well-functioning coop-eration in Washington, D.C. might be the institutional context in which federal agencies are embedded in the region (Feldman, 2001). Our research indicates that the institutional context supports US federal agencies in creating effective partnerships with regional firms. For example, personal linkages between gov-ernment and regional firms are strengthened by intense worker flows. The term "revolving door" was coined to describe how individuals move from one job to another across sectors (White, 2006). While interviewees in Washington, D.C. highlighted the advantages of this institutional context in terms of exchanging knowledge, interviewees in other regions highlighted the disadvantages of such an arrangement in terms of maintaining neutrality and objectivity of national gov-ernment agencies. As regards regional innovation activities, US federal agencies seemed to be far more open to engaging in collaboration with regional actors. Strong regional partnerships facilitated by frequent face-to-face interactions are perceived as an effective way of meeting the agencies' goals. In contrast, national government agencies in Bern, Ottawa, and The Hague are far more reserved in their participation in joint innovation projects with regional partners because they are afraid of being accused of favoring the capital city region over other regions.

Overcoming fragmentation

Overcoming fragmentation is a major issue for all kinds of RIS, but fragmentation is particularly relevant in the context of capital cities, as cooperation across the public and private sectors might present various barriers and hinder partnering, collaboration, etc. We take a closer look at The Hague since the region is experi-encing an interesting transformation from a fragmented RIS into a well-connected RIS. The story of how The Hague is transforming can best be told by looking at the emergence of the HSD. In the previous section, we described how the HSD builds bridges between supply and demand in public procurement. Yet public pro-curement is just one of the instruments that the HSD deals with, and other efforts focus on linking regional actors.

   In the early 2000s, leaders in The Hague noted the concentration of actors in the field of security, but they also noted that there was very little knowledge spillover. The municipality failed to develop the security cluster and spur knowl-edge dynamics for a long time. Interviewees reported a tendency on the part of the municipality to treat the field of security as part of the field of justice. As such, the municipality focused primarily on lawyers and other legal service providers, but refrained from stimulating technology-based entrepreneurship in security. Interviewees indicated that the lack of recognition of security on the part of the municipality as a sector with special characteristics, e.g. highly regu-lated, strong technology focus, was also reflected in city branding. When the municipality launched a new slogan, the actors involved came up with the idea, "The Hague – City of Peace, Justice *and Security*". However, the municipality felt no need to include security, and so cut the word "security" from their slogan.

Between 2006 and 2010, a number of projects in the field of security were initiated to foster partnerships between security actors. These projects were co-financed by the Ministry of Economic Affairs, Agriculture and Innovation through the "Pieken in de Delta" program. Pieken in de Delta was a national program to foster the economic competitiveness of regions in the Netherlands. Interviewees noted that collaborations between various public and private actors took place, but lasted only as long as the projects themselves. On completion of a project, the group fell apart and firms continued with their business as usual. Even though the establishment of long-lasting linkages failed, these projects brought together regional actors in security for the first time and can be seen as the antecedent of what is now called the HSD.

In 2010, The Hague's economic situation deteriorated and the city was increasingly challenged to implement new initiatives to develop the regional economy. The Hague faced a decline in jobs in the public sector, as well as in the telecommunications sector, while the oil industry stagnated. To identify the economic potential of the region, the municipality launched a study and found that the regional innovation capacity could be increased by stimulating knowledge dynamics in security. The study pointed to the fact that The Hague hosts many relevant actors in security at different levels of government. Despite the presence of relevant security actors, there was no venue for contractors, researchers, pro-curement officials, or regional economic developers to meet and share ideas. One interviewee from a think tank stated that the linkages between relevant actors in security were still almost nonexistent and noted that, "actors were just like grains of sand, they were not glued together" (The Hague interview, 7).

In the same year, a group of public and private actors started to organize them-selves and addressed the lack of regional linkages by launching the "The Hague Security Delta – Pieken in the Delta" project. So, instead of applying for financing for single security projects, the idea was to apply for financing to formalize and professionalize the larger network in security. It took another two years before the HSD was officially launched in 2012. To ensure that the organization meets the varying requirements of the actors involved, the HSD was launched as a public–private partnership. Co-founders included the municipality, major security firms (i.e. Thales, Siemens), federal agencies (i.e. Ministry of Security and Justice), and knowledge organizations (i.e. Delft University of Technology (TU Delft), TNO).

At around the same time, a collaborative project in the field of forensics received a lot of attention from policymakers, and therefore contributed to the formation of the HSD. In 2009, the Netherlands Forensic Institute (NFI), an agency of the Ministry of Justice, initiated "CSI The Hague" to develop technology that enables NFI investigators to digitize and visualize a crime scene. This constituted a break-through in forensics as it allows investigators to virtually revisit the crime scene and investigate the crime scene over and over again. NFI drove regional knowl-edge dynamics from the demand side by informing the organizations involved about exactly what their needs were, without predefining possible solutions. At the beginning of the project, the NFI held several seminars that aimed to develop a common understanding of the domain of forensics in general, and the project requirements in particular. While the project involved firms and organizations not only from The Hague, but from all over the Netherlands, much of the work required face-to-face interactions that took place in The Hague. More specifically, a large proportion of the work took place in the CSI laboratory, a facility that was created specifically for the CSI The Hague project and located next to the NFI building. A firm based in The Hague that developed the simulation software for this project noted that the CSI laboratory was the central place for all consortium members to meet and develop ideas. As the project progressed, an NFI program manager noted that

> *CSI laboratory was where all companies came with their technology, so you get a very innovative place where people inspire each other, where you are celebrating new things, and if there are problems, you were also there to fight with each other. It was a very, very tense environment where people are creative.*
>
> (The Hague interview, 32)

The project strengthened the regional security network across firms, research organizations, municipalities, and federal agencies. The Municipality of The Hague and the Ministry of Economic Affairs co-financed the EUR five million project. A consortium of nine firms and four knowledge organizations collaborated with the NFI. The source of innovation in this project was the novel combination of various pieces of technology from different domains. For example, components of mediated reality software were adopted from serious gaming, while heat sensors were adopted from medical research. CSI The Hague served

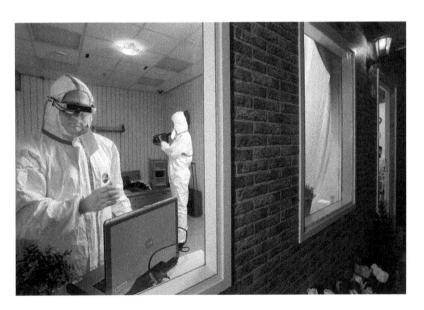

Figure 4.7 Investigators digitalize a crime scene in the CSI laboratory in The Hague (Source: HSD).

as a regional success story and an effective illustration of the value of knowledge exchange across government, industry, and research organizations.

The HSD started as a temporary project but grew into a permanent cluster organization. The "HSD-Pieken in the Delta" project was originally initiated as a two-year venture. As the stakeholders began to realize the potential for collaborations in the field of security as a rapidly-growing market, they decided to establish the HSD as a foundation in 2013. In the first three years, the municipality's investment leveraged additional funds from national government and network partners, as well from the European Regional Development Fund. Along with the formalization of the regional security network, the HSD developed a physical space to facilitate face-to-face interactions, the "HSD Campus." This includes many shared facilities, such as living labs, classrooms, flexible office spaces, and meeting rooms. Linking activities include, for example, the establishment of the Cyber Security Academy, which is again a public–private partnership to ensure regional supply of skilled labor. Collaborating partners include educational organizations such as Leiden University, TU Delft, and The Hague University of Applied Sciences. Partners from the private sector include firms such as Fox-IT (Europe's largest cybersecurity firm), or KPN, a formerly state-owned telecommunications provider.

The HSD was successful in linking regional actors in the field of security and in increasing regional innovativeness. It was also able to organize joint activities that include public-sector organizations at all levels of governments, global security firms, regional SMEs, formerly state-owned firms, educational organizations, research organizations, and NGOs. A crucial success factor was to focus not merely a specific regional competence (security), but also on a specialization with great potential for diversifying the regional economy. Ever since the establishment of the HSD, the municipality has emphasized that an innovation system in security has great potential for firms to win new clients in the private sector. The main argument is that security has traditionally been a topic for the national government to deal with. However, there is knowledge and experience not only in government agencies, but also in firms that have coproduced security systems and in research organizations that operate at the public–private interface. As security has become increasingly important for all kinds of firms across different industries, they are more willing to invest in this field. Thus, firms that have gained security knowledge through interactive learning with government agencies have great potential to exploit their knowledge in their interaction with private-sector clients. The HSD is a fairly new initiative and has yet to materialize and develop any noticeable impact on the regional economy. Nevertheless, in its first three years, more than 500 new jobs were created in the field of security and 18 firms have relocated to The Hague from other regions (The Hague interview, 9).

Start-up dynamics and entrepreneurship in secondary capital cities

SCCs are not generally known as dynamic entrepreneurial cities. The four capital cities share the narrative of a "government town," in some cases even a sleepy one characterized by a bureaucratic environment rather than an entrepreneurial one. Bern, for example, shows the lowest rate of new-firm formation among the five largest agglomerations in Switzerland. While Geneva counted 2.23 start-ups per 1,000 inhabitants in 2013, the figure for Bern is only 1.27 (Swiss Federal Statistical Office, 2015a, 2015b).

One of the reasons for the lack of entrepreneurial dynamics in Bern is the fact that the federal government absorbs much of the talent that could otherwise have the potential to take the risk and start their own firms. After all, the national government in Bern is the largest and most stable employer in the region. Recent graduates of universities in the region and beyond find attractive job opportunities in the public sector. Taking the risks associated with starting a new enterprise may appear unreasonable to public-sector employees in a regional context dominated by job security and a comparably stable and high-salary environment shaped by public administration.

In addition, although we argue that public procurement is a driver for knowledge dynamics in capital cities in general, public procurement is not well suited to stimulating start-up dynamics. First, there are formal mechanisms that technically exclude start-ups. Public procurement is typically carried out in two stages. In the first stage, firms need to meet predefined selection criteria before their proposal will even be taken into account. Selection criteria often relate to human resources and experience of the firm. Since it is in the nature of start-ups not to have any proven track record in public procurement, this criterion basically excludes start-ups. Second, federal agencies tend to be risk-averse. In many interviews, including those with procurement officials, it became apparent that national government agencies hesitate to collaborate with start-ups because they lack trust in the capabilities of start-ups to navigate complex public-sector environments. Even for firms that passed through the early start-up phase, public procurement creates many barriers to the involvement of SMEs (Loader, 2013).

Moreover, the narrative of a government town creates self-reinforcing effects. The public image of the four cities originates in the dominance of the government. While some people relate to the government as an actor that guarantees stability and accountability, many associate it with red tape or regulation frenzy. Such perceptions make it difficult to foster an entrepreneurial environment.

Nevertheless, there are also distinct opportunities for entrepreneurship in SCCs. One type of entrepreneurship relates to spin-off activities from defense system integrators. For example, Washington, D.C. provides an environment that supports these kinds of activities. To promote employee spin-offs, regional economic development agencies have set up accelerators and incubators that provide a supportive entrepreneurial environment. The Entrepreneur Center at the Northern Virginia Technology Council (NVTC) is a prime example of a program that strategically targets employees of government contractors who want to start a new venture. NVTC provides mentoring programs, events, and contacts that aid and enable individuals to leave their employer and start their own firm. The typical entrepreneur of this program is not the 24-year-old coming straight out of school, but a public-procurement-experienced, middle-aged person who has gained technical skills through many years of work in the RIS in Washington, D.C. However, while some new firms are able to enter private-sector industries, the majority sell to government contractors, often to the firms they initially left. Thus, employee spin-offs do not contribute per se to the region becoming less dependent on government spending, but can sometimes be seen as a way of keeping subcontracting activities in the region.

The case of Washington, D.C. also illustrates that there is another distinct type of entrepreneurship that derives from the presence of federal agencies. Located just a few blocks from the White House, 1776 is a prominent example of an incubator for start-ups in the region. In the early 2010s, Evan Burfield, one of the two founders of 1776, realized that "there were these unbelievably useful assets and resources that Washington, D.C. had because of the government, that were not taken advantage of" (Washington, D.C. interview, 12). He noticed that the majority of initiatives to foster start-up dynamics in the D.C. region were still closed to public procurement. What had been overlooked was the concentration of large corporations and organizations that seek proximity to the US government and that this concentration provides opportunities for entrepreneurship beyond traditional subcontracting. Washington, D.C. holds a tremendous amount of expertise in government-dominated markets, such as education, health, energy, sustainability, transportation, and smart cities. In order to take advantage of this unique concentration of experts and decision-makers, 1776 focuses on start-ups in government-dominated markets. Evan Burfield notes that

> *Everybody thinks, for example, "agriculture must be in the Midwest," but a lot of people that are actually thinking through agricultural policy and how do we manage what we are doing and farm subsidies and insurance programs, they are actually all in Washington.*
>
> (Washington, D.C. interview, 12)

The main challenge for start-ups is to tap into these resources and connect with large corporations. It is often globally-operating corporations that co-locate with government agencies. As a result, the gap between start-ups and these organizations is fairly large. 1776 helps here, as it provides an environment in which large firms can interact with start-ups. The incubator has seen several rapid-growth start-ups and is steadily expanding its network. In 2015, 1776 hosted over 260 start-ups and nurtured linkages to large corporations such as MedStar Health and Microsoft. In addition to the concentration of actors that are permanently located in Washington, D.C., there are many firms whose representatives visit the capital on a regular basis. One of the goals of 1776 is to establish itself as an important node in national and international networks.

Washington, D.C. differs from traditional entrepreneurial ecosystems in Silicon Valley or along Boston's Route 128. Entrepreneurs in Washington, D.C. develop innovative solutions from competences in business processes rather than from new or radical technologies. The region's strengths lie in public policy, data analyses, and international relations. Thus, talent keen to engage in these topics moves

Figure 4.8 The 1776 premises provide co-working space for start-ups in government-
dominated industries (Source: Ulrike Dietz).

to Washington, D.C., whereas those interested in technology development (e.g. engineers, programmers) might find other regions more attractive. The orientation of the educational programs of the region's universities, such as Georgetown University, George Washington University, and Virginia Tech, correspond with and reinforce these strengths. For example, Virginia Tech offers programs in data science and collaborates with local and national government agencies that provide data, providing students the opportunity to work on real-world problems. As a result, students engage in problem-solving for the public sector or tackle public-interest challenges. Thus, the types of start-ups that stem from such an environment in Washington, D.C. are mainly the result of business-process innovations. For example, two rapidly-growing start-ups based in Washington, D.C. that became local success stories are eduCanon and Opower. The former provides a platform for teachers to develop interactive video lessons for their students. The latter is a firm that develops energy-saving software for utility companies. In both cases, the firms gained a competitive advantage through domain knowledge. Starting and scaling such firms requires a deep understanding of the structure of specific public sectors, such as education or energy.

We found a similar pattern in The Hague. Strategies to foster entrepreneurship in the region focus on applying established IT components to public-sector domains, as opposed to the development of new technologies. The domains in which The Hague has a competitive advantage are peace, justice, and security. One example for the application of established IT to these domains is the Centre for Innovation at Leiden University. The Centre leverages the region's competences regarding societal challenges and government activities. It operates eight labs, of which HumanityX appears to be the most successful. HumanityX encourages the pursuit of new ideas in peace, justice, and humanitarian affairs through eight-week workshops in which entrepreneurs can transform an idea into a first prototype. Their support includes networking opportunities, methodological insights, business advice, and physical infrastructure. For example, HumanityX encouraged the development of a platform that examines the efficiency of lobbying and advocacy campaigns on Twitter. As NGOs often use Twitter campaigns to reach their audience, the software was developed in cooperation with Human Rights Watch. The emerging product (Impact Tracker) allows NGOs to monitor how their messages spread across Twitter networks. Another example is DiploHack, a team aimed at finding new ways to better prepare government officials for external meetings. To develop software to replace paper-based dossiers, knowledge about public-sector processes and the precise needs of government officials as end users is required. Therefore, the team collaborates with the Ministry of Foreign Affairs and diplomats, as well as with journalists, NGOs, and Microsoft. The Centre for Innovation does not work on solutions by itself, but also coordinates and reaches out to relevant actors. In this way, it is a good example of how knowledge flows are fostered in The Hague's regional innovation system.

Synthesis by regions

Bern

The case of Bern illustrates an RIS that suffers equally from organizational thinness and fragmentation. Firms working on public-procurement contracts often act individually through one-on-one meetings with government officials, for example. This pattern reflects the weak endowment of intermediary actors that are positioned at the interface between public and private sectors and facilitate joint activities. Policymakers and economic developers have not put in place regional initiatives or programs that aim to exploit the presence of national government agencies in terms of innovation. Moreover, innovative actors, such as formerly state-owned firms, display weak interaction with other RIS actors. The lack of public-procurement policies that provide scope for alternative solutions and new approaches demonstrates that Swiss federal agencies do not view public procurement as a tool to stimulate innovation. However, taking into account the fact that capital cities are not only receivers of policies but can engage in policy formulation, one could also turn the argument around: Because of the thin and fragmented structure of Bern's RIS, regional actors have not fostered the emergence of strong associations that speak on behalf of the government contractor community and push for the implementation of public-procurement innovation policies. As such, Bern's RIS is missing an engine for change.

Ottawa

Ottawa provides an interesting case study for a capital city RIS that includes national sector associations that foster knowledge-sharing and work at the interface between the public and private sectors. They give firms a voice in addressing obstacles in public procurement and discuss procurement practices from a supplier's perspective. The Canadian government has shown increasing interest in exploiting public procurement for innovation, for which BCIP can be seen as a prime example. Although there is no strategic vision among regional policymakers to leverage the presence of national government agencies for regional economic development, Ottawa benefits disproportionally from such innovation instruments. Nevertheless, there is evidence of fragmentation in Ottawa's RIS, and the region's endogenous potential associated with hosting national research laboratories seems to be largely untapped. Moreover, many procurement projects are delivered in teams, leading firms to maintain strong relationships with other firms. In searching out partner firms, there is a strong bias toward regional firms, which increases the danger of lock-in.

The Hague

The Hague has long been an important location for organizations and firms specializing in security. It was only recently, however, that the region began to connect different actors in this area. In particular, the HSD links national government agencies, government contractors, international organizations, and specialized knowledge organizations. The cluster organization was established as a direct response to a fragmented regional innovation structure. To create a collaborative environment, the HSD orchestrates joint innovation projects and helps to match firms' innovation agenda with public-procurement agendas, e.g. through the National Innovation Agenda for Security. With strong support from the municipality, the HSD shapes The Hague's RIS to fit the needs of public-sector organizations to better capture the benefits of hosting both national and international organizations. The idea of an RIS that leverages the presence of government agencies and associated competences is supported by various other regional organizations in The Hague.

Washington, D.C.

The case of Washington, D.C. illustrates an RIS characterized by many specialized private- and public-sector organizations that stimulate a cooperative environment and foster joint activities between firms, knowledge organizations, and national government agencies. Intermediary organizations provide collective ground for government agencies and firms to exchange knowledge. Moreover, the strong presence of intermediaries has strengthened the link between public-procurement policies and innovation. As far as overall regional development dynamics are concerned, there are many initiatives that capitalize on the presence of national government agencies. For example, start-up activities draw on the competences

Table 4.1 Case study regions at a glance.

		Bern	Ottawa	The Hague	Washington, D.C.
Federal procurement as a driver of knowledge dynamics	Spatial configurations of knowledge flows	Strong spatial concentration of federal procurement activities; danger of lock-in	Strong spatial concentration of federal procurement activities; danger of lock-in	Strong spatial concentration of federal procurement activities; danger of lock-in	Strong, spatial concentration of federal procurement activities; danger of lock-in
	Partnering activities	Medium degree of partnering activities; projects delivered in teams, but also as a single firm	High degree of partnering activities; projects delivered mainly in teams; bias toward regional partner firms further increases danger of lock-in	Medium degree of partnering activities; projects delivered in teams, but also as single firm	High degree of partnering activities, particularly between SMEs and global system integrators; bias toward regional-partner firms further increases danger of lock-in
Intermediary functions between private and public sectors	Endowment of intermediaries	Organizationally thin; interactions between federal agencies and firms occur in the form of direct, personal one-on-one relationships	High importance of national sector associations as facilitators of knowledge spillovers between public and private sectors	HSD as main organization at the interface between federal agencies and firms	Strong endowment of specialized private and public organizations that facilitate knowledge dynamics between public and private sectors

(continued)

Table 4.1 (continued)

		Bern	Ottawa	The Hague	Washington, D.C.
Holistic view of RIS	Policy link between federal procurement and innovation	Weakly developed (competitive dialogue)	Moderately developed; emergence of innovation support (BCIP, OSME, smart procurement)	Strongly developed (PIANOo, SBIR, NIAS)	Very strongly developed (SBIR, set-asides, preferential treatment of SMEs)
	Cooperative arrangement between various actors	Fragmented structure; formerly state-owned firms as innovative "islands"	Fragmented structure; lack of collaboration between strong knowledge infrastructure and firms	Overcoming fragmentation; HSD coordinates joint innovation projects between government, industry, NGOs, knowledge organizations	Joint innovation projects between all kinds of actors, facilitated by numerous organizations (e.g. Mason Enterprise Center, BRICC)
	Start-up & entrepreneurship	Regular start-up support, independent of capital city functions	Regular start-up support, independent of capital city functions	Capturing benefits of hosting government through combination of IT with public-sector intelligence (Centre for Innovation)	Focusing on government-related sectors (e.g. 1776, NVCT)

that the region provides in government-related sectors. In addition, government agencies anchor many of the regional innovation projects. An important factor of Washington, D.C.'s RIS comes to light here: National government agencies show a willingness to engage in regional collaborations. Government agencies rate the advantages of partnerships with regional universities, NGOs, or firms higher than any possible disadvantages caused by conflicts of interest. This enables the region to develop initiatives that are tailored to the agencies' needs and thereby exploit the benefits of hosting the national government. Nevertheless, the strong focus on regional actors when searching for innovation partners can also create barriers to regional innovativeness. Federal procurement routines and practices for the most part emerge from regional interactions and therefore bear the risk of being "beltway-centric" (Tama, 2015, p. 8) and excluding nontraditional perspectives.

References

Bathelt, H., & Gräf, A. (2008). Internal and external dynamics of the Munich film and TV industry cluster, and limitations to future growth. *Environment and Planning A, 40*(8), 1944–1965.

Bathelt, H., Malmberg, A., & Maskell, P. (2004). Clusters and knowledge: Local buzz, global pipelines and the process of knowledge creation. *Progress in Human Geography, 28*(1), 31–56. https://doi.org/10.1191/0309132504ph469oa

Bettencourt, L. A., Ostrom, A. L., Brown, S. W., & Roundtree, R. I. (2002). Client co-production in knowledge-intensive business services. *California Management Review, 44*(4), 100–128.

Boschma, R. (2005). Proximity and innovation: A critical assessment. *Regional Studies, 39*(1), 61–74.

Bovis, C. (2012). *EU Public Procurement Law.* Cheltenham: Elgar European Law.

Brandenburger, A., & Nalebuff, B. (1996). *Co-opetition.* New York: Currency Doubleday.

CBRE. (2013). The Hague Central Business District. An Insider's View.

Ceruzzi, P. E. (2008). *Internet Alley: High Technology in Tysons Corner, 1945–2005.* Cambridge, MA: The MIT Press.

Congressional Research Service. (2015). *The Federal Acquisition Regulation (FAR): Answers to Frequently Asked Questions.* Retrieved from https://fas.org/sgp/crs/misc/R42826.pdf

Cowell, M., & Mayer, H. (2014). Anchor Institutions and Disenfranchised Communities: Lessons for DHS and St. Elizabeths. In K. Patterson & R. Silverman (Eds.), *Schools and Urban Revitalization: Rethinking Institutions and Community Development* (pp. 86–107). New York and London: Routledge.

Doloreux, D., & Parto, S. (2005). Regional innovation systems: Current discourse and unresolved issues. *Technology in Society, 27*(2), 133–153.

Feldman, M. (2001). The entrepreneurial event revisited: Firm formation in a regional context. *Industrial and Corporate Change, 10*(4), 861–891.

Feldman, M., Francis, J., & Bercovitz, J. (2005). Creating a cluster while building a firm: Entrepreneurs and the formation of industrial clusters. *Regional Studies, 39*(1), 129–141.

Glückler, J. (2011). Islands of Expertise – Global Knowledge Transfer in a Technology Service Firm. In H. Bathelt, M. Feldman, & D.-F. Kogler (Eds.), *Beyond Territory: Dynamic Geographies of Innovation and Knowledge Creation* (pp. 207–226). London: Routledge.

Glückler, J., & Armbruster, T. (2003). Bridging uncertainty in management consulting: The mechanisms of trust and networked reputation. *Organization Studies*, *24*(2), 269–297.

Gordon, D., Donald, B., & Kozuskanich, J. (2000). Unanticipated Benefits: The Role of Planning in the Development of the Ottawa Region Technology Industries. In N. Novakowski & R. Tremblay (Eds.), *Perspectives on Ottawa's High-Tech Sector* (pp. 91–116). Brussels: Peter Lang.

Gordon, D. I. (2012). Reflections on the federal procurement landscape. *The Government Contractor*, *54*(7), 51–58.

Grabher, G. (1993). The weakness of strong ties: The lock-in of regional development in the Ruhr area. In G. Grabher (Ed.), *The Embedded Firm: On the Socio-Economics of Industrial Networks*. London: Routledge.

Hotz-Hart, B., & Rohner, A. (2014). *Nationen im Innovationswettlauf: Ökonomie und Politik der Innovation*. Wiesbaden: Springer.

Hyypiä, M., & Kautonen, M. (2005). Expertise, proximity and KIBS–client relationships. *Conference Proceedings of the International RESER Conference on Growth, Employment and Location of Services*, 125–148.

Jiang, X., Bao, Y., Xie, Y., & Gao, S. (2016). Partner trustworthiness, knowledge flow in strategic alliances, and firm competitiveness: A contingency perspective. *Journal of Business Research*, *69*(2), 804–814.

Kaufmann, D. (2016). *Varieties of Capital Cities: Explaining Locational Policies in Four Secondary Capital Cities*. Thesis submitted to the University of Bern.

Keller, M., & Block, F. (2013). Explaining the transformation in the US innovation system: The impact of a small government program. *Socio-Economic Review*, *11*(4), 629–656.

Loader, K. (2013). Is public procurement a successful small business support policy? A review of the evidence. *Environment and Planning C: Government and Policy*, *31*(1), 39–55. https://doi.org/10.1068/c1213b

Markusen, A., Hall, P., Campbell, S., & Deitrick, S. (1991). *The Rise of the Gunbelt: The Military Remapping of Industrial America*. Oxford: Oxford University Press.

Maskell, P., Bathelt, H., & Malmberg, A. (2004). Temporary clusters and knowledge creation: The effects of international trade fairs, conventions and other professional gatherings. *Spaces*, *4*, 1–34.

Mayer, H., & Zalneraitis, R. (2005). The Homeland Security Industry and Its Impact on the Arlington, Virginia, Economy. Final Report for Arlington Economic Development, Blacksburg, VA: Department of Urban Affairs and Planning, Virginia Polytechnic Institute and State University.

Mazzucato, M. (2013). *The Entrepreneurial State – Debunking Public vs. Private Sector Myths*. London: Anthem Press.

Ministry of Economic Affairs. (2014). Public procurement of innovation: Challenges and opportunities. Presentation at meeting of Industrial Policy Task Force.

Public Services and Procurement Canada. (2016). Pre-Qualified Innovations. Retrieved from   https://buyandsell.gc.ca/initiatives-and-programs/build-in-canada-innovation-program-bcip/pre-qualified-innovations

Roodhooft, F., & Van den Abbeele, A. (2006). Public procurement of consulting services. *International Journal of Public Sector Management*, *19*(5), 490–512. https://doi.org/10.1108/09513550610677799

Scarso, E., & Bolisani, E. (2012). Trust in knowledge exchanges between service providers and clients: A multiple case study of KIBS. *Knowledge Management Research & Practice*, *10*(1), 16–26.

Sedita, S. R., & Apa, R. (2015). The impact of inter-organizational relationships on contractors' success in winning public procurement projects: The case of the construction industry in the Veneto region. *International Journal of Project Management, 33*(7), 1548–1562.

Spigel, B. (2011). Series of Unfortunate Events: The Growth, Decline, and Rebirth of Ottawa's Entrepreneurial Institutions. In G. Libecap & S. Hoskinson (Eds.), *Entrepreneurship and Global Competitiveness in Regional Economies: Determinants and Policy Implications* (pp. 47–72). Bingley, UK: Emerald Group Publishing Ltd.

Sternberg, R. (2007). Entrepreneurship, proximity and regional innovation systems. *Tijdschrift Voor Economische En Sociale Geografie, 98*(5), 652–666.

Swiss Federal Statistical Office. (2015a). *Business Demography 2013.*

Swiss Federal Statistical Office. (2015b). *Municipalities Statistics 2013.*

Tama, J. (2015). *There's No App for That: Disrupting the Military–Industrial Complex.* Washington, D.C.: Center for 21st Century Security and Intelligence at The Brookings Institution.

Thai, K. (2009). *International Handbook of Public Procurement.* Boca Raton, FL: Auerbach Publications.

Tödtling, F., & Trippl, M. (2005). One size fits all? *Research Policy, 34*(8), 1203–1219. https://doi.org/10.1016/j.respol.2005.01.018

Tödtling, F., & Trippl, M. (2011). Regional Innovation Systems. In P. Cooke, B. Asheim, R. Boschma, R. Martin, D. Schwartz, & F. Tödtling (Eds.), *Handbook of Regional Innovation and Growth* (pp. 455–466). Cheltenham, UK: Edward Elgar.

Trippl, M., & Tödtling, F. (2011). Regionale Innovationssysteme und Wissenstransfer im Spanungsfeld unterschiedlicher Näheformen. In O. Ibert & H. J. Kujath (Eds.), *Räume der Wissensarbeit* (pp. 155–169). Wiesbaden: VS Verlag für Sozialwissenschaften.

Trippl, M., Tödtling, F., & Lengauer, L. (2009). Knowledge sourcing beyond buzz and pipelines: Evidence from the Vienna software sector. *Economic Geography, 85*(4), 443–462.

Vonortas, N. S. (2015). Innovation and Public Procurement in the United States. In C. Edquist, N. S. Vonortas, J. M. Zabala-Iturriagagoitia, & J. Edler (Eds.), *Public Procurement for Innovation* (pp. 147–178). Cheltenham, UK: Edward Elgar.

White, R. (2006). *Rolling the Dice in DC.* Bethesda, MD: Wood River Technologies.

5 Locational policies in secondary capital cities

The local governments in the four secondary capital cities (SCCs) formulate very different locational policies agendas. We conceptualize locational policies as policy endeavors of cities and regions designed to strengthen their economic competitiveness in order to sustain and perform in interurban competition. To capture the wide range of potential locational policies, we discuss manifestations of locational policies in four broad categories: Innovation policies, attracting money, coordination, and asking for money. Three lines of inquiry can help to explain this variety of locational policies, namely, the development of the regional innovation system (RIS), institutional factors, and politics. We observe a functional logic, meaning that the RIS, as an economic explanatory factor, influences economic locational policies, while institutional and political factors influence the formulation of political locational policies.

Innovation policies

Cluster policies

KIBS firms in highly-regulated sectors gather in all four SCCs because they profit from the spatial proximity to national government agencies. All SCCs formulate cluster policies that aim to support the development of these highly-regulated sectors and associated knowledge interaction. We found that cluster policies aim, in particular, to stimulate knowledge interaction between the actors from the "triple helix" (Etzkowitz & Leydesdorff, 1995), i.e. firms, knowledge institutions, and public organizations. It is only in SCCs that all three components of this "triple helix" are present. Thus, SCCs provide an arena in which these actors can fruitfully engage in knowledge interactions. However, the specific design and characteristics of cluster policies vary widely.

Cybersecurity is an emerging sector in SCCs due to the fact that national government organizations are at the forefront of demanding innovation in this technology. The nation state needs to remain on the cutting edge of technology development to ensure the safety of its digital activities. Thus, public cybersecurity organizations seek close linkages to the research activities of firms and research institutes. The public sector is also important as a buyer and contracting authority. In such a procurement context, innovation in cybersecurity depends on effective interaction between firms and public organizations. Local governments – and their cluster policies and cluster organizations – can link these two very different actors and, as intermediaries, help to bridge the divide between the public and the private sector.

The Hague provides an excellent example of cluster policies focused on cybersecurity. Local government support for the cybersecurity cluster began in 2010, when The Hague's economic development officials were searching specifically for highly-innovative technologies that could emerge from existing industries. The city realized that there was a consortium of ICT firms in the region focused on security issues, but that these firms lacked crucial links to potential governmental partners and research institutes. The City of The Hague encouraged and facilitated development from a relatively loose consortium into a permanent cluster organization called The Hague Security Delta (HSD). While the City of The Hague was not decisive in stimulating the first innovation activities in cybersecurity, it was instrumental in helping to establish permanent structures to facilitate knowledge interaction within the cluster. Thus, the City of The Hague, together with its partners, succeeded in establishing a prime example of a functioning cluster organization in a knowledge-intensive and highly-regulated sector. The local decision-makers are committed to the HSD and have realigned their locational policies to focus on promoting the HSD (The Hague interview, 9).

Similarly to The Hague, Washington, D.C. focuses on cluster policies in the cybersecurity sector. The District is set to establish an innovation campus in the Anacostia neighborhood to be based in the former psychiatric hospital, St. Elizabeths. The goal is to create an innovative and collaborative environment for academic institutions and firms (Cowell & Mayer, 2016), in which the headquarters of the Department of Homeland Security are to serve as the anchor organization. Many other jurisdictions in the D.C. region also engage in stimulating innovation in the cybersecurity sector. For example, Arlington County, the neighboring jurisdiction in the west of the District belonging to Virginia, initiated the Tandem National Security Innovations (TandemNSI) program that provides a platform for innovative firms to showcase their solutions to security challenges and invites federal agencies to present the security challenges they are facing. Thus, TandemNSI links innovative firms with program managers in the relevant federal agencies.

The economic development organization in Ottawa, Invest Ottawa, has shown great interest in the successful cluster organization HSD. Invest Ottawa, and local economic interest groups, actually sent a delegation to The Hague to learn about their cybersecurity policies, instead of turning to the geographically-closer D.C. (Ottawa interview, 9). As a result, Invest Ottawa and the HSD, with the participation of other public partners, have launched a soft-landing program for cybersecurity firms. These firms are to be encouraged to settle in Ottawa when seeking to enter the North American market, and vice versa for Canadian cybersecurity firms looking to enter the European market (The Hague Security Delta, 2016). Meanwhile,

Figure 5.1 Parts of the old psychiatric hospital of St. Elizabeths are to be transformed into an innovation campus (Source: Heike Mayer).

Bern, as the smallest SCC, is home to a formalized ICT cluster, but has no local or regional innovation policies targeting cybersecurity.

Life sciences, medical and health technology is another knowledge-intensive and highly-regulated sector prevalent in SCCs. Washington, D.C. aims to position itself as the global leader in this area by linking the 16 hospitals and more than ten major universities and colleges in the region (The District of Columbia, 2012). This medical hub is intended to leverage the spatial proximity to important anchor organizations in the Maryland part of the region, such as Johns Hopkins University, the NIH, and the FDA (Washington, D.C. interview, 45). Similar efforts are underway in Bern, which is in the initial phases of establishing a "triple helix" cluster organization in the medical sector called sitem-Insel (Swiss Institute for Translational and Entrepreneurial Medicine). Its goal is to foster and promote translational medical research. The University Hospital of Bern (Inselspital) is the focal point of these activities.

In addition to cybersecurity and life sciences, the four SCCs studied formulate cluster policies in other highly-regulated sectors. The City of The Hague has drafted cluster policies in telecommunication and IT, oil and gas, as well as in the finance sectors. To this end, the economic department of the city hired one account manager to coordinate each of the clusters. However, firms in these three sectors showed little interest in the cluster activities because their ecosystems consist mainly of a small number of large anchor firms (that are competitors) and several small and medium-sized firms (specialized suppliers for these anchor firms). Both a local economic development official and a business actor agree that, in such situations, knowledge diffusion is seen more as a threat to a firm than as a potential driver for innovation (The Hague interviews, 8 & 21).

The Hague also invests in its cluster of international organizations. This cluster has proven fruitful within interaction and is seen as a source of prestige, but lacks economic potential since it is merely budget-driven and does not offer any concrete product innovations (The Hague interview, 3). Hence, the City of The Hague does not formulate cluster policies for this sector, concentrating instead on image-building efforts to market international organizations. Bern also formulates cluster policies for the energy and cleantech cluster. The Canton of Bern obtained government grants to establish one of five Swiss innovations parks in the nearby City of Biel. The successful bid for the innovation park comprised a portfolio of high-tech solutions for the medical sector, 3D metal printing, energy storage, and energy mobility (Bern interview, 41). Ottawa features knowledge-based firms in aerospace, security, and defense, cleantech and life sciences, communications technologies and software, as well as digital media, film, and TV. The first three sectors are highly-regulated sectors and thus specific to a capital city. However, in this context, Invest Ottawa does not formulate targeted cluster policies but instead operates as a broker. As one economic development official explains:

> *We connect the dots. We facilitate and we coordinate. For example, we are doing matchmaking between firms and because we want to bring local firms together. When a firm searches for a specific service, we provide them with lists of firms in Ottawa that can provide this service (...). We run a database with local firms that helps establish this matchmaking (...). We especially help smaller firms in the supply chain by linking them to bigger companies and to the large system integrators.*

(Ottawa interview, 1)

Overall, all four SCCs formulate some sort of cluster policies, but cluster policies can take many forms. We found examples of clusters policies ranging from stimulating knowledge interaction within the "triple helix" in the cybersecurity cluster in The Hague, to organizing events for business leaders in the energy sector in Bern. Thus, the label "cluster policies" does not in itself contain much information about the exact configuration or quality of innovation policies.

Cluster policies in SCCs are often found in knowledge-intensive and highly-regulated sectors such as life sciences, medical technology, security, energy, or education. The knowledge intensity of these sectors points to the capital cities as "information cities" (Castells, 1989), "national information brokers" (Abbott, 1999, 2005), or "knowledge hubs" (Mayer & Cowell, 2014). Bern, Ottawa, The Hague, and Washington, D.C. have no history as industrial cities. These cities have been knowledge-based ever since their selection as the capital. The term "highly-regulated" mirrors the importance of national government organizations for these industries. For example, cybersecurity is a newly-emerging sector and a target for cluster policies in The Hague, in Washington, D.C., and, to a lesser degree, in Ottawa. In cybersecurity, the nation state participates in business activities not only in its role as a regulator, but also as a buyer of cybersecurity technology.

Policies to stimulate entrepreneurial ecosystems

SCCs are not by nature start-up hubs. They are defined by the "government town" narrative, the central administration absorbs much of the talent, the public sector accounts for stability rather than risk, and public procurement is not so conducive to stimulating start-up dynamics and entrepreneurship. However, knowledge-intensive government organizations (such as the health department), or large firms and organizations that seek proximity to government organizations, can provide opportunities for entrepreneurship. We found innovation policies that stimulate start-ups and other entrepreneurial activities primarily in the two North American capital cities.

In Washington, D.C., most entrepreneurs have 15 to 20 years of working experience before becoming an entrepreneur (Washington, D.C. interviews, 3, 14, & 36). As one venture capitalist explains:

> *Such entrepreneurs worked in the public sector where they were the top technical guys. They feel more connected to their technical field than to the government. They become entrepreneurs when they grasp a business opportunity that they are not able to try out in their public organizations.*
>
> (Washington, D.C. interview, 3)

These entrepreneurs tend to be experienced and embedded in technology or business networks and, thus, are not really in need of an incubator (Washington, D.C. interview, 3). Given this demand shortage, the D.C. administration and economic development organizations in the region do not aggressively establish incubators or accelerators in the same way as jurisdictions in the Boston area, for instance, do (Washington, D.C. interview, 9). Nevertheless, there are a few examples where D.C. jurisdictions engage in entrepreneurship policies: D.C.'s city government is a founding partner of the 1776 incubator, although its financial support of the incubator is rather modest (Washington, D.C. interview, 38). There are five incubators in Montgomery County, which support firms in ICT, cybersecurity, and biotechnology (Washington, D.C. interview, 36). The City of Alexandria is developing a small incubator to specifically target veterans as potential entrepreneurs (Washington, D.C. interview, 41). In addition to these incubators, there are a number of venture capital funds in the D.C. region. The states of Maryland and Virginia set up their own venture capital funds (Washington, D.C. interview, 3). However, the availability of venture capital is limited compared to other regions such as Silicon Valley or the Boston area (Washington, D.C. interviews, 3 & 19). Overall, while there are various entrepreneurship policies and initiatives in Washington, D.C., these are not as developed as in other US regions better known for their dynamic entrepreneurial ecosystems.

Ottawa features a vibrant start-up scene in the area of software, but as one entrepreneur explains, this scene is largely detached from the capital city economy (Ottawa interview, 3). There are a small number of incubators and accelerators in Ottawa. Invest Ottawa manages its own modern incubator called Innovation

Center at Bayview Yards (Ottawa interview, 14). Entrepreneurs can participate in an intensive 120-day training program called GrindSpace XL. In 2015, only two venture capital firms were located in Ottawa. However, interviewees noted that venture capital is available, but mostly for products and innovations in the ICT sector (Ottawa interview, 3). Public funds have been established to compensate for the lack of venture capital (Ottawa interviews, 2 & 9). However, one member of the entrepreneurial community assessed public venture capital as rather slow and contingent upon the fulfillment of too many requirements and formalities (Ottawa interview, 3).

In the case of The Hague region, the absence of an entrepreneurial culture and the lack of venture capital are perceived by a variety of interviewees as a major economic weakness of the region (The Hague interviews, 14, 15, & 33). The City of The Hague contributes to the Connectivity Accelerator, an organization that focuses on the development of start-ups in the ICT industry. Another incubator specialized in the creative sector is the Caballero factory (The Hague interview, 8). Furthermore, The Hague tries to link its local competences in international law and conflict resolution to innovation activities (The Hague interviews, 5 & 33). For example, the Center for Innovation, an innovation platform associated with Leiden University's The Hague campus, focuses on technological trends in education and research in the areas of peace, justice, security, and prosperity. Furthermore, the City of The Hague provides a public venture capital fund to support start-ups, research projects, and small and medium-sized firms (The Hague interview, 35). A newer version of the fund aims to spend EUR 6 million over the period 2015–2018, the condition being that start-ups and firms have to focus on societal or technological innovations. An even larger public venture capital fund is managed by InnovationQuarter, the provincial economic development organization, with financial contributions from the central government, the province of South Holland, and the municipalities within the province. The contribution by the City of The Hague to this fund was rather modest, a fact that has been criticized by a public servant from the province (The Hague interview, 39). It seems that the City of The Hague prefers to invest in its own venture capital fund. Thus, The Hague features a variety of activities to stimulate the entrepreneurial ecosystem. Some of them are connected to competences of The Hague's international organizations, whereas others are largely detached from The Hague's function as a capital city.

Jurisdictions in the Bern region do not formulate policies to foster start-ups or to tackle the lack of venture capital funding, and the presence of the innovative state-owned firms is not exploited. In general, the region lacks entrepreneurial spirit and investors oriented toward local opportunities. This may be partially explained by the absence of a technology-oriented university and the absorptive function of the federal government as an employer (Bern interviews, 6 & 41). The Canton of Bern provides a fund of CHF 50,000 annually to support start-ups and small firms (Bern interview, 41). Compared to the other SCCs, it is astonishing that neither local nor cantonal authorities are drafting specific entrepreneurship policies to tackle such a fundamental weakness of the RIS.

Attracting money

Image-building

SCCs present themselves as the capital cities of their nations and utilize this image in strategic ways. Compared to the other capitals, Bern most extensively exploits its capital city status. Local actors in Bern repeatedly argue that a strong capital city is in the interest of the whole nation state. These image-building activities in Bern are consolidated at the regional level. The City of Bern and the Canton of Bern both cooperate with four other cantons and 11 other cities in a partnership of solely-public organizations called Capital Region Switzerland (CRS, Hauptstadtregion Schweiz). Both the city and the canton have been the driving forces behind the establishment of CRS. CRS argues that the capital city should not be measured solely by economic success, but also by its function as the place where political decisions are negotiated and implemented (Kaufmann, Warland, Mayer, & Sager, 2016). This image-building strategy is linked to asking-for-money strategies by arguing that the capital city region is of significance for Switzerland as a whole and, thus, should be favored when awarding public funds (Bern interview, 9).

The Hague's image-building strategies have undergone several transformations over the past two decades. From being traditionally referred to as "The Residence," The Hague once labeled itself the "World City by the Sea," and, later, "International City of Law, Peace and Security." Today, the brand "International City of Peace and Justice" is established, and, according to the interview partners, this brand is not set to change again in the foreseeable future (The Hague interviews, 34 & 38). Clearly, the international organizations are perceived as the source of the city's prestige (Meijers, Hoogerbrugge, Louw, Priemus, & Spaans, 2014). To market the international organizations to the full extent, the city established a Department of International Affairs (Bureau Internationale Zaken) that, among other tasks, assumes promotional activities on behalf of some international organizations (The Hague interview, 34).

Beside image-building strategies that leverage the capital city status or the presence of international organizations, we found that SCCs, with the exception of Bern, try to position themselves as a government city and a business city simultaneously. The Hague aims to transform its image as a city of international organizations toward a truly international (business) city (The Hague interview, 35). The current buzz around the cybersecurity sector, and especially around the HSD, is actively marketed and seen as the cornerstone needed in order to add the term "business" to its image as an international city. Ottawa has a relatively long history of image-building exercises, most of which aimed to overcome the rather negative perceived image of being a government town (Andrew & Doloreux, 2012). The turn of the millennium marked the "zenith moment of Ottawa no longer being perceived as a government town" (Andrew & Doloreux, 2012, p. 1296) when the tagline "Silicon Valley of the North" was used to describe the innovation dynamics in Ottawa (Shavinina, 2004; Spigel, 2011). When Ottawa's high-tech sector crashed in 2001, these branding exercises became obsolete. Currently, Ottawa is trying to position itself as a "G7 capital and high-tech town:" "We fully play this card. We are not using 'either or'" (Ottawa interview, 4).

Similarly, Washington, D.C. utilizes a two-pronged image-building strategy. In respect of international tourists, firms, and investors, D.C. stresses the presence of the US government, the World Bank, the International Monetary Fund, embassies, and global firms (The District of Columbia, 2012). A former economic development official of the D.C. government explains that the singular role of D.C. as the US capital and the fact that it is an international city were both "leveraged to the maximum. It's all about how and when to play the capital city card" (Washington, D.C. interview, 38). This confident image-building is part of a broader international strategy to promote Washington, D.C. as a top North American destination for foreign investors, firms, and tourists (The District of Columbia, 2012). For example, D.C. has an explicit strategy toward China: "The District aims to attract Chinese tourists and identify channels to market the city aggressively" (The District of Columbia, 2012, p. 33). A D.C.-China Center was established in Shanghai in 2012, aimed at helping D.C.-based firms enter the Chinese market and attracting Chinese foreign direct investment (FDI) to Washington, D.C. (Washington, D.C. interview, 45). The capital's efforts also focus on the national US market to showcase its potential as a technological hub on the East Coast. This image-building strategy aims to attract a well-educated workforce by emphasizing, on the one hand, high standards of living in the city and, on the other hand, D.C.'s entrepreneurial ecosystem (The District of Columbia, 2012).

Attracting firms

Similar to image-building, strategies aimed at attracting firms can leverage the capital city status, as well as the economic advantages of the capital city RIS. The capital city status is presented as an asset for firms seeking proximity to national government organizations. However, when formulating strategies for attracting firms and investments in general, greater emphasis is placed on thriving technology-intensive and highly-regulated sectors, such as cybersecurity or life sciences.

Washington, D.C. is very active in acquiring firms and FDI. In order to attract firms, D.C. government officials explicitly liaise with brokers, site locators, accountants, and lawyers, all of whom play a pivotal role in the location decisions of firms (The District of Columbia, 2012). The District wants to "proactively identify and recruit businesses with expiring leases that can benefit from locating in D.C." (The District of Columbia, 2012, p. 25). More specifically, D.C. targets firms that complement the high-tech and life sciences sectors by offering tax incentives for high-technology firms (The District of Columbia, 2012). As regards FDI, the District mainly targets investments from China, but other emerging markets are also increasingly being targeted (Washington, D.C. interview, 45).

Figure 5.2 One example of a large real estate development project in Washington, D.C.
is The Wharf waterfront revitalization project, located in the southwest of the
District (Source: Ulrike Dietz).

D.C. is especially successful in attracting foreign real estate investments. On the
one hand, according to an economic development agent, D.C. is perceived as
a safe investment environment (Washington, D.C. interview, 45). On the other
hand, D.C. has become an attractive location for real estate investments due to a
series of large development projects, such as the Union Station, the Convention
Center, the Wharf, or St. Elizabeths (Washington, D.C. interviews, 34 & 45).
In fact, the "economic development plan of Washington, D.C. heavily relies on
real estate development" (Washington, D.C. interview, 1). While, as a result, the
region added a strikingly high number of jobs in the real estate and construction
sector over recent years, it has also led to gentrification and segregation processes
with especially-negative consequences for less affluent long-term local residents
(Asch & Musgrove 2016; Howell 2016).

In Ottawa, Invest Ottawa is the entity responsible for attracting firms. Its strategy is based on three pillars: First, Ottawa is praised as a "soft landing" spot to tap
into the North American market based on the free trade agreement between the US
and Canada. For example, Invest Ottawa operates a small incubator for Chinese
firms to establish their activities in North America. Second, local key industries are
promoted to entice firms to relocate to Ottawa. Invest Ottawa particularly targets
firms that engage in R & D-intensive activities. Invest Ottawa helps such firms to
gain access to competitive government funding schemes such as tax reductions

based on a firm's R & D intensity (Ottawa interviews, 1 & 4). Finally, the high share of a well-educated workforce is promoted as an opportunity to access a large talent pool (Ottawa interviews, 1, 2, 4, & 12). Beside these specific strategies, Invest Ottawa also pursues more mainstream approaches to attracting firms, such as welcoming trade delegations, attending trade missions, visiting exhibitions and trade shows, and collaborating with site locators.

Compared to their North American counterparts, Bern and The Hague do not implement attracting-firm strategies autonomously. In Bern, neither the city nor the cantonal administration directly acquire firms at the international level (Bern interviews, 36, 41, & 42). Two government organizations are responsible for establishing first contacts with international firms and investors (Bern interview, 41): Namely, the Swiss Global Enterprise (SGE), an organization of the Swiss Confederation, as well as the Greater Geneva Bern Area (GGBa), an initiative of the six cantons in western Switzerland. Once firms express an interest, the Canton of Bern offers competitive bids and package deals to attract them. In a third step, the Canton of Bern reaches out to its municipalities to ask if they have suitable land reserves or real estate to host these firms (Bern interview, 42). The City of Bern is especially interested in attracting firms that fit the medical technology cluster or the energy and cleantech cluster (Bern Wirtschaftsraum, 2012). However, local authorities cannot influence strategies to attract firms at higher levels of government (e.g. the cantonal or national level).

The Hague is similar to Bern as regards its efforts to attract firms. This locational policy is executed mainly by the regional economic development agency, the WestHolland Foreign Investment Agency (WFIA). The WFIA is a partnership of the municipalities The Hague, Leiden, Delft, Zoetermeer, Langsingerland, Haaglanden, and the Chamber of Commerce of The Hague. It aims to attract firms that complement existing clusters in the region. The WFIA operates with standard acquisition instruments such as visiting trade fairs and cooperating with brokers and site locators. Furthermore, the WFIA also serves as the point of contact for firms when they need help with practical tasks such as visa applications, school enrollment, or searching for suitable real estate (The Hague interview, 15). The WFIA is part of the Netherlands Foreign Investment Agency (NFIA) – a national network of regional economic development agencies.

As regards the attraction of international organizations, the City of The Hague is only a junior partner of the Dutch Ministry of Foreign Affairs. The Hague competes to host international organizations with other internationally-oriented European cities such as Brussels, Geneva, and Vienna. Increasingly, there are a variety of globally-connected cities such as Dubai, Nairobi, Singapore, and Seoul that have emerged as competitors in this kind of city competition (The Hague interviews, 1, 34, & 38; Groen, 2014; Meijers et al., 2014). In the case of the Netherlands, the Ministry of Foreign Affairs formulates a general strategy and decides on a case-by-case basis for which international organizations it wants to place a bid. The central government contributes the majority of the funds (e.g. rental real estate) and has room to maneuver to customize specific arrangements for a bid. Because bidding and negotiations with international organizations are in essence a diplomatic task, the Municipal Department of International Affairs joins at a later stage (The Hague interview, 38). The Hague's city government helps mainly with solving practical problems such as logistics and the provision of facilities (The Hague interviews, 34 & 38).

Coordination

The Hague has been coordinating transportation policies and locational policies on the metropolitan scale with the neighboring City of Rotterdam and surrounding municipalities since 2015. Before that time, the City-Region Haaglanden, a council of government organization, was concerned with coordinating environmental, economic development, and spatial planning policies. At the beginning of 2015, the City-Region Haaglanden merged with the City-Region Rotterdam to form a partnership called the Metropolitan Region Rotterdam The Hague (MRTH). This new region has 2.2 million inhabitants, comprises 23 municipalities, employs around 100 staff members, and represents an economic region of international importance. The mayors of Rotterdam and The Hague both initiated the idea for the establishment of MRTH in 2010 (The Hague interviews, 6, 10, 11, & 12). The MRTH coordinates two policy fields: Of first priority are transportation policies and of second priority are locational policies that aim to strengthen the economic competitiveness of the region (The Hague interviews, 11 & 12). The MRTH quickly became a powerful player. For example, the Dutch government redirected parts of its transportation funds from the province to the MRTH (The Hague interviews, 11 & 12; Meijers et al. 2014). The national government supports MRTH's activities because it considers the metropolitan scale most relevant to strengthening the overall international competiveness of the Netherlands (The Hague interview, 36). The MRTH was not established solely to overcome institutional collective action problems. The main interest of the two major cities of The Hague and Rotterdam was to gain more power and, thus, autonomy from the province of South Holland (The Hague interviews, 10, 11, 12, & 37).

In Bern, the local jurisdictions in the region do not coordinate their locational policies. Some interviewees from the private sector see this missed coordination opportunity as one of the major causes for Bern's mediocre economic competitiveness (Bern interviews, 1, 34, & 36). The neglect of regional coordination in this policy field is surprising because municipalities in the Bern region are well embedded in an institutionalized coordination organization called Regional Conference Bern-Mittelland (Regionalkonferenz Bern-Mittelland). Kübler (2009) assesses the regional conference as a progressive tool for tackling institutional collective action dilemmas. A subcommittee (Teilkonferenz Wirtschaft) is responsible for coordinating locational policies. However, there appears to be little willingness and activity as far as coordinating policies at the regional level is concerned in this policy field (Bern interviews, 36 & 37). For example, Köniz, the second-largest municipality in the agglomeration of Bern and the 12th-largest city in Switzerland, does not coordinate any locational policy with neighboring Bern, yet public officials of both Köniz and Bern agree that it is beneficial for their municipality if the economic competitiveness of the whole region increases (Bern interviews, 9 & 42). Echoing our findings, Van der Heiden (2010) finds no coordination of international activities between any municipalities in the Bern region, and this noncooperation appears intentional. In spite of the fact that coordination could enhance the economic competitiveness of the entire region, within the Bern region there is a prevailing resistance toward anything that could potentially constrain local political autonomy (Bern interviews, 36, 37, & 43; Van der Heiden, 2010). At the larger metropolitan level, some locational policies are coordinated within the CRS. Image-building and asking-for-money strategies are linked to a strategy to gain importance at the federal level. However, the CRS is mainly a political vehicle and is not (yet) able to coordinate, for example, innovation policies (Kaufmann et al., 2016).

In the Ottawa-Gatineau region, municipalities refrain from coordinating locational policies. Both the City of Ottawa and the Ville de Gatineau merged with surrounding municipalities in 2001 and 2002, respectively. As a consequence, the cities of Ottawa and Gatineau gained considerable power (Tassonyi, 2009). Siegel (2009) notes that after these amalgamations, for the first time, these cities were able to improve coherent policy implementation in different policy areas, among others in economic development. However, the amalgamations have not encouraged policy coordination between Ottawa and Gatineau (Ottawa interviews, 39 & 41). The economic development agencies, Invest Ottawa and Développement économique – CLD Gatineau, and the economic development departments on both sides of the river do not coordinate their efforts (Ottawa interviews, 4 & 46). Similarly, economic interest organizations like the chambers of commerce and the business improvement districts of Ottawa and Gatineau do not systematically coordinate their efforts (Ottawa interviews, 9, 44, & 45). As a result, one economic development agent says that "people are talking about Ottawa and Gatineau as the two solitudes" (Ottawa interview, 43). However, the current mayors have begun to meet periodically. The National Capital Commission (NCC) – the federal land use agency – has facilitated these conversations, and it is hoped that these top-level talks may trickle down to lower-level city officials (Ottawa interviews, 9 & 40).

In the case of Washington, D.C., we found regional competition instead of policy coordination. Until 2010, the Greater Washington Initiative (GWI) – a public–private partnership and a product of the Greater Washington Board of Trade – was concerned with marketing and attracting firms to the entire D.C. region. The GWI was funded for the most part by the jurisdictions in the region. The larger jurisdictions, such as Arlington, Alexandria, Fairfax, and Montgomery, began their own marketing activities (Washington, D.C. interviews, 14, 32, & 41). As a result, some members stopped their funding, which ultimately led to the dissolution of the GWI in 2010. Since then, no regional organization has been able to fill the vacuum in regional locational policy coordination. The Metropolitan Washington Council of Governments (MWCOG), the regional coordination structure of 22 jurisdictions in the metropolitan region, focuses on transportation, land-use planning, and environmental policies. Even though

Figure 5.3 View from the Peace Tower of the Parliament of Canada overlooking the Ottawa
River. The City of Gatineau is in the background (Source: Martin Warland).

MWCOG's leadership pushed for locational policy coordination, it struggled to
gain the support of its members (Washington, D.C. interview, 47).

Instead of coordinating policies, the interview partners agreed that the jurisdictions in the D.C. region compete fiercely as regards attracting firms, investments,
and residents (Washington, D.C. interviews, 14, 32, 36, 38, 41, & 48). Technically,
there is a no-poaching agreement stating that jurisdictions in the D.C. region are not
allowed to actively contact a firm proposing a relocation unless the firm contacts
the jurisdiction first (Washington, D.C. interviews, 14 & 36). Even though such
"poaching" was condemned by many interviewees, they also recognized that the
no-poaching agreement has limited impact because the interested firms are aware
of the obvious competition and approach individual jurisdictions directly or indirectly via brokers or site locators (Washington, D.C. interviews, 38, 41, & 45). One
economic development agent explains the strategy of jurisdictions in this regional
competition:

> *There is an overlap in the jurisdictions' assets and strengths (...). We did an
> analysis in which we identified our strong clusters and potential clusters that
> are present in other jurisdictions but we do not have. We should have our fair
> share as well in these clusters. So it is a strategy of "guarding" our firms and
> "going after" new firms and organizations.*
>
> (Washington, D.C. interview, 41)

Many interviewees assessed this competition as a zero-sum game that is counterproductive for the economic welfare of the entire region (Washington, D.C. interviews, 36, 38, & 44).

Asking for money

Public funds

In Ottawa and The Hague, public funds constitute an important source of revenue for the local budget. In Ottawa, public funds account for a quarter of annual revenue. In 2015, 19% of the local budget came from conditional and unconditional higher-tier governmental grants (City of Ottawa, 2016). Canadian cities, often supported by local business elites, compete for public funding sources (Horak, 2012). Invest Ottawa is responsible for attracting public economic development funds and competes vigorously for these funds (Ottawa interviews, 1 & 4). For example, the Innovation Center at the Bayview Yards is fully publicly funded by the City of Ottawa, the Government of Ontario, and the Government of Canada. Most of these public funds from higher-tier governments are project-based or program-based and require matching contributions either from other public actors or from the private sector to diversify the risk (Ottawa interviews, 42, 47, & 48).

For The Hague, public funds are even more important than for Ottawa and accounted for 63% of The Hague's municipal budget in 2015 (City of The Hague, 2014). Given this importance, the City of The Hague hired specialists entrusted with the task of tapping into various public funding opportunities (The Hague interview, 35). For example, The Hague attempts to tap into Dutch public funds via national-level cluster programs operated by the Dutch Ministry of Economic Affairs. As a result, The Hague was awarded funding in the cybersecurity sector. The Ministry of Economic Affairs justified the funds because

> [f]urther growth in security must come through interaction between the business community, knowledge institutions and government. The Hague region is seen as a breeding ground for innovation in security and has a track record in cooperation in the triple helix.
>
> (The Hague Security Delta, 2011)

Thus, the HSD is not only an innovation hub, but its triple-helix structure also serves as a tool to tap into various governmental funds. The Hague also tries to attract European public funds such as the EU's European Regional Development Fund or Horizon 2020 in cooperation with its knowledge institutions (The Hague interview, 33).

In Washington, D.C. and Bern, the attraction of public funds is less important than in The Hague and Ottawa. Both D.C. and Bern ask for public funds, justifying these claims with their status as the capital city. In Washington, D.C., local decision-makers are constantly lobbying for public funds but frame this as claims for compensation to offset the various local autonomy constraints resulting from their capital city status. One example are the discussions about the need to invest in D.C.'s outdated infrastructure, such as the regional public-transportation system known as the Washington Metro. The infrastructure debate was launched in 2008 and has still not been resolved. A coalition of D.C.-centric organizations is calling for federal investments in the amount of USD 1 billion to help fund the modernization of the outdated infrastructure (Washington, D.C. interview, 42, 43, & 44). In the case of the Metro, the federal level already pays USD 1.5 billion in subsidies per year because of its interest in a functioning public-transportation system in the D.C. region (Washington, D.C. interviews, 34 & 47). If these federal subsidies decrease, Metro's funding is highly uncertain, since the jurisdictions do not have any agreed financing mechanism (Washington, D.C. interviews, 20 & 33).

In the case of Bern, the region's decision-makers also tried to get public funds from higher-tier governments by stressing Bern's capital city status. The main target are future federal funds that would support Swiss metropolitan regions in strengthening their international economic competitiveness as well as federal support for major infrastructure projects. Currently, the expansion of the main train station in Bern (the second-largest public-transportation hub in Switzerland) (Swiss Federal Railways, 2013) is a major concern for Bern's decision-makers (Bern interviews, 8 & 9).

Compensation payments

Capital cities can also ask for compensation payments for either lost revenue or additional costs attributable to their capital city status. The most prominent compensation payments are the so-called payments in lieu of taxes (PILTs). Of the four cases under scrutiny, only the Canadian government pays PILTs. PILTs account for 6% of the revenue side of Ottawa's budget (City of Ottawa, 2016). Since 1950, a PILTs-system has been in place based on value assessments for tax-exempted properties. The PILT Act of 2000 organizes the establishment of a PILT Dispute Advisory Panel with the mandate of resolving differences between the federal government and local tax authorities based on the fact that the exceptional nature of these properties often poses difficulties in calculating the appropriate value (Tassonyi, 2009). The PILTs do not cover the exact same amount that property tax would: "In the City of Ottawa, for example, there appears to be a considerable gap between PILTs and the amount of property taxes that would be paid, based on the property values set by the Ontario Municipal Assessment Corporation" (Ircha & Young, 2013, p. 159). Because property taxes are the most important revenue source for Canadian local governments – accounting for 47% of the revenue side of the local budget in Ottawa (City of Ottawa, 2016) – the tax exemption for federal premises and diplomatic properties harms Ottawa's financial position. Beside these PILTs, the federal authorities do not compensate for capital city-related costs, such as increasing policing services (Tassonyi, 2009).

No PILTs-systems are in place in The Hague, Bern, or Washington, D.C. The Dutch central government pays no compensation whatsoever for capital city-related costs or capital city-related loss of income. However, in the Netherlands, the majority of capital city-related costs, such as security costs for state visits or events involving the royal family, are directly carried out or directly for paid by the central government. Only in some instances would the Dutch government compensate the local police in The Hague for extra services (The Hague interview, 34). In Bern, the Swiss Confederation pays a lump sum of CHF 1 million to support cultural institutions, activities, and special events that represent the nation state (Tobler, 2013). Police services are under the control of the Canton of Bern and, thus, the canton receives these targeted federal payments for additional security costs (Kübler, 2009). Generally, it is hard to distinguish compensation claims from asking for public funds because asking-for-money strategies are justified by numerous capital city-specific constraints.

Toward explaining locational policies

So far, we have merely described the locational policies formulated and implemented in the four SCCs. Whereas this systematic description is certainly insightful for an understanding of the range of locational policies in SCCs, so far it is unclear *why* these locational policies are formulated and, thus, why SCCs formulate a variety of locational policies. Therefore, the remainder of this chapter focuses on three broad lines of inquiry that can help explain the formulation of locational policies: RIS, three institutional explanatory factors, and regional and urban politics.

Table 5.1 aligns the locational policies and their explanatory factors. As Table 5.1 shows, the two economic locational policies – innovation policies and attracting money – are best explained by economic characteristics, namely, the different configurations of the RIS. In contrast, the two political locational policies – coordination and asking for money – are in each case best approached

Table 5.1 Explanatory factors for locational policies.

Locational policies	Explanatory factors
Innovation policies Attracting money	Regional innovation systems
	Institutional explanatory factors
Coordination	(1) Regional institutional fragmentation and (2) national tax regime
Public funds (asking for money)	(2) National tax regime
Compensation payments (asking for money)	(3) Capital city-specific constraints
Coordination	Regional and urban politics

utilizing three different institutional factors. Regional and urban politics are also important in explaining coordination, but, as we will outline, their influence may go beyond specific locational policies because politics is at the heart of locational policy formulation.

Regional innovation systems

As outlined in Chapter 4, the RIS in the four SCCs feature significant differences in terms of their development. These different characteristics of RIS help explain innovation policies and attracting-money strategies. However, the direction of causality differs: Whereas innovation policies target RIS failures, SCCs apply an image as a business town only if the RIS corroborate this proposed image.

As far as innovation policies are concerned, we found that innovation policies directly address RIS failures in all four case study regions. This finding is most explicit in The Hague. The interview partners were aware of particular RIS shortcomings and formulated innovation policies to ease these shortcomings. The following interview statement from a local economic development official describes the standard procedure when formulating innovation policies in The Hague:

> *When we are formulating strategies, we first look at the economic DNA of The Hague. That means we first analyze which firms are actually present. We then try to find the economic niche within a sector in which The Hague has a comparative advantage. We are willing to spend money in promising niches and prioritize them. Then we facilitate talks and interaction between the companies so that they can find common ground. Then we search for matching knowledge institutions. We always go for the "triple helix".*
>
> (The Hague interview, 8)

It is striking that many interview partners emphasized the importance of fostering interaction between crucial RIS actors. They referred directly or indirectly to the "triple helix" concept (Etzkowitz & Leydesdorff, 1995). Thus, local public actors are keen to address the potential RIS failure of "fragmentation". Another deliberate innovation strategy in The Hague is the stimulation of potential synergies between the existing clusters, as an employee of the municipal economic department explains: "It is not always useful to stick to the cluster approach. Crossovers of clusters now seem more promising for us in triggering innovation" (The Hague interview, 35). In particular, City Hall officials sought out such synergies between the fast-growing and technology-intense cybersecurity cluster and the prestigious international organizations (The Hague interview, 33). The intention is to capitalize on The Hague's position as the seat of international organizations and, at the same time, to become somewhat less dependent on these organizations, since there is not expected to be any substantial growth in this area (Meijers et al., 2014). This seems to be a strategy against RIS lock-in. In a similar vein, we can interpret the efforts to establish public venture capital funds as strategies to ease a specific RIS shortcoming: The lack of private venture capital.

The case of Ottawa highlights innovation policies that tackle the fragmentation between RIS actors, which is a distinctive weakness of the RIS in Ottawa. Ottawa's local government and Invest Ottawa act as brokers between different RIS actors. Their goal is to improve the linkages between the key actors in Ottawa's RIS, such as the different business communities, business interest organizations, the research institutions, and the universities. Interviewees noted several linkages that are not exploited to the full (Ottawa interviews, 4 & 12). For example, there are two ICT communities in Ottawa that operate in relative isolation from each another. On the one hand, firms originating from the old telecoms industry are located in Kanata in the west of Ottawa (Ottawa interviews, 3, 4, & 12). These firms are remnants of the once world-class ICT technology cluster. On the other hand, younger entrepreneurs involved in developing new technologies, such as software products, locate primarily in downtown Ottawa (Ottawa interviews, 3 & 10). Invest Ottawa established initial contacts between key persons in these two communities (Ottawa interviews, 12 & 14). The goal was "to break down the barriers and establish first linkages" (Ottawa interview, 12). Furthermore, Invest Ottawa aims to rebuild the once highly-dynamic entrepreneurial ecosystem by formulating innovation policies that stimulate the local start-up scene. Specific courses are offered for new entrepreneurs to address legal, financial, and strategic issues facing start-up firms, and start-ups are actively brought in contact with venture capital firms. One motive for establishing the Innovation Center at Bayview Yards is to "bring industries together and it should serve as a melting pot" (Ottawa interview, 14). Overall, we found that local economic development officials are clearly targeting RIS weaknesses in Ottawa's case.

In Washington, D.C., innovation policies aim mainly to diversify the RIS as there is an imminent danger of lock-in resulting from a strong dependence on the public sector. In 2012, D.C. officials launched *The Five-Year Economic Development Strategy for the District of Columbia* in a collaborative policy formulation process with private-sector actors, business-sector organizations, civic organizations, and universities (The District of Columbia, 2012). The strategic goal of this economic development strategy is to diversify D.C.'s economy and to educate and prepare the local workforce for the future knowledge-intense economy. Among others, the economic development strategy is seen as a shift from an old economic development paradigm, i.e. attracting firms and workforces, toward an innovation-based paradigm that aims to enhance knowledge transfers and to foster start-ups (Washington, D.C. interview, 45). This policy change stems from the recognition that the long-term decline in federal spending calls for diversification of the regional economy (Washington, D.C. interviews, 1, 45, & 47).

Not many innovation policies are formulated in the case of Bern. However, the establishment of two organizations aimed, on the one hand, at advancing the medical hub (sitem-Insel) and, on the other hand, establishing an innovation park (InnoCampus). This illustrate the efforts to improve the weak linkages between private-sector firms, higher education institutions, and governmental organizations. Thus, both organizations are set up to tackle the RIS failure of "fragmentation."

Innovation policies in SCCc are policy instruments specifically developed to target RIS failures. This finding supports the rather functionalistic take on policy interventions found in the RIS literature, which expects policy interventions only in the case of system failures (Asheim, Smith, & Oughton, 2011; Cooke, 2001; Martin & Trippl, 2014). As put forward by Tödtling and Trippl (2005), it shows that policy actors, such as local governments and economic development agencies, can play a powerful role in shaping a RIS in the context of a capital city. Local public actors are especially well equipped to act as intermediaries that tackle fragmentation within a RIS. Local governments and their economic development organization can thus act as "local brokers to 'connect and cluster' researchers, firms and talent" (Bradford & Wolfe, 2013, p. 13).

As far as image-building strategies are concerned, we found that the state of development of the respective RIS determines whether an SCC puts forward an image as a business city. In particular, weakly-developed RIS do not allow SCCs to showcase themselves as business cities, as this would simply not be credible. Highly-developed RIS, meanwhile, enable such images as business cities. In addition, it is always possible for SCCs to position themselves as government towns, and all four SCCs examined make use of this option. Thus, the development of the RIS determines whether SCCs can simultaneously position themselves as an attractive market place and as a government town.

The case of Ottawa shows most impressively how the RIS and image-building strategies are connected. Ottawa features a relatively-long history of branding exercises, with most strategies aimed at overcoming the image of a government town (Andrew & Doloreux, 2012). The various image-building campaigns coincide with Ottawa's course of economic events. Before the collapse of Ottawa's regional economy in 2001, the local government in Ottawa was able to build an image around its vibrant high-tech sector to the extreme, such that Ottawa was branded "the Silicon Valley of the North." Back then, local elites rejoiced that the end of the government town had come. The crash of the high-tech sector rendered this image obsolete. After the crisis, Ottawa for a long time struggled to build an image because it wanted to copy the business town image of the 1990s and early 2000s (Ottawa interview, 14). According to a city official, it took some time after the economic crash to realize that Ottawa will always be associated with its capital city function (Ottawa interview, 14). Currently, Ottawa employs a two-dimensional image-building strategy by presenting itself as a "G7 capital and high-tech town."

Washington, D.C.'s efforts to present itself as a capital city are prime examples of such a two-dimensional image-building strategy. D.C. presents itself as the US capital city and even goes as far as referring to itself as the "capital city of the free world" (Washington, D.C. interview, 38). Simultaneously, D.C. aims to complement its image as a government town by highlighting the innovation potential of the highly-regulated sectors, such as security and biological and health technology. In addition, Washington, D.C. officials adjust their image-building strategies to fit the target group (Washington, D.C. interviews, 38 & 45). In respect of the federal government, tourists, and foreign investors, D.C. presents itself as the US capital. When dealing with firms, D.C. highlights its dynamic economic sectors and the numerous economic opportunities stemming from the spatial proximity to government agencies.

The Hague has a history of various branding exercises that are closely connected to its most prestigious sectors: The international organizations. The emergence of the dynamic cybersecurity sector supplied the local asset necessary to supplement the image of "International City of Peace and Justice" with an economic angle. The buzz around the HSD is actively marketed because it is a rapidly-expanding sector with clear links to an international business community (The Hague interviews, 3, 8, & 9). Thus, The Hague nowadays pursues a two-dimensional image-building strategy. It is solely on account of the dynamic cybersecurity sector that The Hague's decision-makers are able to credibly put forward an image as an international business city.

Bern's decision-makers put a great deal of effort into positioning Bern as the political center of Switzerland. The capital city image strategy is promoted mainly within the structures of the CRS. The CRS explicitly positions and markets the region as the political center of the nation and, as such, differentiating Bern from the three economically stronger metropolitan areas of Zurich, Basel, and Geneva. This political function, as the initiators of the CRS argue, is important for the prosperity of Switzerland as a whole. Thus, the capital city status is a unique selling proposition that allows Bern to shift the focus away from its economic inferiority and onto its political superiority (Kaufmann et al., 2016). Strategies to position Bern as a business city are not evident, and it seems that the existing industry sectors are not visible enough to be leveraged in image-building strategies.

The four case studies reveal that image-building needs to be linked to functions a capital city is able to perform. Capital cities cannot compete in interurban competition by referring to RIS that have not yet developed, since this is simply not persuasive. Thus, image-building is not primarily about persuasion, but about responsiveness to local conditions (Eshuis, Braun, & Klijn, 2013). Overall, the cases also show that thriving industry sectors seem to be more important than the RIS in its totality. If the capital city possesses internationally-visible sectors, this allows for image-building strategies that focus on the capital as a business city. Yet capital cities possess an essential asset in interurban competition because they can rely on their role as a political center and use this status as a unique selling proposition. As a result, economically weak SCCs can shift the message away from their economic inferiority and onto their political superiority. This is a clear advantage compared to other types of (secondary) cities.

As regards strategies to attract firms, we found that thriving economic sectors are central to understanding this locational policy type in SCCs. Washington, D.C. is very active in acquiring firms and FDI. D.C.'s attracting-firm strategies rest on the combination of a well-developed RIS (especially regarding highly-regulated sectors) and the capital city status. This combination enables a profound and large-scale attracting-firms strategy. Knowledge dynamics in highly-regulated sectors and the presence of national government agencies are good arguments to lure firms to a region. The various jurisdictions in the region of Washington, D.C. that are active in attracting firms also leverage the highly-developed capital city RIS by highlighting the advantages stemming from spatial proximity to government agencies. This dynamic leads to rather intense regional competition in attracting firms, research organizations, and government agencies.

Ottawa is similarly aggressive and international in its strategies to attract firms. However, Ottawa does not attract firms solely by referring to its RIS or to specific economic sectors. Ottawa's economic developers systematically highlight the comparative advantages of the city. For example, it leverages the free trade agreement between Canada and the USA when they present themselves as a soft-landing spot for overseas firms. Furthermore, Ottawa's marketing instruments tailored to firms highlight the high concentration of well-educated professionals who live in the region. In a sense, Ottawa intelligently markets the effects of the capital city function: The presence of a deep talent pool. Finally, key industries are promoted to attract firms to Ottawa that can profit from the spatial proximity to these industries. Firms that engage in R & D-intense activities are especially targeted.

In The Hague, firms and international organizations are acquired by pursuing a cluster approach. For example, the "cluster of judicial organisations was a strategic asset in the attraction of Europol, the International Criminal Court and Eurojust" (Meijers et al. 2014, 96). Another example is the cybersecurity sector: NATO concentrates its activities in the field of information technology, digital security of private networks, and missile defense in The Hague. International organizations such as Europol and Eurojust alongside with the emerging specialized cybersecurity cluster were an important asset in attracting the NATO presence (The Hague interviews, 9, 14, & 15; The Hague Security Delta, 2014).

The City of Bern also tries to employ a cluster approach to add firms to the medical technology or the energy and cleantech cluster, but the local sphere of influence is very limited since the acquisition process is a task incumbent upon the higher-tier governmental levels. Whereas the federal level or consolidated cantonal organizations establish first contacts to international firms or investors, it is the Canton of Bern that hands in competitive bids to attract these firms and investments. The Canton of Bern does not employ a cluster approach, because the cantonal finances do not allow it to be picky about firms. Thus, Bern mainly takes what it can get.

The cases revealed that the strategies to attract firms can be based on a variety of local assets. SCCs compete with what they have and try for the most part to simply get what they can. The RIS is certainly an important asset. However, rather than the RIS in its totality, the dynamic economic sectors are leveraged. For both image-building and attracting firms, dynamic industries with a promising future are assets that can be exploited. Dynamic industries embody the very image of business cities that SCCs often lack. For example, the cybersecurity sector in The Hague is the basis for a lot of locational policies, and, therefore, this sector seems to carry the main weight of The Hague's future as an international business city. Generally, the attraction of firms and investments is a big business in the four SCCs. In the Netherlands and Switzerland, international attractions are the task of consolidated national agencies. Only at a later stage in the process do lower-level, subnational, and local jurisdictions submit their competitive bids. The two North American SCCs acquire rather independently and invest considerable efforts in this task.

Overall, the RIS is a good predictor of economic locational policies both for innovation policies and attracting-money strategies. However, the direction of causality seems to be reversed when explaining the two economic locational policies: Whereas innovation policies target the shortcomings of the RIS, the economic sectors of the RIS influence attracting-money strategies. Image-building as a business town is possible only if the RIS and its economic sectors are well developed. For a city to position itself as the capital city is always possible, given the unique position of capitals in national urban systems. Strategies to attract firms can be based on the economic sectors, yet these strategies can also leverage whatever local assets are to hand and whatever local assets best fit the target groups.

Institutional explanatory factors

We found that three institutional factors are powerful in explaining political locational policies (see Table 5.2). First, the national tax regime determines, among other things, the localities' capacities to raise income (Page & Goldsmith, 1987). The degree of local tax autonomy can be operationalized by the availability of tax instruments for local governments. If the degree of local tax autonomy is low, higher-tier governmental funding compensates for these local financing constraints. The national tax regime explains whether SCCs engage in asking-for-public-funds strategies. Furthermore, the national tax regime, in combination with regional institutional fragmentation, is important in explaining if the jurisdictions in the region coordinate their locational policies. High local tax autonomy unfolds its full negative effect on coordination only in institutionally-fragmented metropolitan regions. Finally, capital cities have to deal with a variety of constraints specific to capitals. The more of these constraints exist, the more SCCs engage in asking-for-money strategies that target compensation payments.

The cities of The Hague and Rotterdam, together with the surrounding municipalities, coordinate some locational policies within the structures of the Metropolitan Region Rotterdam The Hague (MRTH). All municipalities involved

Table 5.2 Institutional explanatory factors for locational policies.

Political locational policies	*Institutional explanatory factors*
Coordination	National tax regime + regional institutional fragmentation
Public funds (Asking for money)	National tax regime
Compensation payments (Asking for money)	Capital city-specific constraints

belong to the province of South Holland, and this structure diffuses a consolidated political order. The Dutch national tax system assigns its municipalities a low degree of tax autonomy because they are allowed to levy taxes on property only. This low degree of local tax autonomy mitigates tax competition on the local level as there is not much tax money at stake. In addition to these two institutional explanatory factors, coordination is furthermore enabled by the polycentric setting of the Randstad because this spatial context provides ample opportunities to "borrow size" (Burger, Meijers, Hoogerbrugge, & Tresserra, 2015). Only together with other cities in the region can The Hague provide sufficient critical mass to support a wide range of metropolitan functions and be competitive in interurban competition (Meijers et al., 2014).

The Bern region does not display any pronounced institutional fragmentation, but the municipalities enjoy a high degree of tax autonomy. All municipalities in the Bern region belong to the same canton. However, high local tax autonomy – meaning that municipalities are allowed to levy personal income tax, corporate income tax, as well as property tax – leads to moderate tax competition in the region (Bern interviews, 34, 35, 36, & 37). High local tax autonomy seems to discourage municipalities from coordinating locational polices because tax revenues are at stake. On the regional level, the City of Bern coordinates image-building and asking-for-money strategies within the structures of the CRS. The CRS incorporates five cantons, and this not only increases the complexity of decision-making, but also increases the differences in their tax rates. This institutional fragmentation creates an unlevel tax competition. In fact, the cantons of Bern and Fribourg are strong competitors in attracting residents (Bern interviews, 1, 8, 9, & 34). Thus, the local and regional politicians view the CRS project as "a tightrope walk". It is a political partnership, but the various jurisdictions are simultaneously competitors in attracting tax revenue (Bern interviews, 33, 35, & 38). This is also reflected by the statement of a high-ranking politician in the City of Bern:

> *Whereas we consider it beneficial for the whole region if a firm relocates to Fribourg, where the new residents are going to live is another question and this issue is more competitive.*
>
> (Bern interview, 9)

The unlevel playing field of tax competition seems to explain why the CRS is successful in coordinating locational policies only on issues that generate few financial consequences (e.g. image-building and asking-for-money strategies).

In Ottawa, we have a setting in which a provincial border cuts through the very middle of the region but the municipalities do not enjoy much tax autonomy. Given the spatial proximity of Ottawa to Gatineau, it is astonishing that we did not detect any coordination mechanism in locational policies. An economic development agent explains that Ottawa and Gatineau refrain from cooperating because this may involve spending taxpayers' dollars from one jurisdiction that would benefit the other jurisdiction (Ottawa interview, 4). Even though Ottawa and Gatineau constitute a functional urban area, the provincial border prevents regional coordination. This is exemplified by the poorly-developed and loosely-connected public-transportation system. The latter is segregated in the middle of the metropolitan region where about 60,000 people commute every day to the other side of the Ottawa River (Champagne, 2011). However, we did not detect regional tax competition because the jurisdictions have only limited local tax autonomy. Ottawa and Gatineau have different tax rates and Gatineau is, for example, able to offer more specific tax incentives (Tassonyi, 2009, Ottawa interviews, 4 & 46). Nevertheless, these different tax settings do not lead to much competition in attracting firms because tax competition between municipalities occurs only around the property tax base.

In the D.C. region, there is a setting with high regional institutional fragmentation and high local tax autonomy. As a consequence, we observed regional competition in locational polices. The core of the region is the District of Columbia, which accounts for only around 10% of the population. The interplay between three states, the District, and the federal government makes regional coordination complicated, especially if we consider that every jurisdiction has its own economic development board (Washington, D.C. interviews, 20 & 44). Regional tax competition is carried out on an unlevel playing field because the different jurisdictions feature different tax settings. A private actor perceives that regional competition is primarily about tax money: "Tax competition underpins everything" (Washington, D.C. interview, 33). Regional tax competition hampers the coordination of locational policies in the region. Thus, there is no impetus to increase the global competitiveness of the D.C. region in a coordinated manner (Washington, D.C. interview, 9). One regional politician sums it up as follows: "We can't change anything about the institutional fragmentation and the different tax system. So we have to accept that and try to work around it" (Washington, D.C. interview, 47).

The cases revealed that second-tier borders (i.e. states, provinces, or cantons) are powerful institutional constraints for regional coordination. In the D.C. region and the Ottawa-Gatineau region, inter-municipal coordination fails due to second-tier borders dividing the regions. The cases of Bern and The Hague illustrate that the vertical structure matters for integration. In these cases, both the canton and the province emulate consolidated spatial orders and play important roles in fostering regional coordination. This finding is bad news for SCCs, as they are prone to be located in a situation with high vertical institutional fragmentation (Slack & Chattopadhyay, 2009). The degree of local tax autonomy also proved meaningful. Generally, tax competition and its underlying rationale of ensuring efficient and lean government entities via competition are different to the underlying rationale of coordination as a welfare theoretical concept (Scharpf, 1994). More specifically, the cases point to an interaction effect of two explanatory factors: High tax autonomy is an obstacle to coordinating locational policies, but it only unfolds its full negative effect in vertically fragmented functional urban areas. The combination of both institutional factors creates an unlevel playing field for local tax competition. This finding supports the argument of Leitner and Sheppard:

> When cities in competition face unequal conditions of possibility [i.e. an unlevel playing field] these not only affect the nature of local initiatives but also work to undermine the putative general benefits of entrepreneurial strategies: (…), and creating zero-sum or negative-sum game of 'beggar thy neighbor.'
>
> (Leitner & Sheppard, 1999, p.242)

Regarding asking-for-public-funds strategies, we found that the degree of local tax autonomy explains whether SCCs actively pursue these kind of strategies. In both Ottawa and The Hague, asking for public funds is an important locational policy. These seem to be linked to their national tax systems. Both countries allow their municipalities to levy only property taxes. Personal income taxes and corporate income taxes are the prerogative of higher-tier governments. However, local governments are compensated for these local tax autonomy constraints by a wide array of public funds.

Invest Ottawa is very active and strategic about tapping into public funds. For example, the whole public–private partnership set-up of Invest Ottawa can be seen as a strategy to attract higher-tier governmental funding because these public economic development funds often need matching funds or private-sector involvement (Ottawa interview, 42). An economic development agent explains:

> *[T]he evolution of the "triple helix" model or public–private partnership models is stimulated by the requirements of the federal or provincial funds to match these funds. It is mostly the private sector that matches these funds.*
>
> (Ottawa interview, 47)

The same mechanism is at work where incubators or accelerators are concerned. One reason why the city established the new start-up facilitator at Bayview Yards is to be attractive for governmental investments (Ottawa interview, 10).

Local governments in the Netherlands are similarly dependent on intergovernmental money transfers. A local public servant explains that the municipal efforts in the cybersecurity sector have been intensified because the Dutch Ministry of Economic Affairs, among other reasons, also supported this sector (The Hague interview, 33). Other economic sectors in The Hague simply do not comply with the national government's funding criteria. Thus, only by focusing on cybersecurity have national economic development funds begun to flow into The Hague.

In D.C. and Bern, asking for public funds is less central to the locational policies agendas. Higher-tier governments do not provide many public funds because both the US and Switzerland grant their local governments high local tax autonomy. For example, Swiss local governments and some US local governments are allowed to levy taxes on personal income and corporate income. As a consequence, these local governments ought to be able to sustain themselves and cannot rely on higher-tier governmental funding. Both D.C. and Bern ask for public funds and justify these claims, citing their status as the capital city. In D.C., local decision-makers are constantly lobbying for public funds but frame this as claims for compensation payments to offset the many local autonomy constraints.

In Bern, the regional coordination organization CRS is mainly a political vehicle for lobbying on the federal level and for positioning the region in the top tier of the Swiss urban system (Kaufmann et al., 2016). The CRS was established following the decision of the Swiss Federal Office for Spatial Development in 2008 to designate three Swiss metropolitan regions as growth centers, namely, Zurich, Basel, and the Geneva/Lausanne region (Bassin Lémanique). Bern is considered to be an urban agglomeration and, thus, of secondary importance for Switzerland. By positioning itself as the political center of Switzerland, Bern was placed in the top tier of metropolitan regions in the revised Swiss Federal Spatial Concept of 2012, albeit with an addendum regarding its function as Switzerland's political center since Bern does not fulfill the formal requirements to be a metropolitan region, such as gateway or corporate functions. This is now referred to as the "3 + 1 formula" – Zurich, Geneva–Lausanne, Basel + Bern – which indicates that Bern and the wider region were added as an additional metropolitan region with a different function (Kaufmann et al., 2016). One issue of major importance for Bern's decision-makers is the expansion of its main train station. To justify federal support for the capital city transportation infrastructure, a Madisonian line of argument (meaning that the national government should guarantee equal access to the seat of government for all citizens) (Engstrom, Hammond, & Scott, 2013) was often pursued. Following this line of argument, as a capital city region, Bern should be favored when awarding federal funds for transportation projects (Bern interview, 9).

In D.C., it is not possible to distinguish between asking for public funds and asking for compensation payments. D.C.'s decision-makers combine these two strategies into a powerful agenda by pointing to the many local autonomy constraints ensuing from the constitutional status as the Federal District. They argue that compensation payments are needed to offset these constraints. The local decision-makers push for federal investments in the District's outdated infrastructure and the regional public-transportation system. In all these negotiations, D.C. decision-makers explicitly referred to the special status as the Federal District. A delegate of a nonprofit interest group explains their strategy:

> *We launched the discussions for the new infrastructure deal because the Obama administration came into power. We thought the Clinton administration gave us the Revitalization Act, the Bush administration gave us some land that we could develop, and so we can also give the Obama administration a choice to improve the District. The commuter tax was always the elephant in the room over the years because states can tax commuters. Also because it is a lot of tax money given the amount of commuters. We thought we are probably not getting the commuter tax but we can negotiate a compensation for it.*
>
> (Washington, D.C. interview, 42)

Thus, the capital city-specific local autonomy restrictions are a good argumentative strategy for justifying federal payments.

As regards asking for compensation payments, we found that the intensity of capital city-specific constraints can explain whether an SCC actively tries to claim capital city-specific compensation payments. In general, compensation payments are claimed based on local autonomy restrictions resulting from the capital city status. As we have already discussed, this is most obvious in D.C., with its long history of negotiations between the federal level and the Federal District. The establishment of payments in lieu of taxes in Ottawa can also be linked to local autonomy restrictions imposed by the federal level. In both The Hague and Bern, locational policies agendas do not focus on compensation payments because the two cities do not face many capital city-specific local autonomy restrictions.

In Ottawa, the establishment of PILTs that compensate for lost property tax income is remarkable from a comparative perspective on financing capital cities. Thus, Ottawa is relatively better off than most other capital cities because of these rather generous PILTs (Chattopadhyay, 2011, vi; Slack & Chattopadhyay, 2009). The PILTs scheme was established in 1950 in the context of the Gréber Plan, which reorganized the relationship between the federal and municipal levels in Ottawa. The same plan led to the creation of the NCC out of its predecessor organization, the Federal District Commission. The area covered by the NCC was greatly expanded by a highly-active program of property acquisition (Andrew, 2013). Thus, the establishment of PILTs may be interpreted as a form of compensation for the capital city-specific constraints of Ottawa's local autonomy. Aside from these PILTs, the federal authorities do not compensate for capital city-related costs, such as increasing policing services (Tassonyi, 2009).

Bern receives compensation payments of CHF 1 million annually to support cultural institutions, activities, and special events that represent the nation state (Tobler, 2013). Furthermore, the Canton of Bern receives compensation for additional policing costs (Kübler, 2009). However, local decision-makers in Bern were not satisfied with these compensation payments and pushed for a new negotiation of compensation payments at the beginning of the 2000s (Bern interview, 34). The federal government agreed to set up a working group, but the working group was unable to agree on a list of positive and negative economic effects for the city attributable to its capital city status. In consequence, the working group commissioned an independent analysis (Ecoplan, 2004) that concluded: The added value and the job growth due to the federal presence has a positive effect overall for the region of Bern and therefore outweighs the tax losses. Given these findings, the federal government unilaterally terminated the negotiations for a new "capital-city legislation" (Kübler, 2009). Thus, in these negotiations also, the effects of the capital city function were the critical criteria when determining possible compensation payments.

The Hague does not pursue any strategies to access compensation payments. Given the established structures of the City Hall to tap into public funds, it seems surprising that The Hague does not pursue compensation claims. However, security costs are directly paid by the central government and The Hague does not face many local autonomy constraints arising out of its capital city status.

The case comparison showed that compensation payments are paid in the two North American capitals. Both of these capitals have a federal agency that represents federal interests over federal land – a feature absent from the two European SCCs. In D.C., the local autonomy constraints are more profound, to the extreme that the Congress has de facto oversight over local policymaking. Both North American cities were built from scratch, or heavily developed to serve as the nation's capital, whereas the European SCCs were already established cities at the time of their selection as the capital. It is unlikely that the latter would have accepted cutbacks in their local autonomy brought along by their capital city status. The case studies suggest that the status of the cities prior to their selection as the capital should be considered as an explanation for capital city-specific constraints and, thus, can explain compensation payments in SCCs. Purpose-built capitals seem to face more capital city-specific constraints in their local autonomy, whereas purposely-selected capitals seem to enjoy more local autonomy. Thus, it is important to differentiate between purpose-built capitals and purposely-selected capitals when studying capital cities. This differentiation enriches the existing political-institutional capital city categorizations, such as Rowat's (1973) distinction between three types of legal statuses or governing structures of capital cities: (1) A capital city that is located in a special district, (2) a capital city as a city state that is simultaneously a constitutive unit of the nation, and (3) a capital city that is located within a province, state, or canton with no special status (Harris, 1995; Rowat, 1973; Slack & Chattopadhyay, 2009).

Regional and urban politics

The four case studies frequently point to political factors that are important for explaining the formulation of locational policies. Political factors are evident in the coordination of locational policies since coordination is in its essence a matter of agency, interests, and power relations. Hence, politics is a factor in its own right since "cooperation results from bargaining and negotiating among the officials of affected jurisdictions" (Dowding & Feiock, 2012, p. 37).

In Bern, a partisan divide exists between the agglomeration municipalities and the core city. Whereas the City of Bern is a stronghold of the social democratic and green parties, moderate-right and conservative-right parties dominate the agglomeration municipalities (Bern interviews, 34, 37, & 43). This leads to – probably politically motivated – suspicion between the core city and the agglomeration municipalities. This partisan divide, intertwined with the deeply-rooted idea of municipal autonomy in Swiss federalism, has led to a resistance toward anything that could potentially constrain the municipal political autonomy (Van der Heiden, 2010).

In The Hague, the establishment of the MRTH was a strategic move on the part of Rotterdam and The Hague to gain more autonomy from the province of South Holland (The Hague interviews, 10 & 37). An employee of the MRTH clarifies the founding intention:

*We have to redefine the relationship with the province. The hierarchical
structure of the three state levels no longer matches the realities. The mayors
of the big Dutch cities have a direct line to the Prime Minister. The provinces
are not as important anymore. That means we have to find new ways of dividing political tasks, we have to find new ways of cooperation between the three
state levels.*

(The Hague interview, 11)

Indeed, the major Dutch cities "often view the provinces as unwelcome representatives of the smaller municipalities that surround them" (Andeweg & Irwin,
2014, pp. 212–213). Consequently, the MRTH is an initiative of the two major
cities with noticeably less political commitment from the mayors of the smaller
municipalities (Meijers, Hollander, & Hoogerbrugge, 2012).

The location of Ottawa at the most symbolic Canadian subnational border
causes two different political systems to meet at the level of regional politics. In
general, Quebec has a more centralized political system, whereas the municipalities in Ontario enjoy more autonomy (Ottawa interviews, 39 & 40). In addition,
there are different languages and legal systems – common law in Ontario and civil
law in Quebec – that further hamper regional coordination (Ottawa interviews, 14,
38, & 49). Furthermore, political conflicts resulting from Quebec's status within
Canada underlie and, thus, complicate regional politics. The very political struggles of Canada are manifested in its National Capital Region (Veronis, 2013). The
problems caused by this extreme type of regional institutional fragmentation leads
one expert to conclude that "Ottawa is probably the hardest capital city-region to
govern" (Ottawa interview, 38).

Similarly to Ottawa, in Washington, D.C., the Federal District is located at a
symbolic subnational border that marks the line between Northern US states and
Southern US states. The three states and the District of Columbia feature different
political settings. Whereas the two Virginias are Southern states with limited local
autonomy, Maryland is a Northern state in which local jurisdictions enjoy more
autonomy (Washington, D.C. interviews, 20 & 41). The District is a very specific
political construct with a unique political structure. This high degree of institutional fragmentation, i.e. the interplay of three states, the District, and the federal
government, makes regional coordination extremely challenging.

Beside the regional coordination of locational policies that are certainly influenced by regional political factors, we have not yet discussed the local formulation
process of locational policies. Locational policy formulation could be approached
by concepts stemming from the urban politics literature, such as urban regimes
(Stone, 1989, 1993) or growth machines (Logan & Molotch, 1987; Molotch,
1976). These concepts help us to analyze the interactions between public and
private actors in their struggles over power or, framed more positively, in their
efforts to find common solutions to urban problems. The growth machine theory
emphasizes the power of land and property owners in local politics that form alliances with other local actors to constantly strive to increase the value of their land
and real estate. The result of such machine politics is that the exchange value of

property and land trumps their use value. The urban regime approach emphasizes the importance of informal arrangements in which public and private actors function together in order to have the "capacity to govern" a city. In a nutshell, popular control (votes) and investments in local development projects (money) are the two decisive factors that constitute the "capacity to govern" in an urban arena.

Both seminal theories emphasize that local decision-making does not follow the formal line of authority, but instead involves a wide array of private actors. Business elites play a crucial role in urban policy-making because they can provide crucial resources, such as money, land, and expertise, in return for political influence. In SCCs, rather few business actors seems to engage in locational policy formulation. In essence, SCCs are government towns that lack an industrial tradition, meaning that resource-rich and powerful business elites never developed in SCCs. The only powerful business actors in government cities are developers. An expert explains the political influence of developers in Ottawa:

> *Here in Ottawa, developers are very important for running the city. I guess that 50 influential developers have something to say in local politics. They chose not to be organized because they do not want to give themselves a face or a name and they are also heavy competitors. Developers have a diffuse form of power. Thus, here in Ottawa we have no urban regime except the developers. Ottawa never was an industrial town. That means that the chambers of commerce have not much to say because they do not have much money and power behind them.*
>
> (Ottawa interview, 38)

An expert in D.C. describes the urban governance system similarly:

> *I would call the local governance structure rather growth machine than urban regime. Growth machine applies better as a concept, because D.C. never had industries, but it has land to develop. (...) Real estate developers are important throughout the whole metropolitan area.*
>
> (Washington, D.C. interview, 44)

In summary, the only powerful business elites that could influence urban politics in SCCs are developers. This central role of developers may be what has led to the growth-oriented urban land-use agenda that prevails in Ottawa and Washington, D.C. (for D.C. see Hyra & Prince, 2016). However, we did not analyze systematically how developers and local political elites align themselves to push for specific locational policies agendas. Such urban politics issues could be investigated further. However, due to the lack of any formalized system of access to informal politics, it is extremely difficult for academics to open the "black box" of local informal political processes.

Different political levels intersect in capital cities with a stronger intensity than in other cities (Campbell, 2000). Many capital city researchers have studied capital cities from the perspective of nation states (e.g. Harris, 1995;

Rowat, 1968, 1973). The strong presence of the nation state certainly influences policy formulation in SCCs. At its most extreme, this was observed in D.C. One the one hand, D.C. has to deal with a number of local autonomy constraints and, on the other hand, American politics is spatially anchored in the District. Examples are the Congressional blockages of local societal policies that are contested at the national scale. Thus, the US capital is simultaneously a place for local politics and a local playing field for American politics in a way that no other jurisdiction in the whole country is. The national government level without doubt exerts some influence on local policy-making in SCCs.

Synthesis by regions

Bern

The City of Bern concentrates mainly on cluster policies in the medical technology, energy, and cleantech sectors. One promising triple helix organization has been established in each of these sectors. The stimulation of an entrepreneurial environment by fostering start-ups or providing venture capital funds is, however, largely ignored. In general, the City of Bern formulates more political locational policies than economic locational policies. The City showcases itself as the political center of Switzerland. This image-building strategy is also pursued in regional coordination organizations (CRS) and is linked to asking-for-money strategies by arguing that a strong capital city is in the interests of Switzerland as a whole. Beside image-building and asking for public funds, the city is not able to coherently coordinate locational policies with jurisdictions in the region.

Ottawa

The locational policies agenda of Ottawa is dominated by three topics: First, there is a strong focus on innovation. Innovation policies aim to strengthen linkages between key actors in the RIS and by providing services for start-ups. Second, Ottawa tries to position itself simultaneously as a government town and as a business hub. This is most evident in its image-building strategy, which is to present itself simultaneously as a G7 capital and a high-tech town. Third, asking for public funds is central to the local budget and, thus, to the locational policies agenda. There is no regional coordination of locational policies, given that the region is divided by a provincial border that cuts through its very center.

The Hague

The Hague tries to position itself as an international business city while still leveraging its standing as the "International City of Peace and Justice". The emerging cybersecurity sector is the crucial cornerstone in this transformation. Cybersecurity capitalizes on the presence of international organizations in the area of law and security or national security organizations. The shift of focus from

Table 5.3 Case study regions at a glance.

Locational policy	Bern	Ottawa	The Hague	Washington, D.C.
Innovation policies	Support of cluster organizations in medical technology and energy & cleantech Two triple-helix organizations Few activities regarding start-ups and venture capital	Focus on technology-intense key industries Local public actors strengthen linkages between key actors of the RIS Various support services for start-ups and entrepreneurs	Focus on cluster policies, adoption of the triple-helix concept, cybersecurity as the most promising cluster Search for diversification of clusters Setting up of public venture capital funds	Stimulating knowledge interactions in the high-tech sector and the medical sector Several individual initiatives to foster start-ups and entrepreneurship
Attracting money	Image as the political center of Switzerland Not much influence in attracting firms, because this is the task of the canton and the Swiss Confederation	Two-dimensional image-building: "G7 capital and high-tech town" Threefold strategy in attracting firms: (1) Soft-landing spot in the North American market, (2) local key industries, (3) local talent pool	Image as the International City of Peace and Justice, plus positioning as an international business town The city is junior partner in attracting international organizations	Two-dimensional strategy: "Capital city of the free world" and highlighting the innovation potential of highly-regulated sectors Profound and wide-ranging strategies to attract firms
Coordination	Coordination organizations in the Bern agglomeration and at the regional level, but not much coordination of locational policies	Absence of regional coordination	Regional coordination between The Hague and Rotterdam at the metropolitan level	Regional tax competition and beggar-my-neighbor behavior
Asking for money	Capital city function is used to ask for public funds No compensation regarding capital city-specific costs or loss of income	High importance of public funds PILTs compensate for loss of property taxes	No compensation for capital city specific costs or loss of income High importance of central government funds	Asking for compensation payments based on capital city-specific constraints

international organization to cybersecurity is a perfect example of the kinds of cluster crossovers that the City of The Hague is actively searching for when formulating innovation policies. Given the limited local tax autonomy, The Hague focuses on attracting a wide array of public funds. We found successful coordination at the metropolitan level between the cities of Rotterdam, The Hague, and surrounding municipalities in the policy fields of transportation, as well as locational policies.

Washington, D.C.

The locational policies agenda of Washington, D.C. is dominated by three topics. First, innovation policies target mainly the medical sector and the high-tech sectors. Both sectors are technology-intense and highly regulated and dominate, together with the defense industry, the economy of the entire region. Second, the D.C. administration tries to leverage the status as the US capital city to the maximum, for example, by using the tagline "capital city of the free world." D.C. is able to unite the government city image-building with an image of an innovative business city by highlighting the economic dynamics in its highly-regulated sectors. This two-dimensional positioning strategy can be detected in both image-building and attracting firms. Third, D.C. decision-makers constantly ask for federal compensation payments based on capital city-specific constraints. There is regional tax competition in attracting residents and firms. However, attempts to ensure regional coordination of locational policies have failed.

References

Abbott, C. (1999). *Political Terrain: Washington, D.C., from Tidewater Town to Global Metropolis*. Chapel Hill & London: The University of North Carolina Press.
Abbott, C. (2005). Washington and Berlin: National Capitals in a Networked World. In A. W. Daum & C. Mauch (Eds.), *Berlin – Washington, 1800–2000: Capital Cities, Cultural Representation, and National Identities*. New York: Cambridge University Press.
Andeweg, R., & Irwin, G. (2014). *Governance and Politics of the Netherlands*. London: Palgrave Macmillan.
Andrew, C. (2013). The Case of Ottawa. In Klaus-Jürgen Nagel (Ed.), *The Problem of the Capital City: New Research on Federal Capitals and Their Territory* (pp. 83–102). Barcelona: Generalitat de Catalunya: Institut d'Estudis Autonomics.
Andrew, C., & Doloreux, D. (2012). Economic development, social inclusion and urban governance: The case of the city-region of Ottawa in Canada. *International Journal of Urban and Regional Research*, *36*(6), 1288–1305. https://doi.org/10.1111/j.1468-2427.2011.01025.x
Asch, C. M., & Musgrove, G. D. (2016). We Are Headed for Some Bad Trouble: Gentrification and Displacement in Washington, DC, 1920–2014. In D. Hyra & S. Prince (Eds.) *Capital Dilemma: Growth and Inequality in Washington, D.C.* (pp. 107–136). New York and London: Routledge.
Asheim, B., Smith, H. L., & Oughton, C. (2011). Regional innovation systems: Theory, empirics and policy. *Regional Studies*, *45*(7), 875–891.
Bern Wirtschaftsraum. (2012). Strategie 2020.

Bradford, N., & Wolfe, D. (2013). Governing regional economic development: Innovation challenges and policy learning in Canada. *Cambridge Journal of Regions, Economy and Society. 6*(2), 331–347.

Burger, M. J., Meijers, E. J., Hoogerbrugge, M. M., & Tresserra, J. M. (2015). Borrowed size, agglomeration shadows and cultural amenities in North-West Europe. *European Planning Studies, 23*(6), 1090–1109.

Campbell, S. (2000). *The Changing Role and Identity of Capital Cities in the Global Era.* Annual Meeting of the Association of American Geographers. Pittsburgh, PA.

Castells, M. (1989). *The Informational City: Information Technology, Economic Restructuring, and the Urban-Regional Process.* Oxford: Blackwell Publishers.

Champagne, E. (2011). Transportation Failure in the Federal Capital Region. In R. Chattopadhyay & G. Paquet (Eds.), *The Unimagined Canadian Capital: Challenges for the Federal Capital Region* (pp. 27–34). Ottawa: Invenire Books.

Chattopadhyay, R. (2011). Foreword. In R. Chattopadhyay & G. Paquet (Eds.), *The Unimagined Canadian Capital: Challenges for the Federal Capital Region.* Ottawa: Invenire Books.

City of Ottawa. (2016). *Budget 2016.* Retrieved from http://ottawa.ca/en/city-hall/budget-and-taxes/budget-2016

City of The Hague. (2014). Programmabegroting 2015–2018.

Cooke, P. (2001). Regional innovation systems, clusters, and the knowledge economy. *Industrial and Corporate Change, 10*(4), 945–974.

Cowell, M., & Mayer, H. (2016). Anchoring a Federal Agency in a Washington, DC Community: The Department of Homeland Security and St. Elizabeths. In D. Hyra & S. Prince (Eds.), *Capital Dilemma: Growth and Inequality in Washington, D.C.* (pp. 207–224). New York and London: Routledge.

Dowding, K., & Feiock, R. (2012). Intralocal Competition and Cooperation. In K. Mossberger, S. E. Clarke, & P. John (Eds.), *The Oxford Handbook of Urban Politics* (pp. 29–50). New York: Oxford University Press.

Ecoplan. (2004). Bern als Bundesstadt: Positive and negative Effekte.

Engstrom, E., Hammond, J., & Scott, J. (2013). Capitol mobility: Madisonian representation and the location and relocation of capitals in the United States. *American Political Science Review, 107*(2), 225–240.

Eshuis, J., Braun, E., & Klijn, E.-H. (2013). Place marketing as governance strategy: An assessment of obstacles in place marketing and their effects on attracting target groups. *Public Administration Review, 73*(3), 507–516.

Etzkowitz, H., & Leydesdorff, L. (1995). The triple helix–university-industry-government relations: A laboratory for knowledge-based economic development. *EASST Review, 14*(1), 14–19.

Groen, R. (2014). Politics and International Organizations: Four cases in The Hague and Geneva. Prepared for the IIAS Congress in Morocco.

Harris, C. W. (1995). *Congress and the Governance of the Nation's Capital: The Conflict of Federal and Local Interests.* Washington, D.C.: Georgetown University Press.

Horak, M. (2012). Conclusion: Understanding Multilevel Governance in Canada's Cities. In M. Horak & R. Young (Eds.), *Sites of Governance: Multilevel Governance and Policy Making in Canada's Big Cities* (Vol. 3, pp. 339–370). Montreal, Quebec and Kingston, Ontario: McGill-Queen's University Press.

Howell, K. (2016). "It's Complicated … ": Long-Term Residents and Their Relations to Gentrification in Washington, DC. In D. Hyra & S. Prince (Eds.) *Capital Dilemma: Growth and Inequality in Washington, D.C.* (pp. 255–278). New York and London: Routledge.

Hyra, D., & Prince, S. (Eds.). (2016). *Capital Dilemma: Growth and Inequality in Washington, DC*. New York and Abingdon: Routledge.

Ircha, M., & Young, R. (2013). Conclusion. In M. Ircha & R. Young (Eds.), *Federal Property Policy in Canadian Municipalities* (pp. 157–180). Montreal, Quebec and Kingston, Ontario: McGill-Queen's University Press.

Kaufmann, D., Warland, M., Mayer, H., & Sager, F. (2016). Bern's positioning strategies: Escaping the fate of a secondary capital city? *Cities, 53*, 120–129. https://doi.org/10.1016/j.cities.2016.02.005

Kübler, D. (2009). Bern, Switzerland. In E. Slack & R. Chattopadhyay (Eds.), *Finance and Governance of Capital Cities in Federal Systems* (pp. 238–262). Montreal, Quebec and Kingston, Ontario: McGill-Queen's University Press.

Leitner, H., & Sheppard, E. (1999). Transcending Interurban Competition: Conceptual Issues and Policy Alternatives in the European Union. In A. Jonas & D. Wilson (Eds.), *The Urban Growth Machine: Critical Perspectives Two Decades Later* (pp. 227–243). Albany, NY: State University of New York Press.

Logan, J., & Molotch, H. (1987). *Urban Fortunes: The Political Economy of Place*. Berkeley, Los Angeles, and London: University of California Press.

Martin, R., & Trippl, M. (2014). System failures, knowledge bases and regional innovation policies. *disP – The Planning Review, 50*(1), 24–32.

Mayer, H., & Cowell, M. (2014). Capital cities as knowledge hubs: The economic geography of homeland security contracting. In S. Coventz, A. DeRudder, A. Thierstein, & F. Witlox (Eds.), *Hub Cities in the Knowledge Economy* (pp. 223–246). London: Ashgate.

Meijers, E., Hollander, K., & Hoogerbrugge, M. (2012). *Case Study Metropolitan Region Rotterdam–The Hague*. The Hague: European Metropolitan Network Institute.

Meijers, E., Hoogerbrugge, M., Louw, E., Priemus, H., & Spaans, M. (2014). City profile: The Hague. *Cities, 41*, 92–100.

Molotch, H. (1976). The city as a growth machine: Toward a political economy of place. *American Journal of Sociology*, 309–332.

Page, E., & Goldsmith, M. (1987). *Central and Local Government Relations: A Comparative Analysis of West European Unitary States*. London: Sage Publications.

Rowat, D. (1968). The problems of governing federal capitals. *Canadian Journal of Political Science, 1*(3), 345–356.

Rowat, D. (1973). *The Government of Federal Capitals*. Toronto: University of Toronto Press.

Scharpf, F. (1994). Games real actors could play: Positive and negative coordination in embedded negotiations. *Journal of Theoretical Politics, 6*(1), 27–53.

Shavinina, L. V. (Ed.). (2004). *Silicon Valley North: A High-Tech Cluster of Innovation and Entrepreneurship*. Amsterdam: Elsevier.

Siegel, D. (2009). Ontario. In A. Sancton & R. Young (Eds.), *Foundations of Governance: Municipal Government in Canada's Provinces* (pp. 20–69). Toronto: University of Toronto Press.

Slack, E., & Chattopadhyay, R. (2009). *Finance and Governance of Capital Cities in Federal Systems*. Montreal, Quebec and Kingston, Ontario: McGill-Queen's University Press.

Spigel, B. (2011). Series of Unfortunate Events: The Growth, Decline, and Rebirth of Ottawa's Entrepreneurial Institutions. In G. Libecap & S. Hoskinson (Eds.), *Entrepreneurship and Global Competitiveness in Regional Economies: Determinants and Policy Implications* (pp. 47–72). Bingley, UK: Emerald Group Publishing Ltd.

Stone, C. (1989). *Regime Politics: Governing Atlanta, 1946–1988.* Lawrence, KS: University Press of Kansas.

Stone, C. (1993). Urban regimes and the capacity to govern: A political economy approach. *Journal of Urban Affairs, 15*(1), 1–28.

Swiss Federal Railways. (2013). Die SBB in Zahlen und Fakten. 2013.

Tassonyi, A. (2009). Ottawa, Canada. In E. Slack & R. Chattopadhyay (Eds.), *Finance and Governance of Capital Cities in Federal Systems* (pp. 55–78). Montreal, Quebec and Kingston, Ontario: McGill-Queen's University Press.

The District of Columbia. (2012). The Five-Year Economic Development Strategy for the District of Columbia.

The Hague Security Delta. (2011). Ministry of Economic Affairs to Support HSD. Retrieved from https://www.thehaguesecuritydelta.com/news/newsitem/82-ministry-of-economic-affairs-decides-to-support-hsd

The Hague Security Delta. (2014). Cyber Service Nato to The Hague because of Presence Security Cluster. Retrieved from www.thehaguesecuritydelta.com/news/newsitem/164

The Hague Security Delta. (2016). Seminar at HSD Campus on Business Building in Canada: Opportunities in Soft Landing. Retrieved from https://www.thehaguesecuritydelta.com/news/newsitem/487-seminar-at-hsd-campus-on-business-building-in-canada-opportunities-in-soft-landing

Tobler, G. (2013). Governance in Hauptstadtregionen: Was kann die Hauptstadtregion Schweiz von Washington lernen? In H. Mayer, F. Sager, A. Minta, & S. M. Zwahlen (Eds.), *Im Herzen der Macht: Hauptstädte und ihre Funktion* (pp. 295–310). Bern: Haupt Verlag AG.

Tödtling, F., & Trippl, M. (2005). One size fits all?: Towards a differentiated regional innovation policy approach. *Research Policy, 34*(8), 1203–1219.

Van der Heiden, N. (2010). *Urban Foreign Policy and Domestic Dilemmas: Insights from Swiss and EU City-regions.* Colchester, UK: European Consortium for Political Research.

Veronis, L. (2013). The border and immigrants in Ottawa-Gatineau: Governance practices and the (re) production of a dual Canadian citizenship. *Journal of Borderlands Studies, 28*(2), 257–271.

6 Conclusion: Deal with it – ten recommendations to ensure secondary capital cities thrive

This book set out to study the economic and political dynamics of secondary capital cities (SCCs), i.e. capitals that are not the economic centers of their countries. This simultaneous economic inferiority and political superiority creates specific challenges. Capital cities for a long time relied on their political importance as seats of national power and representation of the nation as such. This came hand in hand with subsidies from the nation states, which are more ample in centralistic states than in federalist systems with higher political autonomy at the regional and local levels. The decline of the nation state as the core organizational unit of political life in a globalized world, coupled with the economic crisis, meant that sole reliance on national funds for capital city functions became an increasingly precarious strategy for capital cities in general, but particularly for SCCs. Consequently, SCCs today have to reconsider their role in global city competition and develop tailored strategies for success. This conclusion consolidates our key insights on how this objective can best be achieved.

The goal of this book is to understand the political economy of SCCs and what this has to do with their capital city function. We used two perspectives to do so: as economic geographers, we employed the regional innovation system (RIS) framework to study how firms interact with each other and how they connect via knowledge interactions to research organizations and governmental units in an SCC economy; as political scientists and policy analysts, we applied the locational policy framework to understand what kinds of strategies SCCs formulate to develop their RIS and to position themselves in international urban competition. Our findings are derived from our in-depth analysis of the RIS and the locational policies in four SCCs, namely, Bern, Ottawa, The Hague, and Washington, D.C. These cases are relevant and telling for the general issue of SCC economies, as a number of intervening variables have been controlled by case selection: Switzerland, the Netherlands, Canada, and the United States are all liberal Western democracies and OECD members. None of the four SCCs has a history as an industrial city, and all have been knowledge-based ever since being selected as their respective nations' capitals. They thus share basic economic, democratic, and cultural traditions that make them comparable. At the same time, they display various differences at a more specific level in terms of their urban system, institutional order, and policy choices. This makes their comparison interesting and the findings relevant for other SCCs in different contexts, as well as for other secondary cities in similar contexts to the ones observed here.

Implications for the literature

This book makes an important contribution to three different strands of the literature. First, we contribute to the capital city literature by adding a political economy perspective. While traditional accounts of capital cities focus on the political functions and how these influence identity, politics, governance, etc. in the capital city (Gordon, 2006; Gottmann, 1977; Hall, 2010; Rowat, 1968a, 1968b; Slack & Chattopadhyay, 2009; Wolman, Chadwick, & Karruz, 2006), our perspective goes beyond the role of the capital as a political center and takes the capital's role as a modern economy into account.

Second, our inquiry from the economic geography perspective was motivated by the question of how public-procurement-driven innovation activities function as drivers for knowledge dynamics in capital city RIS. We were guided by a set of basic tenets that highlight the dominant role of outsourcing and contracting in the capital city economy across all four countries under study. We found a specific RIS that is characterized by close interactions between national government agencies and contracting firms and by mediating activities on behalf of intermediaries. It seems that capital city RIS function in a similar way to other types of territorial innovation systems in terms of knowledge dynamics and interactions. However, the drivers are different, as it is the public sector, not the private sector, that provides incentives and impulses for innovation through public procurement. Thus, the RIS literature (Asheim, Smith, & Oughton, 2011; Braczyk, Cooke, & Heidenreich, 1998; Doloreux & Parto, 2005; Tödtling & Trippl, 2005) needs to take the public sector on the demand side into account.

Third, the political science perspective was guided by the question of what kinds of locational policies are formulated in SCCs and the rationale behind them. The locational policies framework helped us to categorize the wide range of locational policies formulated by the four SCCs. Various factors emerged as important when explaining the formulation of locational policies. We proposed three broad lines of inquiry that can help make sense of the variety of locational policies in the four SCCs, namely, the development of the RIS, institutional factors, and regional and urban politics. Our findings support neo-institutionalist theories that argue for a diversity of policy responses to global economic pressures. More specifically, it seems that the RIS as an economic explanatory factor influences economic locational policies and that institutional and political factors influence the formulation of political locational policies. This points to a functional logic of locational policy formulation that can be related to the Varieties of Capitalism theory. Hall and Soskice (2001) propose that the political-institutional setting and the economic orientation of a political economy are the two crucial explanatory factors for strategic decisions of localities. This assumes a necessary coherence between the economic and political setting of a locality, which, in combination, makes up the political economy of capital cities. These tentative findings take a stance against theories that assume converging urban policies given the pressures to be competitive in globalized interurban competition. While the motivations behind engaging in locational policies formulation may be similar, i.e. enhancing economic competitiveness, the actual locational policies drafted depend on specific local assets and constraints.

We combine the two perspectives and answer the question as to how capital cities respond economically and politically to their changing roles in terms of their knowledge economy but also in terms of their position in interurban hierarchies. More specifically, capital cities differ in terms of their development (weakly developed, moderately developed, and highly developed) and RIS failures and the formulation of locational policies differ according to the level of development. We found that in Bern, for example, the RIS is fragmented and lacks collaboration between government agencies and firms. Fragmentation also characterized the RIS in Ottawa, while The Hague is set up to overcome fragmentation. Washington, D.C., in contrast, might represent a highly-developed RIS, in which partners cooperate extensively, but may also be under threat of overembeddedness and lock-in. Locational policies in the four capital cities differ. Whereas the political locational policies – coordination and asking for money – are best explained by institutional and political factors, the formulation of economic locational policies – innovation policies and asking for money – interacts with the level of RIS development. We found that innovation policies in SCCs are policy instruments specifically developed to target RIS failures. This finding supports the take on policy interventions prevalent in the RIS literature, that expects policy interventions only in the event of system failures (Asheim et al., 2011; Cooke, 2001; Martin & Trippl, 2014). In the case of asking-for-money strategies, the direction of causality seems to be reversed. Image-building and attracting firms are not aimed at developing the RIS, but these policies want to make use of RIS development. Image-building as a business town and strategies to attract firms are dependent on a well-functioning RIS, as they would otherwise not be credible. The reversed direction of causality makes sense theoretically because the locational policies framework conceptualizes innovation policies as inward-oriented and attracting-money-strategies as outward-oriented.

Recommendations for practitioners

The well-being and prosperity of SCCs are first and foremost a practical endeavor; only in second place are they an academic interest in their own right. In the following, we therefore present our core insights in the form of recommendations. Our recommendations speak primarily to urban practitioners, such as local and regional politicians, economic developers, policy specialists, etc. They are also supported by our theory-driven empirical evidence as presented in this book. The contribution to the academic literature has been mapped in the previous two chapters. We identified considerable potential for SCC-RIS development and strengthening in our cases. We consequently consider this hands-on approach a straightforward contribution to evidence-based policymaking in the urban context.

We organize our recommendations from bottom to top in the order of urban actor levels. We first address economic actors in SCCs, i.e. firms and business individuals; we then move on to the level of urban politics, addressing participants in the urban regime as well as formal decision-makers in the executive and its administration; finally, we move to the national system level where important decisions crucial for SCCs are taken. Our recommendations are not intended to imply that there are single factors that are decisive for the well-being of an SCC. Quite the contrary: An important finding from our comparison is the context-sensitivity of the factors – hardly any single feature exerts unitary explanatory power for success or failure. Nevertheless, we claim that, though the context is decisive, the following recommendations once implemented may contribute to the development of successful SCC-RIS.

Recommendations for firms

Our recommendations for RIS participants in SCCs concern the specific economic opportunities for firms in SCCs and the strategies used to exploit these.

Recommendation 1:

If you want to win a contract from the national government, be spatially proximate.

Public procurement is a core driver of SCC economies. Government contractors profit from the specific needs of federal administrations and tailor their offers accordingly. The cases show how spatial proximity makes a difference. This is especially true for the two large countries, Canada and the US, whereas the Netherlands and Switzerland have a limited size and a somewhat denser urban system by comparison. However, in the latter two SCCs also, firms benefit from spatial proximity to government agencies. Public procurement is a highly-regulated business guaranteeing a level playing field for all potential competitors, near and far. However, the case studies show how firms use proximity to take advantage of the regulated procurement process, building a competitive advantage by entertaining informal contacts with contracting agencies.

These informal contacts do not mean that there are illegal practices at work. Intense relations between government contractors and contracting agencies serve mutual information-sharing and establish a common understanding of the problems addressed in public tenders. If firms and agencies are in contact before the problems at hand are solved and, hence, before the call for tenders is drafted, exchange can be beneficial for both sides of the contract. The agency gets a clearer idea of what is possible in a contract and what issues should be emphasized in a call for bids, while potential contractors profit from knowledge of what calls are about to be published and, more importantly, what the procuring agency's core needs are. In so doing, government contractors gain valuable time in the procurement process since they know what the agency needs before the call is actually published. In turn, based on informal discussions, procurement officers have security that they will receive tenders addressing their actual problems. This mechanism operates in all four SCCs studied and it works very similarly, irrespective of the size of the contracts.

These discussions do not circumvent competition, as informal contacts are not limited to only one contractor. However, as all cases show, spatial proximity is a crucial condition for such informal contacts as they go beyond online contacts and formal Q&A processes. Taking advantage of spatial proximity does not come for free. Contacts are complex and many different units and individuals are involved. Pierre Bourdieu (1986) speaks of social capital when he describes how contacts can be transformed into other forms of capital, such as economic capital in the form of money:

> Social capital is the aggregate of the actual or potential resources which are linked to possession of a durable network of more or less institutionalized relationships of mutual acquaintance and recognition – or in other words, to membership in a group – which provides each of its members with the backing of the collectivity-owned capital, a "credential" which entitles them to credit, in the various senses of the word.
>
> (Bourdieu, 1986, p. 247)

According to this view, social capital is an investment and does not magically fall like manna from heaven, but entails hard work. Relationships need to be built and maintained with all participants in the procurement process in order to build social capital that, once the call is out, can be transformed into economic profit. This investment is easier to make for proximate companies with established contacts with public agencies compared to what would be possible for competitors that lack proximity. In summary, spatial proximity creates a competitive advantage for government contractors by way of informal social relationships.

Recommendation 2:

Increase the competitiveness of your region as well as your own city by cooperating with competitors.

Exchange is important, not only with potential contracting agencies, but also with other firms, i.e. actual competitors. The concept of social capital, where contacts are considered a resource, is captured in the RIS approach by the notion of "local buzz" (Bathelt, Malmberg, & Maskell, 2004): The better a competitor is connected, the better its access to information, rumors and news. Local buzz applies to contacts with competitors as well as contracting agencies. Local buzz fosters partnerships among government contractors and increases the competitiveness of a SCC region as a whole.

Fragmentation is a threat to functioning RIS. As our cases show, firms do not cooperate to the same degree in all SCCs. Due to the larger contract volumes, cooperation is more common in Washington, D.C. and Ottawa than it is in The Hague and Bern. In the US, the preferential treatment of SMEs in public procurement plays an additional role. Cooperation, however, also has very practical advantages for competitors: First, complementarity leads to better tenders. Companies team up to exchange ideas and complement one another. Larger firms can close gaps in their profile with specialized niche companies. From the procurement perspective, this makes the tender more solid as it rests on more shoulders than just one supplier's. Should one partner drop out for whatever reason, the second may step in. Second, the costs of bidding decrease. This applies not only to the actual drafting, but even more so to the investment in building social capital long before the call is published. Tying networks together increases social capital and, correspondingly, the chances of success. Networks are mirrored in the lists of reference projects, and the same cumulative effect is evident. Overall, our study indicates that cooperation is highly beneficial for competing government contractors.

However, the benefit of partnering goes beyond the individual firm. Cooperation is good for the RIS as a whole. The circulation of knowledge increases an SCC's competitiveness because it fosters mutual learning among competitors and, consequently, advances specialization of the entire RIS. The RIS can thus sharpen its focus on government needs. This lends the entire region a comparative advantage. Not all SCCs studied are aware of this effect. As we find, Canadian and US government agencies actively encourage project teams comprising more than one firm. They incentivize horizontal cooperation among competitors and thereby contribute to the competitiveness of the SCC as a whole. Procurement officers in Bern and The Hague do not do so and, hence, leave it to the contractors themselves to realize the advantages of partnerships. The impact on the economic profile of these two SCCs might be stronger if the public calls for tenders were to contain a clause that partnerships are preferred.

In summary, cooperation and partnership prove to be the main countermeasures against RIS fragmentation. As the cases also show, there is an underlying dynamic at work whereby the narrative of a government town has a reinforcing effect; new firms can align to this narrative and more smoothly integrate themselves into the SCC-RIS.

Recommendations for policymakers at the city level

The recommendations we formulate at the city level address the issues of how to domestically manage an SCC-RIS, on the one hand, and how to externally position an SCC in international city competition and in respect of the more senior federal levels, on the other.

Recommendation 3:

Enhance economic dynamics through innovation and entrepreneurship policies in knowledge-intensive and highly-regulated sectors.

Innovation and entrepreneurship policies aim at developing and diversifying RIS by promoting interaction between economic actors such as industry, academia, and government agencies. The preconditions for such strategies in SCCs exist in particular in sectors where the government plays a strong regulating role, such as medical technology, energy, education, and defense. All of the SCCs studied engage in summoning expertise and entrepreneurship in one or more of these sectors. Highly-regulated sectors are the obvious choice for support policies since the relevant knowledge and expertise are already present in the competent units of the national administration. The flipside of this situation is that the administration tends to absorb a great deal of the innovative potential. The strategies for translating this knowledge into economic dynamics therefore differ considerably.

The Hague presents itself as the most determined SCC in terms of actively linking industry, academia, and government agencies to promote innovation in specific subfields identified in a collaborative effort. This strategy proves to be effective and outplays less engaged approaches. Bern's strategy relies on the voluntary engagement (driven by self-interest) of businesses, which can be undermined by lack of resources and may constitute an entry barrier for new firms. An active involvement of official city authorities in the promotion of innovation and entrepreneurship has a number of advantages. The official commitment to these economic dynamics renders the endeavor more binding for all participants. This leads to planning security on both the private supplier and the public demand side, which is an important asset for long-term planning and investment. The common elaboration and definition of future fields of demand for R & D activities also strengthen the involvement of government units who have a long-term interest in solutions for their identified problems and future objectives. Finally, an important opportunity for start-ups and new firms is to profit from domain knowledge. This expertise may come from contracting with government agencies or from mobility of civil servants who transition into the private sector. Moderated network structures may contribute to this form of binding exchange between the private and the public sectors.

On the whole, we recommend that SCC authorities opt for innovation and entrepreneurship policies, especially in highly-regulated sectors where mutual learning on both the public- and the private-sector side has the greatest potential to stimulate economic dynamics.

> *Recommendation 4:*
>
> Establish and make use of intermediary organizations to bring together government contractors and federal agencies.

The connection between government contractors and public agencies is crucial for SCC-RIS. Consequently, in all four SCCs studied we observe semipublic organizations that act as intermediaries between market providers and federal agencies. Local public agencies can bridge the cultural divide between the private sector and the public sector, but do so to varying degrees. All SCCs have regional economic development agencies that promote the unique opportunities of the capital city. Only two of them, however, namely, Washington, D.C. and The Hague, actively leverage innovation. These organizations are strategic about how to use public procurement as a means to foster innovation. In The Hague, a single organization stimulates innovation by orchestrating private supply and public demand in the field of security. This strategy has a very concrete structure based on the identification of 16 focus areas for future innovation activities within which private firms can orient their R & D strategies. In Washington, D.C., this coordination is more dispersed, with several economic development organizations serving the same task. Given the diversity in specialization in the region's counties, the intermediaries also differ as to strategy and performance. There is less focus on innovation in Ottawa and Bern. The semipublic intermediaries there act more as promoting agencies than proactively taking advantage of the specific SCC opportunities. This is due mainly to the federal agencies' reluctance to take part in such activities since this could be perceived as preferential treatment of the SCC-RIS. However, as the two cases also illustrate, the organizations' own strategies are not fully geared toward sharpening the economic focus of the supply side to fit the government's needs. The promotion of the SCC with national government agencies as a unique advantage thus remains largely lip service.

However, the local public sector is not the only body that can initiate intermediary organizations. As our cases show, national sectoral associations are also important in this context. National associations are sector-specific and bring together the interests of individual firms that are naturally dispersed across the whole country. They therefore cannot be accused of favoring regional enterprises. With their sector-specific expertise, national associations are attractive information providers and discussion partners for procurement officers in their field. They can assemble the views of the represented firms and coordinate with the needs of the national government units without promoting one firm over the other. The combination of expertise and neutrality is an important advantage. National sectoral associations can also compensate for the deficiencies of semipublic place-bound intermediaries. Such a combination of intermediaries allows firms to deepen their domain knowledge and increase their competitive advantage. This is particularly important for new competitors and start-ups entering the SCC-RIS.

We therefore recommend that semipublic intermediaries that fail to incorporate the national government units collaborate more intensively with sector associations representative of a nationwide market, in order to provide platforms of knowledge-sharing through which SCC-RIS actors can gain access to public-procurement officers.

Recommendation 5:

Build your city image on the current assets of your SCC.

Image-building is an important part of attracting firms, taxpayers, and tourists. Unlike other locational policies, image-building is a straightforward marketing measure open to any city at relatively low cost and requiring no internal restructuring measures. Correspondingly, all SCCs take advantage of this tool not only to attract tourists, but also to attract capital and to place themselves on the federal agenda.

Bern deploys the image-building strategy with considerable success to make itself heard at the federal level and was able to shift the SCC region upward in the federal spatial planning concept to the same level as the metropolitan regions. Bern successfully used the argument that the capital city function equals economic importance. The Hague has coupled the capital city image with the image of the home of international organizations. It translates its brand of "International City of Peace and Justice" into concrete services for international organizations. Ottawa also promotes itself with the capital city function, but adds the G7 label to underscore its importance. All these strategies build upon the core assets of the SCCs.

The capital city narrative also proves to be conducive to RIS development, as has been shown in Washington, D.C. The clustering of government-related services and industries attracts more of the same. The security industry in D.C. best illustrates this implementation of the "Matthew effect" of accumulated advantage, which applies to several jurisdictions in the Washington, D.C. region, such as Arlington County, VA, or Alexandria, VA. Washington, D.C. itself, beside being the "capital city of the free world" with the World Bank, the International Monetary Fund, global companies, and over 170 embassies, also pushes its economic positioning strategy to become a top North American destination for foreign investors, businesses, and tourists. This strategy finds its concrete implementation in the recent focus on China through the establishment of the DC-China Center in Shanghai. The corresponding city image, on the national scale, is to become the technological hub on the East Coast.

Image-building is easy to combine with other strategies and rarely contradicts other elements of locational policy. On the contrary, as our cases illustrate, it can lead to synergies with present locational policies. We therefore recommend that SCC authorities develop image-building strategies that both generally focus on the capital city function while at the same time leveraging the structure of the present RIS as an asset in order to attract more of the same and promote the sectors that already cluster in the region. However, image-building cannot market any assets that SCCs wish to have. Instead, image-building strategies should refer to concrete local assets, such as the existing capital city functions or thriving economic sectors.

Recommendation 6:

Design your firm-attraction strategy in line with your RIS potential.

Firm attraction is an important part of locational policy in all four SCCs. This importance is mirrored in the specialized agencies established for this task and the professional manner in which firms from outside the region are attracted. However, the strategies employed and the implementation structure for those strategies vary. In all four cases, firm attraction is quite an opportunistic endeavor in that all four SCCs take whatever they can get. While this is not wrong, a more focused strategy is likely to be more fruitful. For example, Washington, D.C. and Ottawa target firms that fit existing clusters. While Washington, D.C. pursues a general demand-oriented strategy by approaching firms with an expiring lease to convince them to move to the SCC area, it also specifically targets so-called qualified high-technology companies by offering tax incentives. This latter strategy is an integrative element of Washington, D.C.'s cluster policy. In the same vein, Ottawa targets Chinese firms, presenting itself as a suitable landing spot in the North American market, and promotes its cluster as a favorable environment for R & D-intense activities. These companies are offered support in applying for government funding.

It is no coincidence that these focused firm-attraction strategies are defined and implemented by agencies run by the two North American SCCs themselves, whereas the less defined and broader strategies of the two European SCCs are part of national and larger regional development agencies. In the case of The Hague, this is the regional WestHolland Foreign Investment Agency (WFIA), which is part of the national Netherlands Foreign Investment Agency (NFIA). In the case of Bern, international contacts are established by Swiss Global Enterprise (SGE), a national organization, and the Greater Geneva Bern Area (GGBa), an initiative of the six cantons in western Switzerland, while the City of Bern itself does not have any international outreach. All these agencies serve an area much larger than the narrow SCC region. Consequently, their acquisition strategies are not tailored specifically to the two SCCs.

Attracting firms is welcomed either way. However, in the context of SCC-RIS, a focused attraction strategy is a sound idea. In addition to new taxpayers and employers, a strategy aligned with the RIS structure increases economic leverage in this system and contributes to innovation and entrepreneurship dynamics.

Given this advantage, we recommend that SCCs invest in development agencies of their own and pursue targeted attraction strategies in order to allow for synergies in the RIS. These agencies can base their strategies on the capital city function and the existing highly-regulated sectors stemming from this function. Such organizations demand coordinated action from all political entities of the RIS, which leads to the next recommendation.

Recommendation 7:

Coordinate your municipalities as far as possible.

Like any other metropolitan area, SCCs consist not only of their core cities but extend to the whole region. And, just like any other region, challenges are not limited to city boundaries but need common solutions. In SCCs, this situation is nuanced, first, in that SCCs are typically found in federalist systems, which grant more political autonomy to their lower-tier entities than centralized systems. In our cases, local autonomy, and in particular local tax autonomy, differs to a large extent, but still constitutes a challenge for coordinated solutions in all SCCs. Second, SCCs are often located close to subnational, politically-contested borders to attenuate these conflicts, such as at Ontario/Quebec in Canada or at the border between the Northern and Southern US states in the case of Washington, D.C. This tendency impairs regional coordination. Third, different interests of suburban residential areas and business-oriented core cities are normal; in the case of SCCs, the contrast is underscored by the capital city function, which focuses only on the city center, and not necessarily its suburban belt, even though it does so in Washington, D.C.

Coordination is impaired or supported by the political system context. First, second-tier entities such as member states, provinces, and cantons can emulate institutional consolidation and structuring occasions and incentives for local governments to coordinate their economic development policies. The comparison shows that second-tier borders are powerful institutional constraints for horizontal coordination. Second, tax competition and its underlying rationale of ensuring efficient and lean government entities via competition contradicts coordination. More specifically, our cases point to an interaction between two institutional factors: High tax autonomy is an obstacle to coordination of economic development policies but unfolds its full negative effect only in SCC regions fragmented at the second-tier level. The combination of both institutional factors creates an unlevel playing field for local tax competition in which local jurisdictions compete fiercely.

Coordination comes with a political price tag. Coordination means curtailing a political entity's decision-making autonomy and, thus, interferes with local government. Promoters of coordination may want to invest in a common-problem understanding before starting to set up coordination bodies. This common-problem understanding could rest on the threats and opportunities inherent in dependence on the nation state. This strategy may be fruitful when the jurisdictions throughout the entire region profit from the presence of the national government. In regions in which the capital city functions are concentrated mainly in the city center, the capital city function could be seen as a welcome complement to other economic functions of the region, as the example of The Hague suggests.

Our case studies illustrate the need for coordination. Image-building, firm and taxpayer attraction, RIS development, as well as innovation and entrepreneurship policies are all regional tasks. The fierce competition in Washington, D.C. is consistently evaluated as a zero sum game leading to beggar-thy-neighbor strategies, whereas the region-wide cooperation in The Hague has proved to be a great success. SCCs can overcome their constraints only by coordinating their policies and presenting and promoting themselves as consolidated capital city areas. However, SCCs have an ace up their sleeve that they may not even be aware of: If central government is reminded of the interest it has in a well-functioning capital, it may direct resources to coordinating bodies within SCCs. The capital city function is a good argument for treating capital cities well. We therefore consider it a core task of SCC authorities to seek political collaboration and develop a common strategy for the entire region in order to become serious competitors in international city competition.

Recommendation 8:

Ask for compensation payments and public funds regardless of your other locational policy choices.

Compensation is paid for either lost revenue or costs incurred as a result of the capital city status. The form of these compensation payments by the federal government differs among the four SCCs and is largely contingent on the local tax autonomy of the SCCs. Ottawa is the only one of the studied SCCs to receive payments in lieu of taxes (PILTs). The Canadian PILTs system is quite generous. It is limited to property tax loss, however, and does not include expenses due to the capital city function, which are compensated in addition to tax losses.

The three other SCCs are not compensated within a PILTs system. The Hague receives no compensation whatsoever, but the central government pays for capital city-related costs directly. In Bern and Washington, D.C., capital city expenses are directly compensated to varying degrees. These payments are easier to negotiate than general compensation based on estimations of positive and negative economic effects for the city ensuing from the capital city status. In Bern, a working group mandated to estimate these effects failed as the negotiation took the form of a political discussion rather than econometric model-based deliberation. Moreover, in Washington, D.C., compensation payments are subject to constant negotiations. Washington, D.C. has succeeded on a few occasions in negotiating capital city-specific payments by pointing to the manifold local autonomy constraints stemming from its special constitutional status as the Federal District. As the cases of Washington, D.C. and Ottawa showed, compensation payments could be successfully demanded when it is argued that they offset local autonomy constraints.

Asking for general public funds is an alternative strategy. We found two strategies that SCCs employ in the competitive process to receive these funds. First, in national tax regimes that restrict municipalities' tax capacities (such as in Canada and the Netherlands), asking-for-public-funds strategies do not leverage the capital city function. In such a tax regime, strategies involving asking for economic development public funds showcase local cluster organizations in highly-regulated sectors that foster interactions between KIBS firms, research institutions, and governmental organizations. Given the presence of the national administration, the full integration of the "triple helix" into a cluster organization, which certainly is an asset in asking for public funds, is facilitated in capital city regions. Second, in national tax regimes in which municipalities enjoy a high degree of tax autonomy, public funds are awarded as sporadic tools to steer lower-tier governments. In such a context, we found that SCCs put forward their importance as the political center of the nation when asking for public funds. Both Washington, D.C. and Bern leverage their capital city status to access public-transportation infrastructure funds by arguing that the capital city needs to be accessible to all its citizens.

Ultimately, however, asking for compensation payments for the capital city function is fully compatible with any other strategy. Lobbying for federal money makes sense in any case and does not constitute a zero sum game with other measures. Asking for compensation payments can therefore be considered a useful element of SCCs' locational policy if used to complement other strategies. It does not constitute a full locational strategy on its own, as history has shown. However, asking for federal compensation does not harm other efforts and, thus, is recommended as an additional political element in the multilevel setting of SCCs that ought not to be neglected.

Recommendations for decision-makers at the national level

The recommendations for actors at the national level relate to both public-procurement officers and public authorities. Procurement officers influence SCC-RIS with their procurement decisions, whereas national government agencies set the conditions for an SCC to prosper as a region.

Recommendation 9:

Take action against lock-in.

Firms and SCC-RIS profit from proximity to government agencies, as well as close networks among competitors circulating knowledge and exchanging information. Such inward-oriented density runs the risk of resulting in lock-in, which goes together with a loss of openness and flexibility. Such "sclerosis" is bad for firms and RIS to the same degree.

The problem for the firm is that individual contacts too close to government agencies tend to become risky. If a specific employee then leaves, not only the current contract knowledge, but also networks and information access accumulated by that worker are lost. This mainly affects SMEs. However, in large companies also, there can be a tendency to interact within specific divisions rather than within locations. In the case of public procurement, this means that even global firms cannot fully compensate lock-in with knowledge circulation among different public- and private-sector divisions at one location. Thus, lock-in is also a problem for innovation capacity in the firm; this, in turn, impacts upon the RIS. Fundamentally, lock-in impairs RIS openness. As we find, barriers to new firms from outside the regions are numerous and high. The better attuned to the procurement process the established competitors are, the higher the threshold for new firms to attain the procedural and regulatory know-how necessary for successful bidding. The closer the existing contacts and the denser the network among competitors, the harder it is for new firms to acquire the social capital necessary to enter the marketplace. Lock-in can lead to RIS failure by diminishing the innovation part of the system. This is damaging to the SCC's economy.

Nevertheless, as the case studies show, no action is taken against this risk of RIS failure. While this seems counterintuitive, it is attributable to a mismatch of policy competences and problem affectedness. The SCC as a whole is affected by the problem; the SCC authorities have a core interest in a functioning RIS and the resulting economic well-being of the region. Public-sector dependency is a key threat to an SCC-RIS, as the case of Washington, D.C. demonstrates. However, competition policy is not in the competence of the regional and local levels. SCC authorities have limited possibilities to actively interfere in the behavior of competitors within the RIS since market regulation is not within their remit.

Firms then can individually counteract lock-in by cooperating with new competitors and thereby making RIS borders more hybrid. However, the individual firm has to weigh utility against risk and, from a short-term perspective, there is not much that speaks in favor of the invitation of new competitors. In fact, firms would need to actively build up competition to the benefit of the RIS as a whole. A firm's interest in such endeavor is likely to be too indirect for a company to risk taking such a step. It would require common effort by the RIS as a whole. In the event of lock-in, this cannot be expected because the firms profit in this situation from their existing partnerships. Following a functionalist approach, the costs of lock-in may simply not be great enough for firms to take action to prevent it.

Finally, the actors with the highest leverage are the ones at the national level: First, the contracting agency can prevent lock-in by drafting rules of the game and by actively selecting new suppliers, despite the fact the existing supplier's service may be equally good. Such strategy is not free of risk, as a new player may, in fact, lack the full knowledge to sufficiently perform. Contracting agencies, however, can incentivize partnership tenders with new companies from outside the RIS. They can also demand system openness in IT and infrastructure projects in order to prevent path dependency and secure compatibility with other systems. National authorities are then responsible for market regulation. If the competition is impaired by RIS lock-in, the regulation of public procurement must be adjusted accordingly. The national level has no immediate interest in the SCC-RIS in particular, but must be concerned with the national economy as a whole. This general orientation, however, does not contradict RIS failure prevention if the solution is seen in market openness as opposed to lock-in. The damage of lock-in for public procurement is more evident for national government authorities than for individual firms. First, service quality may suffer due to a restricted circle of tenderers; second, the less transparent public-procurement procedures, the more likely the specter of corruption is to make an appearance.

In summary, action against lock-in must be taken by national government authorities since they not only have a more obvious interest in a functioning RIS than the individual firm does, but, unlike the local- and regional-level SCC authorities, they also have the political competence to regulate the market in order to secure competition.

Recommendation 10:

Honor your SCC – commit to your SCC-RIS.

SCC-RIS depend on their governments. As we have seen, the administrations' choices to engage with SCC-RIS crucially determine the development and success of the latter. SCCs are in a special situation, which they tackle in diverse ways and with varying degrees of success. They are bound to serve their capital city function and are compensated for this. Some SCCs take advantage of their situation and successfully translate it into an economic asset. Others succeed to a limited degree only, not least due to institutional constraints both at the city level, in the form of limited discretion, and at the national level, in the form of reluctance to afford the local economy any preferential treatment. As we have also shown in our study, national governments profit from a well-functioning RIS because this allows for the fruitful discussion of its needs and participation in developing tailored solutions on a long-term basis.

As secondary cities, SCCs are not the economic centers of their countries. However, SCCs face constraints due to their capital city function. They represent the nation, they provide political infrastructure, and they host the administration, which absorbs much of the local brainpower. This, in turn, limits the innovation potential of SCC-RIS. Compensation for this situation may go beyond financial indemnification, and governments may acknowledge the capital city function, as well as the benefit they gain from functioning SCC-RIS, by committing themselves to these RIS, as showcased by the Netherlands. Governments that actively participate in exchange with the multitude of actors involved in the RIS are rewarded with a prospering capital city. All SCCs deserve a win-win arrangement like this to enable them to prosper.

By following these recommendations, policy- and decision-makers in SCCs like Bern, Ottawa, The Hague, and Washington, D.C. may be better able to contribute to the economic dynamics and prosperity of their capital cities.

References

Asheim, B., Smith, H. L., & Oughton, C. (2011). Regional innovation systems: Theory, empirics and policy. *Regional Studies*, *45*(7), 875–891.

Bathelt, H., Malmberg, A., & Maskell, P. (2004). Clusters and knowledge: Local buzz, global pipelines and the process of knowledge creation. *Progress in Human Geography*, *28*(1), 31–56. https://doi.org/10.1191/0309132504ph469oa

Bourdieu, P. (1986). The Forms of Capital. In J. Richardson (Ed.), *Handbook of Theory and Research for the Sociology of Education* (pp. 241–258). New York: Greenwood.

Braczyk, H.-J., Cooke, P., & Heidenreich, M. (1998). *Regional Innovation Systems: The Role of Governances in a Globalized World*. London: UCL Press.

Cooke, P. (2001). Regional innovation systems, clusters, and the knowledge economy. *Industrial and Corporate Change*, *10*(4), 945–974.

Doloreux, D., & Parto, S. (2005). Regional innovation systems: Current discourse and unresolved issues. *Technology in Society*, *27*(2), 133–153.

Gordon, D. (2006). *Planning Twentieth Century Capital Cities*. London and New York: Routledge.

Gottmann, J. (1977). The role of capital cities. *Ekistics: The Problem and Science of Human Settlements*, *44(264)*, 240–243.

Hall, P. A., & Soskice, D. W. D. (2001). *Varieties of Capitalism: The Institutional Foundations of Comparative Advantage*. Oxford: Oxford University Press.

Hall, T. (2010). *Planning Europe's Capital Cities: Aspects of Nineteenth Century Urban Development*. New York: Routledge.

Martin, R., & Trippl, M. (2014). System failures, knowledge bases and regional innovation policies. *disP – The Planning Review*, *50*(1), 24–32.

Rowat, D. (1968a). *The Government of Federal Capitals*. Toronto: University of Toronto Press.

Rowat, D. (1968b). The problems of governing federal capitals. *Canadian Journal of Political Science*, *1*(3), 345–356.

Slack, E., & Chattopadhyay, R. (2009). *Finance and Governance of Capital Cities in Federal Systems*. Montreal, Quebec and Kingston, Ontario: McGill-Queen's University Press.

Tödtling, F., & Trippl, M. (2005). One size fits all?: Towards a differentiated regional innovation policy approach. *Research Policy*, *34*(8), 1203–1219.

Wolman, H., Chadwick, J., & Karruz, A. (2006). *Capital Cities and Their National Governments: Washington, D.C. in Comparative Perspective*. Washington, D.C.: George Washington University, Institute of Public Policy.

Appendix

This study of secondary capital cities used a variety of sources, and we have triangulated primary and secondary data in four different national contexts. The following provides details on the data and definitions used.

Defining capital city regions

In Chapter 3, we present profiles of the four secondary capital cities using data from a variety of sources. We present these data both for the central jurisdiction and for the jurisdictions that make up the functional region (usually referred to as the metropolitan area or metropolitan region).

The metropolitan area of Bern refers to MS region 11, as defined by the Swiss Federal Statistical Office. MS region 11 comprises the following 29 munici-palities: Allmendingen, Bäriswil, Belp, Bern, Bolligen, Bremgarten bei Bern, Deisswil bei Münchenbuchsee, Diemerswil, Frauenkappelen, Iffwil, Ittigen, Jegenstorf, Kehrsatz, Kirchlindach, Köniz, Mattstetten, Meikirch, Moosseedorf, Münchenbuchsee, Muri bei Bern, Ostermundigen, Stettlen, Urtenen-Schönbühl, Vechigen, Wiggiswil, Wohlen bei Bern, Worb, Zollikofen, and Zuzwil.

The metropolitan area of Ottawa-Gatineau refers to the census metropolitan area Ottawa-Gatineau, as defined by Statistics Canada. The census metro-politan area Ottawa-Gatineau includes the following 15 cities, townships, and municipalities: Bowman, Cantley, Chelsea, Clarence-Rockland, Denholm, Gatineau, La Pêche, L'Ange-Gardien, Mayo, Notre-Dame-de-la-Salette, Ottawa, Pontiac, Russell, Val-des-Bois, and Val-des-Monts.

The metropolitan area of The Hague (Agglomeratie 's-Gravenhage) refers to the COROP region (=NUTS NL332) as defined by Statistics Netherlands (CBS). The metropolitan area includes the following six municipalities: The Hague ('s-Gravenhage), Leidschendam-Voorburg, Pijnacker-Nootdorp, Rijswijk, Wassenaar, and Zoetermeer.

The metropolitan area of Washington, D.C. refers to the Washington-Arlington-Alexandria, DC-VA-MD-WV metropolitan statistical area (FIPS MSA Code 8840), which is delimited by the United States Office of Management and Budget (OMB). The metropolitan area includes the following 23 counties and cities, plus the District of Columbia: Alexandria, Arlington, Calvert, Charles,

Clarke, Culpeper, District of Columbia, Fairfax (City), Fairfax (County), Falls Church, Fauquier, Frederick, Fredericksburg, Jefferson, Loudoun, Manassas, Manassas Park, Montgomery, Prince George's, Prince William, Rappahannock, Spotsylvania, Stafford, and Warren.

Employees in knowledge-intensive sectors

In Chapter 3, we compare the structure of the knowledge economies in the four case studies with the structure of the knowledge economies of the largest, second-largest, and third-largest cities in their respective countries. In particular, we distinguish between knowledge-intensive business services (KIBS) and high- and medium-tech manufacturing. This comparison draws on several different classification systems (see below).

Canada and USA

In Canada and the USA, economic activities are classified based on the North American Industry Classification System (NAICS). We identify the KIBS sector and the high- and medium-tech sector in line with previous KIBS studies that draw on NAICS, e.g. Doloreux and Mattson (2008).

The KIBS sector is defined as legal services (NAICS 5411), accounting, tax consultancy, bookkeeping, and payroll services (NAICS 5412), architectural, engineering, and related services (NAICS 5413), specialized design services (NAICS 5414), computer systems design and related services (NAICS 5415), management, scientific, and technical consulting services (NAICS 5416), scientific research and development services (NAICS 5417), advertising, public relations, and related services (NAICS 5418), and other professional, scientific, and technical services (NAICS 5419).

The high- and medium-tech sector is defined as chemical manufacturing (NAICS 325), machinery manufacturing (NAICS 333), computer and electronic products (NAICS 334), electronic equipment and components (NAICS 335), and transportation equipment (NAICS 336).

Switzerland

In Switzerland, economic activities are classified by the Nomenclature générale des activités économiques (NOGA). NOGA is based on Nomenclature statistique des activités économiques dans la Communauté européenne (NACE). Therefore, we utilize the identification as suggested by Schnabl and Zenker (2013).

Pursuant to this, the KIBS sector is defined as the provision of computer programming, consultancy services, and related activities (NOGA 62), information service activities (NOGA 63), legal and accounting activities (NOGA 69), activities of head offices and management consultancy activities (NOGA 70), architectural and engineering activities, technical testing, and analysis (NOGA 71), scientific research and development (NOGA 72), and advertising and market research (NOGA 73).

The high- and medium-tech sector is defined as manufacture of the following: Coke and refined petroleum products (NOGA 19), chemicals and chemical products (NOGA 20), basic pharmaceutical products and pharmaceutical preparations (NOGA 21), rubber and plastic products (NOGA 22), computer, electronic, and optical products (NOGA 26), electrical equipment (NOGA 27), machinery and equipment not elsewhere classified (n.e.c.) (NOGA 28), motor vehicles and vehicle components (NOGA 29), and other transport equipment (NOGA 30).

The Netherlands

In the Netherlands, economic activities are classified by the Dutch Standaard Bedrijfsindeling (SBI 2008). SBI is based on NACE. As in the case of Switzerland, we therefore utilize the identification as suggested by Schnabl and Zenker (2013).

The KIBS sector is defined as information technology activities (SBI J62), other information service activities (SBI J63), legal services, accounting, tax consultancy, administration (SBI M69), holding companies/management and business consultancy (SBI M70), architects, engineers, and technical design and consultancy; testing and analysis (SBI M71), research and development (SBI M72), advertising and market research (SBI M73).

The high- and medium-tech sector is defined as the manufacture of the following: Chemicals and chemical products (SBI C20), basic pharmaceutical products and pharmaceutical preparations (SBI C21), computers, electronic, and optical products (SBI C26), electrical equipment (SBI C27), machinery and equipment n.e.c. (SBI C28), motor vehicles, trailers, and semitrailers (SBI C29), and other transport equipment (SBI C30).

Identification of IT KIBS utilizing public procurement data

To identify KIBS firms that are active in public procurement with national government agencies, we utilized national-level databases. While the differing data collection obligations and practices of the four governments mean that the databases are somewhat problematic when used for direct comparison, they are ideal for identifying KIBS firms for interviews. We then describe the data in more detail for each country. Differences in our data collection strategies between the four countries (for example, regarding the period of investigation) can be explained by the fact that this book builds on several studies that, in parts, have been published as single-case studies.

Switzerland

In Switzerland, we gathered data about national procurement contracts between 01.01.2010 and 31.12.2013 from the Système d'information sur les marchés publics en Suisse (SIMAP), Switzerland's official national procurement database system. If an IT service contract reaches the threshold of CHF 230,000, the federal administration reports the contract through SIMAP. The data include information on the name and location of the requesting agency, the name and location of the supplying company, and the date and volume of the procurement contract. Moreover, the content of every contract is described with a title and a code from the so-called common procurement vocabulary (CPV) classification[1]. Of the initial 7,028 procurement records, a total of 2,792 records were excluded because of duplicated entries in a second or third language (due to the fact that Switzerland has four official languages).

To distinguish between knowledge-intensive and regular services and products, we created a table of correspondence between the NACE and the CPV classifications. While empirical studies of KIBS usually draw on the NACE classification (Muller & Doloreux, 2009; Schnabl & Zenker, 2013), Swiss procurement data employ the CPV classification. Since the latter was originally developed from the NACE classification (European Commission, 2008), we applied NACE Revision 1.1 instead of the more recent NACE Revision 2 classification. Thus, IT KIBS are defined as the CPV codes 503, 721, 722, 723, 724, 725, 726, 727, 728, and 729.

Canada

In Canada, the identification of KIBS firms is based upon federal procurement data from Canada's authoritative federal procurement organization, Public Works and Government Services Canada (PWGSC), which purchases on behalf of federal agencies. The database includes 268,478 federal procurement records, accounting for a total of CAD 87.38 billion awarded between 2009 and 2014. The records provide information about the contract number, contract subject in the form of Goods and Services Identification Number (GSIN), contract value, supplier name, supplier location, number of employees, procurement entity, and end-user entity. Drawing on the GSIN classification, IT-KIBS are defined as follows: Automated data processing system development services (GSIN D302), automated information system design and integration services (GSIN D307), and programming services (GSIN D308), as such activities were identified as KIBS in prior studies (Huggins, 2011; Simmie & Strambach, 2006).

United States

In the US, we gathered data about public-procurement contracts between 01.01.2010 and 31.12.2013 from www.fpds.gov. In contrast to other national procurement database systems, the US system allows the user to apply filters. We downloaded 451,817 contract records that exclusively represent IT KIBS. Based on the assumption that contract volume correlates with the complexity of IT government systems, contractors with the highest contract volume were contacted first.

The Netherlands

In the Netherlands, we gathered data about national public-procurement contracts between 01.01.2010 and 31.12.2013. Based on the assumption that contract volume positively corresponds to the complexity of IT government systems, contractors with the highest contract volume were contacted first for interviews.

Both the data and the methods suffer from a number of limitations that need to be addressed. First, our analysis draws solely on prime contracts with KIBS firms. There are no data on the extension and geography of subcontracting activities. The interviews and survey have addressed this issue by asking about the extent to which services are provided by in-house staff, through partner firms or independent consultants. Second, this study provides only limited comparability to other KIBS studies. This is because KIBS firms were identified based on the service they provided, as opposed to the main activity as reported in industrial classifications. However, identification based on the supplied service leads to a more accurate group of KIBS firms, whereas identification based on industrial classifications can be incorrect due to false registrations or strategic redirections (Thomi & Böhn, 2003).

Interviews

A total of 179 semistructured, face-to-face expert interviews provide the main data source for this study (see also Chapter 1). The interview partners were carefully selected to ensure sufficient variety within the cases and the necessary consistency between the cases. We started the interview process in each locality with a first set of explorative interviews conducted with academics and experts. Semistructured, face-to-face interviews are well suited to studying an actor "embedded in a complex network of internal and external relationships" (Schoenberger, 1991). Rathbun (2008) adds that interviewing is best suited to tackling political processes that, for the most part, are not written down on paper. The main purpose of the interviews with KIBS firms was to uncover how they organize knowledge-generation processes with their public-sector clients. The main objective of the interviews with other RIS actors was to establish how federal procurement policies, rules, and regulations shape regional knowledge dynamics. The political actors were interviewed to find out the rationale behind the formulation of locational policies. Interviews by and large lasted between 40 and 90 minutes and were typically conducted in meeting rooms, with a few carried out in coffee shops due to limited facility access on account of security requirements.

Note

1 KIBS definition based on CPV: IT services (503, 721–729), R & D (731–734), economic services (791, 792, 794), marketing and advertising (793), and technical services (712–717).

References

Doloreux, D., & Mattson, H. (2008). To what extent do sectors "socialize" innovation differently? Mapping cooperative linkages in knowledge-intensive industries in the Ottawa region. *Industry & Innovation, 15*(4), 351–370.

European Commission. (2008). Public Procurement in the European Union – Guide to the Common Procurement Vocabulary (CPV).

Huggins, R. (2011). The growth of knowledge-intensive business services: Innovation, markets and networks. *European Planning Studies, 19*(8), 1459–80.

Muller, E., & Doloreux, D. (2009). What we should know about knowledge-intensive business services. *Technology in Society, 31*(1), 64–72. https://doi.org/10.1016/j.techsoc.2008.10.001

Rathbun, B. C. (2008). Interviewing and Qualitative Field Methods: Pragmatism and Practicalities. In J. M. Box-Steffensmeier, H. E. Brady, & D. Collier (Eds.), *The Oxford Handbook of Political Methodology*. Oxford: Oxford University Press.

Schnabl, E., & Zenker, A. (2013). *Statistical Classification of Knowledge-Intensive Business Services (KIBS) with NACE Rev. 2*. Karlsruhe: Fraunhofer ISI.

Schoenberger, E. (1991). The corporate interview as a research method in economic geography. *Professional Geographer, 43*(2), 180–189.

Simmie, J., & Strambach, S. (2006). The contribution of KIBS to innovation in cities: An evolutionary and institutional perspective. *Journal of Knowledge Management, 10*(5), 26–40.

Thomi, W., & Böhn, T. (2003). Knowledge intensive business services in regional systems of innovation – the case of southeast-Finland. Paper presented at the 43rd European Congress of the Regional Science Association.

Index

1776 incubator 109, 110, 122

accelerators 27–8, 122–3
Acquisition Reform Working Group
    (ARWG) 94
actor-centered perspective 2, 5
actors 16–18
additional expenses/services 32
Aerospace Industries Association of
    Canada 95
American Council for Technology and
    Industry Advisory Council (ACT-IAC)
    94–5
Amsterdam 11
analytical framework 10, 14–42; regional
    innovation systems 14–24; linking RIS
    with locational policies 33–6; locational
    policies 23–33
Andrew, C. 24
Arlington County 77, 78, 92
Arlington Economic Development 92
asking for money 26, 31–6, 131–3, 156;
    compensation payments 26, 32–3,
    132–3, 139, 143–5, 165–6; institutional
    explanatory factors 133, 139, 142–5;
    public funds 26, 31–3, 131–2, 133, 139,
    142–3, 166; recommendations 165–6
attracting money 26, 28–30, 33–6,
    124–8, 156; attracting firms 26, 28,
    29–30, 125–8, 137–9, 163–4; image-
    building 26, 28–9, 124–5, 136–7,
    162–3; recommendations 162–4; RIS as
    explanatory factor 133, 136–9
autonomy, local 46–9

Basic Research Innovation and
    Collaboration Center (BRICC) 102–3
Bern 8–10, 154–5, 156, 170; asking for
    money 131, 132, 133, 142, 142–3,

144, 149; attracting money 124, 127,
137, 138, 149; coordination 128–9,
140, 141, 145, 149; economy 57–60;
entrepreneurship 108; fragmentation
100–2; innovation policies 120, 121,
123, 135, 149; intermediaries 93, 96;
knowledge-based economy 61, 62,
63–5; knowledge infrastructure 70; local
autonomy 48; lock-in 87; overview
of knowledge dynamics 111, 113–14;
overview of locational policies 148, 149;
partnering 86; profile 49–51, 56; public-
procurement policies 99–100; purposely-
selected capital 43–5, 145; spatial
expressions of public procurement 79
bidding costs 84–5
Bourdieu, P. 158
Build in Canada Innovation Program
    (BCIP) 99
Burfield, E. 109
business cities 124
business-process innovations 110

Campbell, S. 3, 4
Canada: KIBS sector 62–8, 171, 173;
    Ottawa see Ottawa
Canadian Association of Defence and
    Security Industries 95
Caniëls, M.C.J. 18
capital city conflict (Rowat thesis) 4
capital city function 7
capital city-specific constraints 133, 139,
    143–5
Capital Region Switzerland (CRS) 93, 124,
    129, 137, 140, 143
Carleton University 102
case studies 10, 43–75; defining capital
    city regions 170–1; economies 57–60;
    knowledge-based capital city economy

60–71; local autonomy 46–9; profiles
49–57; selection as capital cities 43–6;
see also under individual cities
Centre for Innovation, Leiden University
111, 123
China 125
city-level policymakers, recommendations
for 159–66
cluster policies 26, 27, 118–21
clusters, highly-regulated 60–2
common-problem understanding 164–5
comparative advantage 25
compensation payments 26, 32–3, 132–3;
institutional explanatory factors 133,
139, 143–5; recommendations 165–6
competition 19; and cooperation in public
procurement 85; instead of coordination
in Washington, D.C. 129–31, 141, 149;
worst-case scenario for coordination 31
competitive dialogue procedure 99–100
competitiveness 24–5, 158–9
Conference for IT Procurement 96
Congressional oversight 46
Connectivity Accelerator 123
contract proposal teams 82–3
cooperation 19, 84–6, 102–4, 158–9
coordination 26, 30–1, 33–6, 128–31, 156;
institutional explanatory factors 133,
139–42; recommendations for 164–5;
regional and urban policies 133, 145–8
councils of governments 26, 30
'CSI The Hague' project 105–7
CSI Laboratory 106
cybersecurity 118–20, 121

defining capital cities 2–6
developers 147
DiploHack 111
Doloreux, D. 14, 15, 24

economic development organizations 16,
17–18
economic geography perspective 4, 6, 155;
see also knowledge dynamics, regional
innovation systems (RIS)
eduCanon 110
education levels of the workforce 70
entrepreneurship 107–11; policies to
stimulate entrepreneurial ecosystems 26,
27–8, 122–3, 160
entry barriers 88, 90
European Regional Development Fund 32
European Union (EU) funds 32, 131
ex-imperial capitals 2

Federal Institute of Technology (ETH) 70
Feiock, R.C. 30
firm-attraction policies 26, 28, 29–30,
125–8, 137–9, 163–4
*Five-Year Economic Development Strategy
for the District of Columbia* 135
foreign direct investment (FDI) 125–8
former capitals 2
formerly state-owned firms 100–1
fragmentation 22–3, 24, 100–2;
overcoming 104–7; regional institutional
fragmentation 133, 139–42

Gatineau 129, 130, 140–1
General Service Administration (GSA) 94
global capitals 2
global cities 5
global intra-firm linkages 88–90
Gordon, D. 1
Gordon, I. 6
Gottmann, J. 2
government agencies 15, 16–17, 18–19, 48;
action against lock-in 167–8; benefits of
spatial proximity to 80–4; differences in
approaches to procurement 98; reports 82
government cities 124–5
government contractors 15, 16–17; benefits
of spatial proximity to government
agencies 80–4; cooperation between
84–6; recommendations for 157–9;
specialised proposal teams 82–3
government IT systems 21
government officials 20
Government Technology and Services
Coalition (GTSC) 95
'government town' narrative 107–8
Greater Washington Initiative (GWI) 129
Gréber Plan 144
growth machine theory 146–7

Hague, The *see* The Hague
Hague Security Delta (HSD) 80, 91–2, 93,
119, 131; emergence of 104–7; HSD
Campus 107
Hall, P.G. 2–3
Harper, R. 2
high- and medium-tech manufacturing
62–3, 171–2
highly-developed CC-RIS 23, 24, 34, 35–6
highly-regulated clusters 60–2
highly-regulated sectors 160
Home Rule Act 1973 47
HSD Campus 107
HumanityX 111

ICT cluster 62
image-building 26, 28–9, 124–5, 136–7; recommendations for 162–3
Impact Tracker 111
incubators 26, 27, 109, 122–3
industry associations 16, 17, 93–7, 161–2
informal contacts 26, 30–1, 81, 157–8
information asymmetries 17
information cities 4, 121
information and communication technology councils 16
information gathering 81–2
Innovation Center at Bayview Yards 122–3, 131, 135
innovation parks 121
innovation policies 26–8, 33–6, 118–23, 156, 160; cluster policies 26, 27, 118–21; RIS as explanatory factor 133, 134–6; stimulation of entrepreneurial ecosystems 26, 27–8, 122–3, 160
Institute for Innovation 95
institutional explanatory factors 133, 139–45
interdisciplinary perspective 3–4
intermediaries 16, 17, 90–7, 161–2; national sectoral associations as 16, 17, 93–7, 161–2; semipublic organizations as 91–3, 161–2
international cities 125
Interstate 495 beltway 76–7
intra-firm linkages 88–90
Invest Ottawa 92–3, 120, 121, 126–7, 135, 142
investment, attraction of 125–8
IT KIBS subsector 63–6, 67, 172–4

K Street, Washington, D.C. 77, 78
Kanata, Ottawa 78–9
knowledge application and exploitation subsystem 14–15, 16
knowledge-based economy 60–71; highly-regulated clusters 60–2; increased tertiarization 62–6; KIBS firms in public procurement 66–8; knowledge infrastructure 68–71
knowledge dynamics 10–11, 76–117; bridging the public sector–private sector gap 90–100, 113–14; driven by public procurement 18–20, 76–90, 113; holistic perspective on RIS 100–11, 114; overview of case study cities 111–15
knowledge generation: intrafirm linkages and 89; spatial proximity and 20–2
knowledge generation and diffusion subsystem 15–16
knowledge hubs 121

knowledge infrastructure 68–71
knowledge-intensive business services (KIBS) 5–6, 15, 62–8, 171–4; composition 63–6; employment in 62–3, 171–2; firms in public procurement 66–8; IT KIBS subsector 63–6, 67, 172–4
knowledge-intensive sectors 160
Köniz 128–9

large system integrators 95–6
Leigh Instruments 68–9
Leitner, H. 141–2
life sciences, medical and health technology 120
linkages 16–18; intra-firm 88–90; presence or absence of 100–4
local autonomy 46–9
local buzz 21, 86, 158–9
locational policies 1, 9, 10, 11, 118–53, 154, 155–6; analytical framework 23–33; asking for money *see* asking for money; attracting money *see* attracting money; coordination *see* coordination; explaining 133–48; formulating 146–7; innovation policies *see* innovation policies; institutional explanatory factors 133, 139–45; linking with the concept of RIS 33–6; regional and urban politics 133, 145–8; RIS development as explanatory factor 133, 134–9
locational substitutability 29
lock-in 22–3, 24; danger of 86–90; need to take action against 166–8
Lucerne 44

Madison, J. 45–6
market opportunities 18–19
Markusen, A. 15
Mason Enterprise Center (MEC) 103
Maurice, Prince 44
mediating organizations *see* intermediaries
metropolitan government 26, 30
Metropolitan Region Rotterdam The Hague (MRTH) 128, 139–40, 145–6
Metropolitan Washington Council of Governments (MWCOG) 129–30
moderately-developed CC-RIS 23, 24, 34, 35
Muller, E. 15
multifunctional capitals 2

nation states 7
National Capital Commission (NCC) 47, 144

national government agencies *see* government agencies
national information brokers 4, 121
National Innovation Agenda for Security 2015 91–2
national policymakers, recommendations for 166–9
National Research Council (NRC) 68–9
national sectoral associations 16, 17, 93–7, 161–2
national tax regime 133, 139–43
NATO 138
negative coordination 31
Netherlands, the: KIBS sector 62–8, 171–2, 173–4; The Hague *see* The Hague
Netherlands Forensic Institute (NFI) 105–6
Nortel 69
Northern Electric 69
Northern Virginia Technology Council (NVTC) Entrepreneur Center 108–9

Office of Small and Medium Enterprises (OSME) 99
oil industry 61
Opower 110
Organisation for Economic Co-operation and Development (OECD) 8–9
organizational thinness 22–3, 24
Ottawa 8–10, 48, 130, 154–5, 156, 170; asking for money 131, 132, 142, 144, 149; attracting money 124–5, 126–7, 136, 138, 149; coordination 129, 140–1, 146, 149; economy 57–60; fragmentation 102; importance of developers 147; innovation policies 119, 122–3, 135, 149; intermediaries 92–3, 95–6; knowledge-based economy 60–1, 62, 63–5; knowledge generation subsystem 15; knowledge infrastructure 68–9, 70; local autonomy 47; lock-in 87; overview of knowledge dynamics 112, 113–14; overview of locational policies 148, 149; partnering 86; profile 51–3, 56; public-procurement policies and programs 99; purpose-built capital 43, 45, 145; spatial expressions of public-procurement activities 78–9

partnering 84–6, 158–9
Parto, S. 14
payments in lieu of taxes (PILTs) 32, 132, 144
PIANOo 98
'Pieken in de Delta' program 105

place marketing 26, 28–9; *see also* image-building
policy domain 26
policy orientation 26
policymakers, recommendations for 159–69; city level 159–66; national level 166–9
political capitals 2
political cities 5
political science perspective 4, 6, 155–6; *see also* locational policies
population dynamics 49–50, 51, 53, 56–7
positioning strategies 7–8
positive coordination 31
pre-bid conferences 86
precommercial procurement 20
private sector–public sector gap, bridging 90–100, 113–14
private supply 7, 20, 91
procurement knowledge 21–2
Professional Service Council (PSC) 94
project references 85
project teams 85–6
provincial capitals 2–3
public demand 7, 20, 90–1
public funds 26, 31–3, 131–2; institutional explanatory factors 133, 139, 142–3; recommendations 166
public procurement 1, 7; activities in the case study cities 59–60; benefits of spatial proximity between contractors and government agencies 80–4; cooperation between government contractors 84–6; danger of lock-in 86–90; as a driver of knowledge dynamics 18–20, 76–90, 113; KIBS firms in 66–8; policies and programs 97–100; RIS driven by 16–22; spatial expressions of public-procurement activities 76–80; stages of the process 20, 80–1; and start-up dynamics 108
public procurement for innovation (PPI) 18–20
public sector: bridging the gap between the private sector and 90–100, 113–14; employment in 57–8
public venture capital 26, 28, 122–3
purpose-built capitals 43, 45–6, 145; *see also* Ottawa, Washington, D.C.
purposely-selected capitals 43–5, 145; *see also* Bern, The Hague

Randstad, the 53
recommendations 11, 154–69; for firms 157–9; for policymakers at the city level

159–66; for policymakers at the national level 166–9

Regional Conference Bern-Mittelland 128

regional innovation systems (RIS) 1, 5, 7, 9, 10, 154, 155, 156; actors and linkages 16–18; analytical framework 14–24; development of a capital city RIS (CC-RIS) 22–4; firm-attraction strategies should be aligned with RIS potential 163–4; holistic perspective 100–11; linking the concept with locational policies 33–6; need for national governments to commit to 168–9; overcoming fragmentation 104–7; overview of the case study cities' RIS 111–15; presence/absence of linkages 100–4; public procurement as a driver of 16–22; RIS development and explaining locational policies 133, 134–9; spatial proximity and knowledge generation 20–2; start-up dynamics and entrepreneurship 107–11

regional institutional fragmentation 133, 139–42

regional policy 7

regional politics 133, 145–8

relationship building 81–4

request for proposals 80–1

research organizations 15, 16, 18, 101–3

research universities 28

revolving door 104

risk 19

risk aversion 108

Rowat, D. 4, 49, 145

Royal Dutch Shell 61

Scharpf, F. 31

sectoral associations 16, 17, 93–7, 161–2

security clearance requirements 88

security sector 62, 104–7; cybersecurity 118–20, 121

selection of capital cities 43–6

selection criteria 108

semipublic organizations 91–3, 161–2

Sheppard, E. 141–2

Small Business Innovation Research (SBIR) programs 97–8, 98–9

small and medium-sized enterprises (SMEs) 20, 84, 95

Smart Cities and Communities European Innovation Partnership 32

smart procurement 99

social capital 158–9

spatial expressions of public-procurement activities 76–80

spatial proximity 157–8; benefits of 80–4; and knowledge generation 20–2

spin-off activities 108–9

St. Elizabeths former psychiatric hospital 119, 120

stakeholders 82–3

start-up dynamics 107–11

state-owned firms, former 100–1

stimulation of entrepreneurial ecosystems 26, 27–8, 122–3, 160

super capitals 3

Swiss Federal Railways (SBB) 100, 101

Swiss Post 100–1

Swisscom 100–1

swissICT 96

Switzerland: Bern *see* Bern; KIBS sector 62–8, 171–3

Tandem National Security Innovations (TandemNSI) program 92, 119

tax: constraints on local autonomy 47, 48; national tax regime as explanatory factor for locational policies 133, 139–43; PILTs 32, 132, 144

teamwork 17, 82–3, 85–6

technical knowledge 21–2

technical requirements/specifications 80–1

tertiarization 62–6

The Hague 8–10, 154–5, 156, 170; asking for money 131, 133, 144, 149; attracting money 124, 127–8, 137, 138, 149; coordination 128, 139–40, 141, 145–6, 149; economy 57–60; entrepreneurship 110–11; innovation policies 119, 120–1, 123, 134, 149; intermediaries 91–2, 93, 96; knowledge-based economy 61, 62, 63–5; knowledge infrastructure 69–70; local autonomy 48; lock-in 87; overcoming fragmentation 104–7; overview of knowledge dynamics 112, 113–14; overview of locational policies 148–50; partnering 86; profile 51, 53, 54, 56; public-procurement policies and programs 98–9; purposely-selected capital 43–4, 145; spatial expressions of public-procurement activities 79–80

TNO (The Netherlands Organization of Applied Scientific Research) 69–70

Tödtling, F. 22–3

tourism 58–9

traditional capital city research 4–5, 43–9
transactional cities 4
triple helix 27, 118
Trippl, M. 22–3
two-dimensional positioning strategy 7–8

unemployment rates 60
United States (US): Constitution
    45–6; KIBS sector 62–8, 171, 173;
    Washington, D.C. *see* Washington, D.C.
United Nations 61
universities 28; *see also* research
    organizations
urban politics 133, 145–8
urban regime theory 146–7

Van den Bosch, H. 18
venture capital 26, 28, 122–3
Victoria, Queen 45

Washington, G. 46
Washington, D.C. 8–10, 154–5, 156,
    170–1; asking for money 131–2,
    142–3, 144, 149; attracting money
    125–6, 136–7, 137–8, 149; competition
instead of coordination 129–31, 141,
    149; economy 57–60; entrepreneurship
    108–10; innovation policies 119, 120,
    122, 135, 149; intermediaries 91, 92,
    94–5; knowledge-based economy 61–2,
    62–5; knowledge infrastructure 69, 70;
    linkages 102–4; local autonomy 46–7;
    lock-in 87; overview of knowledge
    dynamics 112–15; overview of
    locational policies 149, 150; partnering
    86; profile 51, 53–7; public-procurement
    policies and programs 97–8; purpose-
    built capital 43, 45–6, 145; regional
    and urban politics 146, 147–8; spatial
    expressions of public-procurement
    activities 76–8
Washington Metro 132
weakly-developed RIS 23, 24, 33–5
WestHolland Foreign Investment Agency
    (WFIA) 127
Wharf waterfront project 126
workforce education levels 70

Zuidas 87
Zurich 44–5, 70

Taylor & Francis eBooks

Helping you to choose the right eBooks for your Library

Add Routledge titles to your library's digital collection today. Taylor and Francis ebooks contains over 50,000 titles in the Humanities, Social Sciences, Behavioural Sciences, Built Environment and Law.

Choose from a range of subject packages or create your own!

Benefits for you

>> Free MARC records
>> COUNTER-compliant usage statistics
>> Flexible purchase and pricing options
>> All titles DRM-free.

REQUEST YOUR **FREE** INSTITUTIONAL TRIAL TODAY

Free Trials Available
We offer free trials to qualifying academic, corporate and government customers.

Benefits for your user

>> Off-site, anytime access via Athens or referring URL
>> Print or copy pages or chapters
>> Full content search
>> Bookmark, highlight and annotate text
>> Access to thousands of pages of quality research at the click of a button.

eCollections – Choose from over 30 subject eCollections, including:

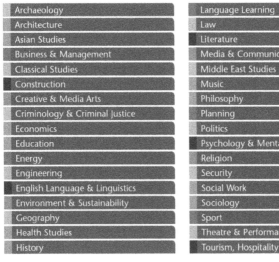

Archaeology	Language Learning
Architecture	Law
Asian Studies	Literature
Business & Management	Media & Communication
Classical Studies	Middle East Studies
Construction	Music
Creative & Media Arts	Philosophy
Criminology & Criminal Justice	Planning
Economics	Politics
Education	Psychology & Mental Health
Energy	Religion
Engineering	Security
English Language & Linguistics	Social Work
Environment & Sustainability	Sociology
Geography	Sport
Health Studies	Theatre & Performance
History	Tourism, Hospitality & Events

For more information, pricing enquiries or to order a free trial, please contact your local sales team:
www.tandfebooks.com/page/sales

Routledge
Taylor & Francis Group

The home of
Routledge books

www.tandfebooks.com

For Product Safety Concerns and Information please contact our EU
representative GPSR@taylorandfrancis.com
Taylor & Francis Verlag GmbH, Kaufingerstraße 24, 80331 München, Germany

www.ingramcontent.com/pod-product-compliance
Ingram Content Group UK Ltd.
Pitfield, Milton Keynes, MK11 3LW, UK
UKHW020953180425
457613UK00019B/665